编委会

普通高等学校"十四五"规划旅游管理类精品教材

总主编

马 勇　教育部高等学校旅游管理类专业教学指导委员会副主任
　　　　中国旅游协会教育分会副会长
　　　　中组部国家"万人计划"教学名师
　　　　湖北大学旅游发展研究院院长，教授、博士生导师

编　委（排名不分先后）

田　里　教育部高等学校旅游管理类专业教学指导委员会主任
　　　　云南大学工商管理与旅游管理学院原院长，教授、博士生导师
高　峻　教育部高等学校旅游管理类专业教学指导委员会副主任
　　　　上海师范大学环境与地理学院院长，教授、博士生导师
韩玉灵　北京第二外国语学院旅游管理学院教授
罗兹柏　中国旅游未来研究会副会长，重庆旅游发展研究中心主任，教授
郑耀星　中国旅游协会理事，福建师范大学旅游学院教授、博士生导师
董观志　暨南大学旅游规划设计研究院副院长，教授、博士生导师
薛兵旺　武汉商学院旅游与酒店管理学院院长，教授
姜　红　上海商学院酒店管理学院院长，教授
舒伯阳　中南财经政法大学工商管理学院教授、博士生导师
朱运海　湖北文理学院资源环境与旅游学院副院长
罗伊玲　昆明学院旅游学院副教授
杨振之　四川大学中国休闲与旅游研究中心主任，四川大学旅游学院教授、博士生导师
黄安民　华侨大学城市建设与经济发展研究院常务副院长，教授
张胜男　首都师范大学资源环境与旅游学院教授
魏　卫　华南理工大学旅游管理系教授、博士生导师
毕斗斗　华南理工大学旅游管理系副教授
蒋　昕　湖北经济学院旅游与酒店管理学院副院长，副教授
窦志萍　昆明学院旅游学院教授，《旅游研究》杂志主编
李　玺　澳门城市大学国际旅游与管理学院执行副院长，教授、博士生导师
王春雷　上海对外经贸大学会展与传播学院院长，教授
朱　伟　天津农学院人文学院副院长，副教授
邓爱民　中南财经政法大学旅游发展研究院院长，教授、博士生导师
程丛喜　武汉轻工大学旅游管理系主任，教授
周　霄　武汉轻工大学旅游研究中心主任，副教授
黄其新　江汉大学商学院副院长，副教授
何　彪　海南大学旅游学院副院长，教授

普通高等学校"十四五"规划旅游管理类精品教材

New Tourism English Alive

新编旅游情景英语

程丛喜 ◎ 编著

精品教材

华中科技大学出版社
http://press.hust.edu.cn
中国·武汉

内 容 提 要

本教材是根据"十四五"规划,为适应我国旅游业发展的需要,满足教育部教育教学改革要求和教材建设目标编写的。主要内容分为四个部分。第一部分共八个单元,每个单元包括三段实用情景对话及一篇相关的英文课文,内容涉及导游迎接游客,带领游客吃、住、行、游、购、娱及欢送游客八个方面的工作程序及相关语言点。第二部分共八个单元,每个单元包括若干实用情景对话及一篇相关的英文课文,内容涉及领队带领出境游客在海外旅游的工作程序及相关语言点。第三部分共九个单元,内容涉及与实际英语导游工作密切相关的海外游客感兴趣的旅游专题。第四部分共三个附录,包括国家级风景名胜区名单、国家历史文化名城名单和中国世界遗产名录。本教材与翻译导游和海外领队实际工作紧密结合,既可作为高等院校旅游管理专业、外语专业和旅游职业教育的教学用书,又可作为广大导游及领队等旅游从业人员、英语导游资格证培训或相关专业的参考用书。

图书在版编目(CIP)数据

新编旅游情景英语/程丛喜编著. —武汉:华中科技大学出版社,2022.4(2024.8重印)
ISBN 978-7-5680-8120-7

Ⅰ.①新… Ⅱ.①程… Ⅲ.①旅游-英语 Ⅳ.①F59

中国版本图书馆 CIP 数据核字(2022)第 057300 号

新编旅游情景英语 程丛喜 编著
Xinbian Lüyou Qingjing Yingyu

策划编辑:李　欢
责任编辑:陈　然
封面设计:廖亚萍
责任校对:阮　敏
责任监印:周治超

出版发行:华中科技大学出版社(中国•武汉)　　电话:(027)81321913
　　　　　武汉市东湖新技术开发区华工科技园　　邮编:430223
录　　排:华中科技大学惠友文印中心
印　　刷:武汉市籍缘印刷厂
开　　本:787mm×1092mm　1/16
印　　张:16
字　　数:459 千字(含二维码内容字数)
版　　次:2024 年 8 月第 1 版第 2 次印刷
定　　价:56.80 元

本书若有印装质量问题,请向出版社营销中心调换
全国免费服务热线:400-6679-118　　竭诚为您服务
版权所有　侵权必究

总序

伴随着我国社会和经济步入新发展阶段,我国的旅游业也进入转型升级与结构调整的重要时期。旅游业将在推动形成以国内经济大循环为主体、国内国际双循环相互促进的新发展格局中发挥出独特的作用。旅游业的大发展在客观上对我国高等旅游教育和人才培养提出了更高的要求,同时也希望高等旅游教育和人才培养能在促进我国旅游业高质量发展中发挥更大更好的作用。

《中国教育现代化2035》明确提出:推动高等教育内涵式发展,形成高水平人才培养体系。以"双一流"建设和"双万计划"的启动为标志,中国高等旅游教育发展进入新阶段。

这些新局面有力推动着我国高等旅游教育在"十四五"期间迈入发展新阶段,未来旅游业发展对各类中高级旅游人才的需求将十分旺盛。因此,出版一套把握时代新趋势、面向未来的高品质和高水准规划教材成为我国高等旅游教育和人才培养的迫切需要。

基于此,在教育部高等学校旅游管理类专业教学指导委员会的大力支持和指导下,教育部直属的全国重点大学出版社——华中科技大学出版社——汇聚了一大批国内高水平旅游院校的国家教学名师、资深教授及中青年旅游学科带头人,在成功编撰出版"普通高等院校旅游管理专业类'十三五'规划教材"的基础上,再次联合编撰出版"普通高等学校'十四五'规划旅游管理类精品教材"。本套教材从选题策划到成稿出版,从编写团队到出版团队,从主题选择到内容编排,均做出积极的创新和突破,具有以下特点:

一、基于新国标率先出版并不断沉淀和改版

教育部2018年颁布《普通高等学校本科专业类教学质量国家标准》后,华中科技大学出版社特邀教育部高等学校旅游管理类专业教学指导委员会副主任、国家"万人计划"教学名师马勇教授担任总主编,同时邀请了全国近百所开设旅游管理类本科专业的高校知名教授、博导、学科带头人和一线骨干专业教师,以及旅游行业专家、海外专业师资联合编撰了"普通高等院校旅游管理专业类'十三五'规划教材"。该套教材紧扣新国标要点,融合数字科技新技术,配套立体化教学资源,于新国标颁布后在全国率先出版,被全国数百所高等学校选用后获得良好反响。编委会在出版后积极收集院校的一线教学反馈,紧扣行业新变化,吸纳新知识点,不断地对教材内容及配套教育资源进行更新升级。"普通高等学校'十四五'规划旅游管理类精品教材"正是在此基础上沉淀和提升编撰而成的。《旅游接待业(第二版)》《旅游消费者行为(第二版)》《旅游目的地管理(第二版)》等核心课程优质规划教材陆续推出,以期为全国高等院校旅游专业创建国家级一流本科专业和国家级一流"金课"助力。

二、对标国家级一流本科课程,进行高水平建设

本套教材积极研判"双万计划"对旅游管理类专业课程的建设要求,对标国家级一流本科课程的高水平建设,进行内容优化与编撰,以期促进广大旅游院校的教学高质量建设与特色化发展。其中《旅游规划与开发》《酒店管理概论》《酒店督导管理》等教材已成为教育部授予的首批国家级一流本科"金课"配套教材。《节事活动策划与管理》等教材获得国家级和省级教学类奖项。

三、全面配套教学资源,打造立体化互动教材

华中科技大学出版社为本套教材建设了内容全面的线上教材课程资源服务平台:在横向资源配套上,提供全系列教学计划书、教学课件、习题库、案例库、参考答案、教学视频等配套教学资源;在纵向资源开发上,构建了覆盖课程开发、习题管理、学生评论、班级管理等集开发、使用、管理、评价于一体的教学生态链,打造出线上线下、课堂课外的新形态立体化互动教材。

在旅游教育发展的新时代,主编出版一套高质量规划教材是一项重要的教学出版工程,更是一份重要的责任。本套教材在组织策划及编写出版过程中,得到了全国广大院校旅游管理类专家教授、企业精英,以及华中科技大学出版社的大力支持,在此一并致谢!衷心希望本套教材能够为全国高等院校的旅游学界、业界和对旅游知识充满渴望的社会大众带来真正的精神和知识营养,为我国旅游教育教材建设贡献力量。也希望并诚挚邀请更多高等院校旅游管理专业的学者加入我们的编者和读者队伍,为我们共同的事业——我国高等旅游教育高质量发展——而奋斗!

总主编

2021 年 7 月

随着世界经济的发展与人民生活水平的提高,旅游日益成为人们的一种主要社会经济活动。《中华人民共和国国民经济和社会发展第十四个五年规划和2035年远景目标纲要》《中国教育现代化2035》等文件对旅游业的下一步发展提出了更高的要求。"十四五"期间,我国将全面进入大众旅游时代,旅游业的发展仍处于重要的战略机遇期,但机遇和挑战都有新变化。高速发展的旅游业对旅游业的相关研究和旅游教育均提出了较高的要求。

我国自1978年改革开放以来,旅游经历了起步、发展和日趋成熟几个阶段,来华旅游的海外游客逐年增加,尤其是20世纪90年代以来,我国旅游业进一步快速增长,旅游业的产业地位不断提升,逐步成为我国国民经济的主要组成部分和我国经济新的增长点之一。中国旅游研究院发布的《中国出境旅游发展报告2020》显示,2019年我国的出境旅游市场仍然保持了增长态势,规模达到1.55亿人次,相比2018年同比增长了3.3%。另据中国旅游研究院发布的《中国入境旅游发展报告2020》,2019年我国接待入境过夜游客6573万人次,外国人入境游客3188万人次,分别同比增长4.5%和4.4%。无论是入境过夜市场占比还是外国人入境旅游市场占比均继续保持上升趋势,客源市场结构持续优化。

旅游业的迅速发展客观上为旅游学科的发展提供了良好的机遇,旅游教育得到了前所未有的发展。随着旅游业的迅速发展,我国旅游从业人员队伍不断壮大,他们在传播我国的先进文化、宣传社会主义精神文明、展示社会主义建设成就和宣传我国旅游业等方面发挥着积极作用。为了适应新形势下高等教育旅游相关专业学生以及翻译导游、海外领队等旅游从业人员的实际应用需要,编者在总结三十余年的翻译导游实践、二十余年的旅游教学科研经验和参考大量相关资料的基础上,在华中科技大学出版社及有关专家的精心指导下,主持编著了《新编旅游情景英语》教材。

本教材主要包括以下四个部分。

第一部分:共八个单元,每个单元包括三段实用情景对话及一篇相关的英文课文,内容涉及导游迎接游客,带领游客吃、住、行、游、购、娱及欢送游客八个方面的工作程序及相关语言点。

第二部分:共八个单元,每个单元包括若干实用情景对话及一篇相关的英文课文,内容涉及领队带领出境游客在海外旅游的工作程序及相关语言点。

第三部分:共九个单元,内容涉及与实际英语导游工作密切相关的海外游客感兴趣的旅游专题。

第四部分:共三个附录,包括国家级风景名胜区名单、国家历史文化名城名单和中国世界遗产名录。

本教材与翻译导游和海外领队等实际工作紧密结合,既可作为高等院校旅游管理专业、外语专业和旅游职业教育的教学用书,又可作为广大导游及领队等旅游从业人员、英语导游资格证培训或相关专业的参考用书。在本教材的编写过程中,邱国清、王文浩、刁宝石、邱战平、胡延华、林华英、陈顺良、罗琳、向兰、肖横溢、李红丹、朱飞、彭琛、张银燕、车前亮、刘保丽、严丽、蒋潞、苏兰兰、张阳阳、程骄阳、魏格、胡宽、程琼琳、李文娟、杨文静、何宇聪、周亚轩、李文浩、彭雪婷、邹林翰、刘开元、徐文瑾、曹国辉、王春慧、张逸飞、刘广澳、徐心娱、郭丽等提供了丰富的资料,毛焱、冯玮、李玲、胡冰霞、李莺莉、李良辰、王晓巍、李忱、王军、王勇、徐光木、魏日、吴丽、龚小龙、李霞、王丹、程领、刘丽莉、吴丽慧、叶晨瑜、徐曼、孙婧婍、濮琼等老师提供了悉心的指导和帮助,在此特向他们表示衷心的感谢。同时,编者还参考了大量的网络资源及书籍,在此对参考资料的作者和单位一并表示感谢。

本教材也得到了湖北省文化和旅游厅,武汉市文化和旅游局,湖北省旅游学会,汉江师范学院,武汉轻工大学管理学院、国际交流与合作处、教务处、科学技术处,湖北县域经济发展研究中心相关领导及专家的大力支持和帮助,在此表示衷心的感谢!

由于编者水平有限,书中难免有疏漏之处,恳请读者、专家批评指正。

程丛喜

2022 年 3 月

二维码资源目录

单元	名称	页码
Unit 1	Conversation 1　Meeting the New Arrivals at the Airport	3
	Conversation 2　Going Through the Customs Formalities	4
	Conversation 3　On the Way to the Hotel	6
	Text　A Welcome Speech	8
	Keys	11
Unit 2	Conversation 1　Checking in	12
	Conversation 2　Handling Complaint about the Housekeeping Service	13
	Conversation 3　Checking out	14
	Text　Lily Hotel	16
	Keys	19
Unit 3	Conversation 1　Seating the Guests	20
	Conversation 2　At the Chinese Restaurant	21
	Conversation 3　At the Western Restaurant	22
	Text　Beijing Roast Duck	24
	Keys	28
Unit 4	Conversation 1　Asking the Way	29
	Conversation 2　Booking Tickets	30
	Conversation 3　Leading a Tour Group to Take the Train	31
	Text　Public Transportation of Beijing	33
	Keys	38
Unit 5	Conversation 1　Conducting a Sightseeing Tour in Hangzhou	39
	Conversation 2　Taking a Natural Scenery Tour in China	40
	Conversation 3　Visiting the Jade Buddha Temple	42
	Text　The Yangtze Three Gorges	44
	Keys	49
Unit 6	Conversation 1　At the Arts and Craft Store	50
	Conversation 2　At the Department Store	51
	Conversation 3　At the Souvenir Department	53
	Text　Shanghai Carpet Factory	55
	Keys	62

续表

单元	名称	页码
Unit 7	Conversation 1　Talking about the Recreation and Fitness Center	63
	Conversation 2　Booking Tickets for Beijing Opera	64
	Conversation 3　Making Appointment	65
	Text　Peking Opera	66
	Keys	72
Unit 8	Conversation 1　Bidding Farewell to the Tourist	73
	Conversation 2　Checking in at the Airport	74
	Conversation 3　Seeing the Tourist off	75
	Text　A Farewell Speech	77
	Keys	80
Unit 9	Conversation 1　At the Information Desk	83
	Conversation 2　At the Check-in Counter	84
	Conversation 3　Going Through Security Check	85
	Conversation 4　At the Transfer Desk	86
	Conversation 5　Flight is Delayed	87
	Conversation 6　Luggage Claim	88
	Conversation 7　Handling the Immigration Procedures	89
	Conversation 8　Handling the Emigration Procedures	90
	Text　The Duty of a Tour Leader	91
	Keys	96
Unit 10	Conversation 1　Asking for Drinks	97
	Conversation 2　Meals on Board	98
	Conversation 3　Airsickness	99
	Conversation 4　Feeling a Little Cold	99
	Conversation 5　Asking for Entry Cards & Customs Declarations	100
	Conversation 6　Inquiry	101
	Text　Air Travel Tips to Make Your Flight Easier	102
	Keys	106
Unit 11	Conversation 1　Check in	107
	Conversation 2　Room Service	108
	Conversation 3　Wake-up Call Service	109
	Conversation 4　Laundry Service	110
	Conversation 5　Check Out	111
	Conversation 6　Reservation	112

续表

单元	名称	页码
Unit 11	Text　Classifications of Hotel	114
	Keys	118
Unit 12	Conversation 1　Arranging the Tour Group to Have Meal	119
	Conversation 2　Ordering Dinner	120
	Conversation 3　Bill Payment	121
	Conversation 4　At the Bar	122
	Text　Western Table Etiquettes	124
	Keys	128
Unit 13	Conversation 1　Buying Cosmetics	129
	Conversation 2　Buying Watches	130
	Conversation 3　Buying Some Fish Oil and Sheep Oil Skin Care Items	131
	Conversation 4　Buying Fruits	132
	Conversation 5　Returning Goods for a Refund	133
	Conversation 6　In the Duty Free Shop	134
	Conversation 7　Inquiring about Tax Refund	135
	Text　Hong Kong—The Shopping Paradise	136
	Keys	141
Unit 14	Conversation 1　Taking a Taxi	142
	Conversation 2　Taking a Bus	143
	Conversation 3　Taking the Subway	144
	Text　London's 5 Airports	145
	Keys	149
Unit 15	Conversation 1　Buying Admission Tickets	150
	Conversation 2　Watching a Song and Dance	151
	Conversation 3　Taking a Group Picture	151
	Conversation 4　Enjoying at the Recreational Center	152
	Text　The Floating City without Auto	154
	Keys	159
Unit 16	Conversation 1　Reporting to the Police	160
	Conversation 2　About Security in the Hotel	161
	Conversation 3　The Passport of a Tourist Is Lost	162
	Text　Safety Tips in Rome	164
	Keys	167

续表

单元	名称	页码
Unit 17	Introduction to China	171
	Keys	177
Unit 18	History of China	178
	Keys	181
Unit 19	Population and Nationalities of China	182
	Keys	187
Unit 20	Political System of China	188
	Keys	192
Unit 21	Education	193
	Public Health	195
	Keys	198
Unit 22	Traditional Chinese Medicine	199
	Keys	204
Unit 23	Wushu	205
	Taijiquan	208
	Keys	212
Unit 24	Religions of China	213
	Keys	220
Unit 25	Chinese Tea	221
	The Chinese Porcelain	224
	The Chinese Embroidery	227
	The Cloisonne Enamel of China	228
	The Chinese Painting	230
	Silk	233
	Keys	235

目录
Contents

PART I ENGLISH FOR INBOUND TOUR GUIDES

Unit 1	Meeting the Tourists	/3
Unit 2	Accommodation	/12
Unit 3	Dining	/20
Unit 4	Transportation	/29
Unit 5	Sightseeing	/39
Unit 6	Shopping	/50
Unit 7	Entertainment	/63
Unit 8	Farewell	/73

PART II ENGLISH FOR OUTBOUND TOUR LEADERS

Unit 9	Practicalities at the Airport and the Duty of a Tour Leader	/83
Unit 10	Practicalities on Board the Plane & Air Travel Tips	/97
Unit 11	Practicalities at the Hotel and Classifications of Hotel	/107
Unit 12	Practicalities at the Restaurant & Bar and Western Table Etiquette	/119

Unit 13 Practicalities on Shopping and Hong Kong—
         The Shopping Paradise /129
Unit 14 Practicalities on Traffic and London's 5 Airports
                                  /142
Unit 15 Practicalities on Sightseeing and Entertainment
         and the Floating City without Auto /150
Unit 16 Practicalities about the Safety Abroad and
         Safety Tips in Rome /160

PART III ENGLISH TOPICS FOR FOREIGN TOURISTS

Unit 17 Introduction to China /171
Unit 18 History of China /178
Unit 19 Population and Nationalities of China /182
Unit 20 Political System of China /188
Unit 21 The Present Status of Education & Public
         Health in China /193
Unit 22 Traditional Chinese Medicine /199
Unit 23 Wushu and Taijiquan /205
Unit 24 Religions of China /213
Unit 25 Local Products /221

PART IV Appendixes /237

参考文献 /239

PART I
ENGLISH FOR INBOUND TOUR GUIDES

Unit 1
Meeting the Tourists

Section 1 Situational Conversations

➢ Conversation 1 Meeting the New Arrivals at the Airport

(At the airport, Wang Hai, a guide from China Youth Travel Service, is to meet a tour group from the United States headed by the tour leader, Mr. Smith. The travel service has received the notice beforehand about their arrival.)

G=Tour Guide   L=Tour Leader   P=Passenger   M=Member of the Tour Group

G: Excuse me, are you Mr. Smith?

P: No, I am afraid you have made a mistake.

G: I'm so sorry.

P: Never mind.

M: (Listening to their talk) Oh, I'm a member of the tour group from America. Mr. Smith is our tour leader. He is over there.

G: Thank you.

G: Excuse me, but aren't you Mr. Smith from the United States?

L: Why, yes.

G: Oh, Mr. Smith, welcome to China. My name is Wang Hai. I am the guide from China Youth Travel Service.

L: Glad to meet you. Thank you for coming to meet us.

G: Glad to meet you, too, Mr. Smith. How was your trip?

L: Fine. We had a very pleasant trip.

G: You have a group of 14, right?

L: Yes.

G: How many pieces of luggage do you have altogether?

L: 28 in all. And here are the luggage checks.

G: I see. When you pick up your luggage, please put it on these trolleys. I'll ask the porter to take care of it.

扫码听听力

L：Thank you very much.

G：Is everybody here now? Our bus is in the parking lot.

L：Oh, let me see. Yes, everybody is here.

G：Mr. Smith, we've made reservations for your group at Lake View Garden Hotel. Your luggage will be delivered to your rooms in the hotel.

L：That is wonderful!

G：Shall we go now?

L：Yes, I think so.

G：Attention, please. Now please follow me to the bus.

Questions:

(1) Where is the tour group from? What is the name of the tour leader of this group?

(2) How many tourists does this group have?

(3) Where does the guide ask the tourists to put their luggage? Who will take care of their luggage?

(4) Where is their bus?

(5) Which hotel will this group live in?

Notes

(1) China Youth Travel Service 中国青年旅行社

(2) tour leader 旅行团领队

(3) Why, yes. 噢(呃)，对的。("why"在这里是感叹词，表示惊奇、不耐烦、抗议、赞成、犹豫等)

(4) How was your trip? 一路还好吗？

(5) luggage check 行李牌

(6) porter 行李员

(7) parking lot 停车场

(8) make reservations 预订

➤ Conversation 2 Going Through the Customs Formalities

(A foreign tour group is about to go through the customs formalities. The tour guide, Wu Jun, is telling the tour leader, Mr. Hans, what has to be done at the Customs Office.)

G＝Tour Guide   L＝Tour Leader

G：Here we are at the Customs Office. I have to leave you here now, but I'll be waiting for you at the exit.

L：Hold on a minute, please. You see, this is my first trip to China and I'm not quite sure about the procedures here.

扫码听听力

PART I ENGLISH FOR INBOUND TOUR GUIDES

G: Well, firstly, you must go through the Immigration Office, and then proceed through the Quarantine Inspection and finally the Customs Office. You have to present your passport and disembarkation card to the immigration officer. At the Customs Office you should show your customs declaration form. On the form you must list the belongings you have taken with you.

L: The customs declaration form looks rather complicated and I'm not sure how to fill it out.

G: Let me have a look. Now, what you need to do is to simply look through the two lists—the Prohibited Articles List and the Duty free Quota List. Right here.

L: What things do I have to declare on this form?

G: You must declare such articles as electric equipments, foreign currency, jewellery, gold, silver, antiques and other treasures.

L: I have nothing but personal belongings.

G: Have you got any valuables?

L: I have a camera with a zoom lens.

G: Then you should put a check mark here. Have you got any foreign currency?

L: Yes, I've brought some U.S. dollars with me.

G: Then you should fill in this foreign currency declaration form.

L: Oh, it's not easy to pass the customs!

G: You bet!

Questions:

(1) Where does the tour guide leave the tourists? Where will he be waiting for the tourists?

(2) Has the tour leader ever come to China?

(3) What do the foreign tourists have to present to the immigration officer?

(4) What do the foreign tourists must list on the customs declaration form?

(5) Does the tour leader have any valuables?

Notes

(1) customs formalities 报关手续

(2) the Customs Office 海关

(3) Hold on a minute, please. 请等一等。

(4) the Immigration Office 入境管理处

(5) the Quarantine Inspection 检疫处

(6) To present your passport and disembarkation card 出示你的护照和入境卡（表）

(7) customs declaration form 海关申报表

(8) prohibited articles 禁运（违禁）物品

(9) Duty free Quota List 免税配额表

(10) electric equipment 电器

(11) foreign currency 外币

(12) personal belongings 个人行李、财物

(13) valuables 贵重物品

(14) zoom lens 变焦镜头

(15) You bet! 的确,当然!

➢ Conversation 3　On the Way to the Hotel

(The tourists get into the coach, the guide is taking the tour group from the airport to the hotel. The coach is about to start.)

G＝Guide　T＝Tourist　L＝Tour Leader

G: After you, Madam.

T: Thank you. (They get into the coach.)

G: (Counting the tourists) Is everybody here, Mr. Hurt?

L: No. One lady hasn't come yet. Poor Lillie, she has been throwing up all the way because of airsickness.

G: Oh, I'm sorry to hear that. I hope she feels better now.

L: Oh, there she comes.

G: Shall we go now?

L: Yes, please.

G: It must be much colder here than it is in England, I suppose.

T: Oh, yes. We have rather mild winters. It was very foggy when I left three days ago. I knew it would be colder here, but I thought there would be a lot of snow.

G: We don't have that much snow in Beijing. In fact, we haven't had any so far this winter.

T: What is the temperature today, do you know?

G: About freezing point, I think. But this morning's forecast said we're going to have a cold spell in the next few days—the temperature will probably drop to 10 or 15 degrees centigrade below zero.

T: It's a good thing that I've brought a heavy overcoat. Of course, I come from Hong Kong today. It was very warm there. What's this place we are passing through?

G: This is the Embassy Quarter, now we are just coming to Tian'anmen Square. This is Tian'anmen, the Gate of Heavenly Peace. The Great Hall of the People is over there. The building we've just passed on the other side of the Square is the Museum of Chinese Revolution and the Museum of Chinese History.

T: What's the monument I saw in the center of the Square?

G: That's the Monument to the People's Heroes, built in memory of those who died for the revolution over the past century. And behind it is the Memorial Hall of Chairman Mao.

T: There are a lot of buildings going on in Beijing.

G: Yes, that's true. But it still isn't as fast as we would like it to be. You see those old, one-storey buildings over there? They were built before the founding of the People's Republic of China. I'm afraid we haven't built enough new houses to replace them all yet. Is there any place you'd particularly like to visit while you're here?

T: Well, I would like to see the Great Wall. I'm also very keen to visit an university.

G: I see. (The car pulls up in front of the hotel) Here is your hotel. Shall we go in? The porter will see to your bags and send them up to your rooms.

Questions:

(1) Why has the tourist Lillie been throwing up all the way?

(2) According to this morning's forecast, how about the weather of Beijing in the next few days?

(3) What's the monument in the center of the Tian'anmen Square? What's its function?

(4) When were those old, one-storey buildings built over there?

(5) Which places would the tourists particularly like to visit in Beijing?

Notes

(1) coach 长途客运汽车

(2) She has been throwing up all the way because of airsickness. 因为晕机，她一路上呕吐。

(3) I suppose. 我以为。

(4) We haven't had any (snow) so far this winter. 到目前为止，还没下过雪。

(5) about freezing 大约 0 ℃

(6) cold spell 寒潮

(7) the Embassy Quarter 使馆区

(8) The Great Hall of the People 人民大会堂

(9) the Monument to the People's Heroes 人民英雄纪念碑

(10) the Memorial Hall of Chairman Mao 毛主席纪念堂

(11) I'm also very keen to visit an university. 我也非常想参观一所大学。

(12) pull up 停下

(13) see to 照看，照料

New Words & Expressions

trolley ['trɒlɪ] n. 电车，手推车，台车

porter [ˈpɔːtə] n. 门房，搬运工，行李员
reservation [ˌrezəˈveɪʃən] n. 保留意见，预订，预约
deliver [dɪˈlɪvə] vt. 递送，交付
attention [əˈtenʃən] n. 注意，关心，关注，注意力，（口令）立正
exit [ˈeksɪt] n. 出口，太平门，退场
belonging [bɪˈlɒŋɪŋ] n. 所有物，财产，行李
jewellery [ˈdʒuːəlrɪ] n.（＝jewelry）珠宝，首饰
antique [ænˈtɪːk] n. 古物，古董　adj. 古董的，古老的
treasure [ˈtreʒə] n. 财宝，财富，珍宝　vt. 珍爱，珍视，珍藏
valuable [ˈvæljuəbl] n. 贵重物品　adj. 贵重的，有价值的，有价值的
camera [ˈkæmərə] n. 照相机
suppose [səˈpəʊz] vt. 假设，猜想
mild [maɪld] adj. 温和的，轻微的
foggy [ˈfɒgi] adj. 有雾的
temperature [ˈtemprətʃə] n. 温度，气温
forecast [ˈfɔːkɑːst] vt. 预测，预报
monument [ˈmɒnjumənt] n. 纪念碑
revolution [ˌrevəˈluːʃən] n. 革命，旋转
throw up 呕出，呕吐

Section 2　Text

A Welcome Speech

Good afternoon! Ladies and gentlemen,

Welcome to Beijing!

Now sit back please and don't worry about your luggage. Your luggage will be sent to the hotel in another bus.

First, let me introduce myself. My name is Gao Xiaoming, but you can just call me Ming. I'm from the China International Travel Service, Beijing Branch. On behalf of my travel service, my colleagues and myself, I warmly welcome you to Beijing, our capital city. Confucius, the great ancient Chinese sage, once said "Isn't it a pleasure to have friends coming from afar?" So it is the great happiness of mine to be your host here in Beijing.

During your stay here, I'll be your local guide and I'll do everything possible to make your stay the most comfortable and enjoyable. Be sure to let me know when you have any questions, any problems or any requests, no matter what they are.

We are going to stay in China World Hotel, a very comfortable and luxurious hotel in downtown. We shall spend a lot of time in this limousine, our only

扫码听短文

"transportation". We'd better remember its number and its features so that we won't get a wrong bus. The bus number is 84176. Now I'd like to introduce our driver to you. Mr. Li has been working as a professional driver for over 15 years and he is surely experienced and responsible.

You have just completed such a long flight from San Francisco to Beijing. The time difference between the two cities is 16 hours. Now take your watch and reset the time. It is 4:27, Beijing standard time. Although China spans five time zones, the whole country follows Beijing standard time.

There is one thing I must remind you that you mustn't drink the water from the tap here because the unboiled water might cause you sick. However, boiling water for making tea is available in the hotel rooms.

Notes

(1) sit back（在紧张活动之后）舒舒服服地休息
(2) China International Travel Service, Beijing Branch 中国国际旅行社北京分社
(3) the great ancient Chinese sage 中国古代的伟大圣人
(4) "Isn't it a pleasure to have friends coming from afar?" "有朋自远方来不亦乐乎？"
(5) limousine 豪华轿车,（往返机场接送旅客的）中型客车
(6) reset the time 重设时间
(7) the unboiled water 没烧开的水

New Words & Expressions

sit back 休息一下
on behalf of 代表
colleague [ˈkɒliːg] n. 同事，同僚
Confucius [kənˈfjuːʃəs] n. 孔子（公元前551—公元前479年，中国春秋末期思想家、政治家、教育家）
sage [seɪdʒ] n. 圣人，智者
comfortable [ˈkʌmfətəbl] adj. 安逸的，使人舒服的
enjoyable [ɪnˈdʒɔɪəbl] adj. 愉快的，快乐的
luxurious [lʌgˈʒʊəriəs] adj. 奢侈的，豪华的
limousine [ˈlɪməziːn] n. 豪华轿车,（往返机场接送旅客的）中型客车
responsible [rɪˈspɒnsəbl] adj. 负责的，责任重大的
experienced [ɪkˈspɪəriənst] adj. 有经验的，老练的
reset [ˌriːˈset] vt. 重新放置或安置，将……恢复原位
tap [tæp] n. 水龙头，电话窃听 vt. 轻敲，轻拍
boiled [bɔɪld] adj. 煮沸的
available [əˈveɪləbl] adj. 可用的或可得到的，有空的

Exercises

1. Read and recite the following special terms

(1) tourist generating country 旅游客源国

(2) tourist destination country 旅游目的地国

(3) visitor arrivals 旅游到达人数

(4) package tour 包价旅游

(5) certificate of tourist guide 旅游导游证书

(6) tourism marketing 旅游市场营销

(7) the World Tourism Organization (UNWTO) 世界旅游组织

(8) outbound tour 出国旅游

(9) inbound tour 入境旅游

(10) tour leader (conductor, manager) 旅游团领队

(11) national guide 全陪(导游)

(12) local guide 地陪(导游)

(13) the customs formalities 海关手续

(14) entry visa 入境签证

(15) passenger passage 旅客通道

(16) unaccompanied baggage (check luggage) 托运行李

(17) customs luggage declaration form 海关行李申报单

(18) reception program 接待计划

(19) luggage check-in counter 行李过磅处

(20) time difference 时差

2. Complete the following dialogues

(Mr. Alex White and his colleagues have just arrived in Beijing. Mo Jun, from the China International Travel Service, Beijing Branch, has met them at the airport.)

　　G＝Tour Guide　　L＝Tour Leader　　T＝Tourist

　　G：Good morning! Mr. White, ＿＿＿＿＿(1)＿＿＿＿＿(团队的每个人都到了吗)?

　　L：Yeah. There are five of us.

　　G：Good. Now, let's go to the baggage claim to get our baggage. (After some time, all have got their baggage except Miss Lois Thompson.)

　　T：I haven't seen my suitcase. I hope it's not lost.

　　G：＿＿＿＿＿(2)＿＿＿＿＿(你的行李是什么颜色), Miss Thompson?

　　T：It's blue. Please call me Lois. First names are more friendly than last names.

　　G：OK, Lois. Don't worry. ＿＿＿＿＿(3)＿＿＿＿＿(我们会尽力找到你的行李). ＿＿＿＿＿(4)＿＿＿＿＿(请把你的行李牌给我).

　　T：Here you are.

(Mo goes to check with the Lost Baggage Office. After a while, he returns.)

　　G：I'm terribly sorry, Lois. ＿＿＿＿＿(5)＿＿＿＿＿(昆明机场弄错了).

PART I   ENGLISH FOR INBOUND TOUR GUIDES

_____(6)_____（他们装行李时把你的行李给遗漏了）.

T：Oh, dear. What can I do?

G：_____(7)_____（我已经和昆明机场取得了联系）and they said they were awfully sorry and _____(8)_____（他们将把你的行李放在下一个来北京的航班上）.

T：When will it arrive here?

G：Around six o'clock this evening. _____(9)_____（这里的机场将把行李直接送到你所在的酒店）.

T：Thank you, Mr. Mo.

G：Don't mention it. OK, everybody, we will drive directly to your hotel. I believe you will look refreshed and revitalized after a good sleep.

3. Translate the following sentences into English

（1）常言道："有朋自远方来，不亦乐乎？""海内存知己，天涯若比邻。"

（2）你们总共有多少件行李？大家取到行李后，请放到这几辆手推车上。我会让行李员看管行李的。

（3）欢迎大家来到武汉！希望大家在这里玩得愉快！如果有什么特别的要求，请告诉我。

（4）现在是北京时间下午四点三十分，请大家根据这个时间对一下自己的手表。

（5）在海关检查处你得出示你的海关申报表，在表上一一列出你随身携带的物品。

Unit 1   Keys

Unit 2
Accommodation

Section 1 Situational Conversations

➢ Conversation 1 Checking in

(A tour guide and his tour group come to the reception desk of the hotel. They have made a reservation through the travel service in advance. A receptionist is attending to them.)

G=Tour Guide L=Tour Leader R=Receptionist T=Tourist

R: Good afternoon! Welcome to our hotel.

G: Good afternoon! I'd like to have two suites and ten single rooms, please.

R: Have you made a reservation?

G: Yes, we have booked them for our tour group from the United States. I'm Wang Hai. I'm from China International Travel Service, Shanghai Branch.

R: Oh, I'm sorry. There is no reservation from your service.

G: I'm sure we have made a reservation. Could you check again a reservation for Friday for the tour group from the United States?

R: All right. Let me check again. Ah, yes, two suites and ten single rooms from China International Travel Service, Shanghai Branch.

T: Do the rooms have a bath? I feel like taking a bath right now.

R: Yes, every room is equipped with a bath, a telephone and an air-conditioner.

T: That's good.

R: Can I see your passports, please?

L: Yes, these are our passports.

R: Thank you. Here are your passports. Please fill in these registration forms.

L: The registration forms are finished. Shall we have our keys to the rooms?

R: Of course. Here are the keys to your rooms. Your rooms are on the third floor. The bellboy will take you to your rooms.

L: Thanks!

G: I think it's time for you to take a good rest. If there's nothing else you want, I will be leaving. I will meet you at the lobby on the ground floor at seven o'clock tomorrow morning for your breakfast. You can take a good rest tonight.

L: I don't think there is anything else. You have been very considerate. Thank you very much.

G: You are welcome. Enjoy your stay. See you tomorrow!

L: See you tomorrow!

Questions:

(1) How many suites and single rooms would the tour guide like to have?

(2) Where is the local guide from?

(3) What is every room equipped with?

(4) Who will take the tourists to their rooms?

(5) Where and when will the tour guide meet the tourists for their breakfast?

Notes

(1) make a reservation 预订

(2) two suites 两个套间

(3) reception desk 接待处

(4) in advance 提前

(5) take a bath 洗个澡

(6) be equipped with 装备，安装

(7) air-conditioner 空调

(8) Please fill in these registration forms. 请填写这些登记表。

(9) considerate 周到的，体贴的

➤ Conversation 2   Handling Complaint about the Housekeeping Service

(Sue, a member of a tour group, is knocking at the door of Mr. Tang, the tour guide.)

G＝Tour Guide   T＝Tourist   M＝Manager

G: Oh, good morning, Sue. Anything wrong?

T: Well, I hate to disturb you, but I really can't stand it any more.

G: What's the trouble exactly?

T: I need to change the room. It's too noisy. I was woken up several times by the noise the baggage elevator made. It was too much for me.

G: I'm sorry to hear that. Let me check with the front office and I'm sure they will come up with a satisfactory solution.

(After a while)

G: Well, Sue, they are awfully sorry for the inconvenience. They will change the

扫码听听力

room for you. There comes the manager.

M: I'm terribly sorry, miss. I do apologize. We will move you to another room. I'll send a porter up to your room and help you with the luggage.

T: Thank you. I hope I'll be able to enjoy my stay in a quiet room tonight and have a sound sleep.

M: You can count on that. And if there is anything else you need, please let us know.

T: Ah, yes, the room is too cold for me. I felt rather cold when I slept.

M: Did you turn off the air-conditioning?

T: Yes. Maybe I'm getting a cold.

M: I'll get you an extra blanket.

T: Thank you. And thank you, too, Mr. Tang.

G: You're welcome. I hope you'll be more comfortable in your new room.

Questions:

(1) Why does the tourist Sue need to change the room?

(2) What was the tourist Sue woken up several times by?

(3) What does the tour guide do after he has heard the complaint of the tourist Sue?

(4) How does the manager handle the complaint?

(5) What does the manager do when Sue tells him that maybe she is getting a cold?

Notes

(1) Anything wrong? 有什么问题吗?

(2) But I really can't stand it any more. 但我确实再也不能忍受了。

(3) wake up 弄醒，唤醒

(4) baggage elevator 行李升降梯

(5) It was too much for me. 我确实忍无可忍。

(6) check with 与……相符合，与……联系，与……核实

(7) help you with the luggage 帮你拿行李

(8) a sound sleep 酣睡

(9) count on 期望，指望

➤ Conversation 3 Checking out

(A tour group is going to check out. The tour guide and the tour leader are busy with the checking out procedure.)

G＝Tour Guide　　L＝Tour Leader　　R＝Receptionist

G: Good morning, everyone! We are going to check out this morning. Is everybody here?

L: Yes.

G: Is everybody's luggage ready?

L: Yes, everything is all right.

G: Thank you for being so punctual. The bellboy will take your luggage to the bus. Ten minutes later, please meet at the dining room. Breakfast is to be served at 7:45. After you have your breakfast, please meet on the bus. We will set off to the airport at 8:30. The departure time of the flight is ten o'clock this morning. Is this schedule all right?

L: Yes, thank you.

G: Would you please come with me to check the luggage?

L: Yes, of course.

G: There are altogether 16 pieces of luggage.

L: Yes. That is 16.

G: Are they all locked?

L: Yes, they are. Now can you go with me to the front desk to check out?

G: Sure.

(At the front desk)

R: Good morning, sir. Do you want to check out?

L: Yes, our rooms are 501, 502, 503, 504 and my name is John Smith.

R: Here is your bill. Two nights at 300 yuan each, and here are the meals that you had at the hotel including the breakfast this morning. That makes total of 4500 yuan. Is that right?

L: Yes, I think so.

R: How would you like to pay?

L: I'd like to pay in cash.

R: Here is your receipt. We look forward to seeing you again.

L: Thank you. Goodbye.

Questions:

(1) What does the tour guide tell the tourists when he meets them in the morning?

(2) Where will the bellboy take their luggage?

(3) What time is breakfast to be served? When will they set off to the airport?

(4) How many pieces of luggage are there altogether for the tour group?

(5) How much does John Smith have to pay the hotel? How would he like to pay?

Notes

(1) be busy with 忙于

(2) check out 退房,结账离开
(3) punctual 守时的,准时的
(4) set off 出发
(5) departure time 启程时间
(6) to pay in cash 付现金
(7) look forward to seeing you again 期待着再次见到你们

New Words & Expressions

lodging [ˈlɒdʒɪŋ] n. 寄宿处,寄宿,租住的房间
bellboy [ˈbelbɔɪ] n. (旅馆的)行李员
lobby [ˈlɒbi] n. 大厅,大堂
considerate [kənˈsɪdərət] adj. 考虑周到的
stand [stænd] v. 经受,忍受
inconvenience [ˌɪnkənˈviːniəns] n. 不方便之处
blanket [ˈblæŋkɪt] n. 毯子 vt. 覆盖
punctual [ˈpʌŋktʃuəl] adj. 严守时刻的,准时的
bill [bɪl] n. 账单,钞票,票据 vt. 给(某人)开账单,用海报宣传
receipt [rɪˈsiːt] n. 收条,收据,收到
turn off 关掉
look forward to doing sth. 期望做某事

Section 2 Text

Lily Hotel

Featured for fresh air, quiet and secluded surroundings, Lily Hotel, is located in the southwest of Shanghai on the northern shore of Hangzhou Bay in the East China Sea.

Covering an area of 48000 square meters with a floor space of 30000 square meters, the hotel is composed of the south and north buildings. The 8-storey south building with 250 guestrooms was built in 1974, while the 9-storey north building with 110 guestrooms was built in 1983.

All the rooms are equipped with central air-conditioning, closed-circuit TV, program controlled telephones, refrigerators, smoke detector and alarm systems, etc. There are three combinations for suites: 2-room suites, 3-room suites and 4-room suites, each accompanied by a mini kitchen.

The hotel is furnished with a choice of 15 restaurants, banquet halls and bars. The Cantonese and Beijing dishes are highlights for Chinese meal, while Sichuan and Shanghai specialities, western and Japanese cuisines are also cooked here to meet the customer's tastes. There are a variety of 10 conference rooms and a grand function hall seating 200 persons.

Available in the hotel are an outdoor swimming pool, a golf driving range, a tennis court, a billiard room, a dancing hall and other recreational facilities. In addition, Lily Hotel offers such services as post office, barber shop, clinic, sauna, souvenir shop, taxi, foreign exchange and ticket reservation for domestic flights.

Notes

(1) be composed of 由……组成
(2) central air-conditioning 中央空调
(3) closed-circuit TV 闭路电视
(4) program controlled telephones 内线电话
(5) smoke detector and alarm systems 烟感器报警系统
(6) each accompanied by a mini kitchen 配有小厨房
(7) banquet hall 宴会厅
(8) grand function hall 大礼堂

New Words & Expressions

featured ['fiːtʃəd] v. 以……为特色
secluded [sɪ'kluːdɪd] adj. 与世隔绝的，隐居的
storey ['stɔːrɪ] n. 层
furnish ['fɜːnɪʃ] vt. 供应，提供，装备，布置
be furnished with 装备有……
banquet ['bæŋkwɪt] n. 宴会
cuisine [kwɪ'ziːn] n. 烹饪
conference ['kɒnfərəns] n. 会议，讨论会，协商会
guestroom ['gestrʊm] n. 客房
circuit ['sɜːkɪt] n. 电路，线路，环行，环行道
barber ['bɑːbə] n. 理发师
combination [ˌkɒmbɪ'neɪʃən] n. 合作，结合，组合，联合体，组合物，密码组合，排列
suite [swiːt] n. 套房，套间，一套家具，（一批）随员，随从
highlight ['haɪlaɪt] vt. 强调，突出，使显著 n. 最精彩的部分，最重要的事情
speciality [ˌspeʃɪ'ælɪtɪ] n. 专门研究，专业，特长，特制品，特产
billiard ['bɪlɪəd] adj. 台球的
refrigerator [rɪ'frɪdʒəreɪtə] n. 冰箱

Exercises

1. Read and recite the following special terms

(1) five-star hotel 五星级饭店

(2) well-appointed hotel 设备完善的旅馆

(3) group guests 团体客人

(4) individual guests 散客

(5) late arrival (late-show) 在预订保留期以后到达的客人

(6) checkroom (package and trunk room) 行李寄存处

(7) inquiry office (enquiries, information desk) 问讯处

(8) taxi counter 出租汽车服务台

(9) keyless lock system 无钥匙锁门系统

(10) emergency exit 紧急出口

(11) registration form (registration card) 旅客登记表

(12) deposit valuables 储存贵重物品

(13) hold mail 留交邮件

(14) check out time (hour) 离店手续办理时间

(15) understay 提前离店

(16) one bill for all 合单结账

(17) twin room with private bath 带浴室两张单人床客房

(18) double room with private bath 带浴室双人房(双人大床)

(19) change slip 客人住房变动单

(20) basement car park 地下停车场

2. Complete the following dialogues

(The tourist Mrs. Graham wants to have her laundry washed, she asks the guide Li Ming how to get the laundry service at the hotel.)

G＝Tour Guide   T＝Tourist

G: Good morning, Madam. May I help you?

T: Yes. ＿＿＿＿＿(1)＿＿＿＿＿(我想知道这里洗衣服务的时间).

G: ＿＿＿＿＿(2)＿＿＿＿＿(如果洗衣房在上午十点钟以前收到您要洗的衣服，那么当天晚上十点钟以前就可将衣服送到您的房间). If it is received before 3:00 p.m. you will get it back by noon the next day.

T: What's the rate?

G: ＿＿＿＿＿(3)＿＿＿＿＿(在梳妆台抽屉的文件夹里有一个价格表), Madam.

T: I see. Well, can you send someone up to room 202 to get some laundry for me?

G: Yes, I'd be glad to. ＿＿＿＿＿(4)＿＿＿＿＿(不过您可以给洗衣房打电话). The phone number is on the chart.

T: That's good enough. I'll make the phone call myself.

G: Well, there is a bit of trouble. It is 7:15 a.m., and the laundry is not open yet. ＿＿＿＿＿(5)＿＿＿＿＿(在梳妆台上面的抽屉里有个洗衣袋). If you put your clothes in the bag, and leave it outside your door, ＿＿＿＿＿(6)＿＿＿＿＿(客房服务员将在九点钟左右来取).

PART I ENGLISH FOR INBOUND TOUR GUIDES

T: That's good. But I want to have my dress washed and sent back to me before 6:00 this afternoon. I'll have to wear it at the party at 7:00 this evening.

G: Usually it takes about one day to have laundry done. _____(7) (请不要着急,酒店里有快洗服务)。

T: What's the difference in price?

G: _____(8)_____ (快洗服务额外加收15%的费用), but it only takes three hours.

T: And for the same day? _____(9)_____ (今晚我可以拿回衣服吗)?

G: Yes, Madam.

T: All right. _____(10)_____ (我就选快洗服务). Thank you for all the information.

G: It's my pleasure.

3. Translate the following sentences into English

(1) 这是诸位的钥匙卡。除了那一套间外,其他的房间都在四楼。行李员会帮诸位把行李送到各自的房间。

(2) 您的房间号是8018。请您填一下这张登记表好吗?请您把护照号码写在这儿。

(3) 这种药用来降血压,每天三次,每次两片。

(4) 酒店对在任何客房内遗失的钱币或贵重物品不负任何责任。接待处备有免费使用的寄存物品的保险箱。

(5) 请各位注意!我们明天早上七点半办理离店手续,请各位在早餐之前将托运行李准备好并放在门外。

Unit 2 Keys

Unit 3
Dining

Section 1 Situational Conversations

➤ Conversation 1 Seating the Guests

扫码听听力

(A tour guide and his tour group go to a restaurant. A waiter is attending to them. The tour guide seats his guests.)

G=Tour Guide　W=Waiter　T=Tourist

W: Good evening. Welcome to our restaurant.

G: Good evening. We want a private room with two tables, each table for eight.

W: I'm sorry, sir. The private rooms are not available now. But would you like to have your dinner in the dining hall? I can find two tables by the window for you.

G: No, thanks. We have made a reservation before.

W: Let me check the reservation list. Can I have your name, please?

G: My name is Wang Bo, I'm from China International Travel Service.

W: Yes, a reservation through China International Travel Service, The Rose Dining Room. I'll ask a waitress to show you the way.

G: Thanks.

T1: Is this the dining room?

G: Yes. Please come in.

T1: After you.

G: After you.

(All the guests are in the dining room now.)

G: Ladies and gentlemen, here we are in the Rose Dining Room. This is the coat rack, you can leave your coats here. This is the TV set and you can sing Karaoke after you enjoy your dinner.

T2: That's great!

G: Now, please be seated. Each table is for 8 guests.

T3: Excuse me, Mr. Wang, can I have a high chair for my son? He is too short.

The chair is too low for him.

G: Yes, I'll ask the waitress to bring a high chair for him.

(After a few minutes, the waitress comes in with a high chair.)

W: Is this chair all right?

T3: Yes, It's so good and comfortable. Thank you very much.

W: You're welcome.

Questions:

(1) What dining room does the tour group want?

(2) When the waiter tells the guide the private rooms are not available, what does the guide say?

(3) Which travel service is the guide from?

(4) How many guests is each table for?

(5) Why does the tourist want to have a high chair?

Notes

(1) The private rooms are not available now. 现在没有包间。

(2) Karaoke 卡拉OK

(3) We have made a reservation before. 我们先前已经预订了。

(4) reservation list 预订单

(5) coat rack 衣帽架

(6) You're welcome. 别客气。

➢ Conversation 2 At the Chinese Restaurant

(Li Qing, the tour guide, is with her two guests Mr. and Mrs. Black in a Chinese restaurant.)

扫码听听力

G=Tour Guide   W=Waiter   T=Tourist

W: Good evening, sir. Here is the menu.

T1: Thank you. Let me see what you have.

T2: Miss Li, can you show me how to use chopsticks?

G: With pleasure.

T2: Oh, it is not easy to learn!

G: I think you are a quick learner.

T2: Well, I don't think I can manage.

G: In that case, shall I ask the waiter to bring you a knife and fork?

T2: That's good, thank you.

T1: Miss Li, this is our first visit in China. To tell the truth, I have no idea of Chinese food. Do you, darling?

T2: I am afraid I don't either. Miss Li, could you give us a brief description of

Chinese food?

G: Yes. The Chinese food can be divided into four styles. They are Beijing style, Cantonese style, Sichuan style, Shanghai style.

T1: What are the different features of them?

G: Beijing food is heavy and spicy. Shanghai food is oily. Sichuan food is spicy and hot. This restaurant is famous for its Cantonese food.

T2: Would you tell us the features of Cantonese food?

G: Well, it pays much attention to the freshness, tenderness and smoothness of the dishes. The Cantonese food is light.

T1: I think we shall try the Cantonese food. Can you recommend some dishes to us?

G: How about "blanched chicken"? It is a famous dish in Guangzhou.

T1: That sounds nice.

T2: Can you order some vegetable dishes for us? I'm afraid I'm putting on weight these days.

G: Then how about these two dishes, "fried mushrooms and bamboo shoots" and "bean curd with hot pepper"?

T2: That is very good!

Questions:

(1) Why does the guide ask the waiter to bring the tourist a knife and fork?

(2) Do the tourists know Chinese food well?

(3) How many styles can the Chinese food be divided into? What are they?

(4) What are the features of Cantonese food?

(5) What dishes do the tourists decide to order?

Notes

(1) With pleasure. 很荣幸。

(2) in that case 假使那样的话

(3) Chinese food 中国菜

(4) freshness, tenderness and smoothness 鲜、嫩及爽滑

(5) blanched chicken 白斩鸡

(6) put on weight 体重增加，长胖

➢ Conversation 3　At the Western Restaurant

(Li Qian, the tour guide, recommends a western restaurant to Mr. and Mrs. Smith. The couple are having their dinner in the western restaurant.)

G＝Tour Guide　W＝Waiter　T＝Tourist

T2: Darling, these days we have tasted different Chinese dishes of different styles. I want to have western food for a change today.

PART I ENGLISH FOR INBOUND TOUR GUIDES

T1: Oh, Miss Li, do you have any good western food restaurants around here?

G: Yes, very near the hotel, there is the Red Rose Restaurant which serves western food. I'd like to make a reservation for you if you want.

T1: Thank you. Please make a reservation for seven o'clock tonight.

G: All right.

(At the Restaurant)

W: Good evening!

T1: Good evening! I'm John Smith. We have a reservation.

W: This way, please. Your table is near the window.

T2: Thank you.

W: Here is the menu.

T1: Thank you.

W: May I take your order?

T1: We haven't decided yet. Could you give us a little longer?

W: Yes, take your time, please.

T1: Can we get something to drink? I want a bottle of beer. My wife wants a cup of coffee.

W: Fine.

T1: Could you tell us your specials today?

W: The special today is steak.

T1: I'll take this steak dinner. My wife will have the same.

W: How would you like your steak?

T1: I'd like it medium-rare.

T2: I'd like it well-done.

W: What would you like to go with your steak?

T2: Peas and carrots.

T1: The same for me, please.

W: What would you like for dessert?

T1: Ice cream, please.

T2: No, thanks.

T1: Could I have the check, please?

W: Here's the check.

T1: Can I pay for the bill by credit card?

W: Yes, of course. Here's your receipt.

Questions:

(1) Why does the tourist want to have western food for a change today?

(2) What time does the tourist want to make a reservation for?

(3) What would the tourists like to drink?

(4) How would the tourists like their steak?

(5) What would the tourists like to go with their steak?

Notes

(1) Could you tell us your specials today? 你们今天有哪些特色菜？

(2) I'd like it medium-rare. 我要三分熟的。

(3) I'd like it well-done. 我要全熟的。

(4) pay for the bill 结账

(5) credit card 信用卡

New Words & Expressions

make a reservation 预订
menu ['menju:] n. 菜单
attend [ə'tend] v. 出席，参加，照顾，照料
rack [ræk] n. 行李架，刑架，拷问台　vt. 使痛苦
chopsticks ['tʃɒpstɪks] n.（常用复数）筷子
be divided into 可分为
Cantonese [ˌkæntə'ni:z] n. 广东人，广东话　adj. 广东的
freshness ['freʃnɪs] n. 气味清新，精神饱满
tenderness ['tendənɪs] n. 嫩，亲切，柔和，敏感，棘手
smoothness ['smu:ðnɪs] n. 平滑，柔滑，光滑，平坦
spicy ['spaɪsi:] adj. 加香料的，辛辣的
oily ['ɔɪli] adj. 油的，油滑的，油腔滑调的
hot [hɒt] adj. 热的，辣的
recommend [ˌrekə'mend] vt. 推荐
steak [steɪk] n. 牛排
pea [pi:] n. 豌豆
carrot ['kærət] n. 胡萝卜
dessert [dɪ'zɜ:t] n. 餐后甜点
blanch [blɑ:ntʃ] vt. 使变白，漂白
mushroom ['mʌʃrʊm] n. 蘑菇　vi. 迅速生长
shoot [ʃu:t] n. 嫩芽，幼苗　v. 开枪，射击，拍摄，打猎

Section 2　Text

Beijing Roast Duck

It would be a shame to leave Beijing without trying Beijing Roast Duck. It's Beijing's most famous dish and its taste is unique. Now let me tell you a bit about

PART I ENGLISH FOR INBOUND TOUR GUIDES

扫码听短文

how it became a popular dish and how it is prepared and served.

Beijing Roast Duck dates back to more than three hundred years ago, and originated in the Ming imperial kitchen. The recipe for roasting ducks was first developed by a chef in the service of a Ming emperor. Later, the method was passed down to the common folks by the old chefs retired from the royal kitchen. In 1835, a man from Hebei Province called Yang Quanren came to Beijing and began selling cooked chickens and ducks. Thirty years later in 1864, he opened a roast duck restaurant outside the Qianmen Gate and named it Quanjude. His ducks sold well because he used the recipe once used by royal chefs. Later, he began to use a new breed of duck known as the specially bred Beijing crammed (force-fed) duck. This sort of duck grew fast and had thin skin and tender flesh. He further improved the way of roasting ducks by using the open oven to replace the close oven. As a result, his duck became more tasteful and his restaurant soon became famous.

Beijing Roast Duck is prepared with a unique roasting process which gives it a perfect combination of color, aroma and taste, a crisp skin and a mouth-melting, delicious flavor.

Beijing duck is roasted in a specially constructed oven, which is square outside, has a crescent-shaped door, and is round inside, where there are two racks for hanging the ducks for roasting. Underneath is a fire pit where hardwood such as date, peach and pear is used as fuel. The fruit tree branches are supposed to be able to impart a fruity fragrance to the duck. Nowadays, however, electric ovens are used for environmental and sanitary reasons.

To prepare the duck for roasting, the duck is plucked and gutted and air pumped in. Then it is brushed with a maltase solution and dried in an airy place. The duck is then plugged, half filled with water and then it is ready for roasting. The knack of roasting is the time and temperature. A steady temperature must be maintained in the oven. Experienced chefs are able to regulate the heat and turn each duck so that it is evenly roasted. While the outside of the duck is roasted, the inside of the duck is steamed by the evaporating water. It takes about 50 minutes to roast. The duck is done when the skin turns crisp and golden brown. It is said that it usually takes one to five years to complete apprenticeship and fifteen years to learn all the tricks about roasting the duck.

When serving, the chef brings the whole duck to the table to let the guests have a look at its appetizing appearance, then takes it away and cuts it into about 120 thin pieces, each with both skin and meat. Diners dip each piece of duck meat into the sweet soybean paste placed in front of them. Then, wrap the meat together with stalks of shallots in a sheet of pancake and eat the roll with the hands.

Notes

(1) Beijing Roast Duck 北京烤鸭

(2) date back to 追溯至

(3) originated in the Ming imperial kitchen 产生于明朝的御厨房

(4) pass down 流传

(5) common folk 民间

(6) the recipe 秘方

(7) Beijing crammed (force-fed) duck 北京填鸭

(8) a unique roasting process 一个独特的烘烤过程

(9) color, aroma and taste 色、香、味

(10) mouth-melting 爽口

(11) a crescent-shaped door 一扇月牙形的门

(12) impart a fruity fragrance to the duck 将果香传递到鸭肉里

(13) the duck is plucked and gutted and air pumped in 将鸭子去毛、开膛、打气

(14) a maltase solution 一种麦芽糖溶液

(15) dried in an airy place 放在通风处晾干

(16) the knack of roasting 烘烤的诀窍

New Words & Expressions

unique [juːˈniːk] adj. 唯一的，独特的

originate [əˈrɪdʒɪneɪt] vt. 起源，发端于，创立

recipe [ˈresəpɪ] n. 配方，食谱，秘诀

royal [ˈrɔɪəl] adj. 王室的，皇家的，高贵的

breed [briːd] v. 繁殖，培育　n. 品种

tasteful [ˈteɪstfəl] adj. 高雅的，雅致的，优美的

fame [feɪm] n. 名声，名望　vt. 使闻名，使有名望，盛传

combination [ˌkɒmbɪˈneɪʃn] n. 结合，联合，组合

crisp [krɪsp] adj. 脆的

fuel [ˈfjuːəl] n. 燃料　vt. 加燃料，给……提供燃料

pluck [plʌk] n. 胆识，胆量　v. 拔去（鸡、鸭等的）毛

maltase [ˈmɔːlteɪs] n. 麦芽糖酶

knack [næk] n.（天生的或学会的）技能

steady [ˈstedɪ] adj. 稳固的，稳定的　v.（使）稳定，（使）稳固

evaporating [ɪˈvæpəreɪtɪŋ] v.（使）蒸发

apprenticeship [əˈprentɪʃɪp] n. 学徒制，学徒期，学徒身份

appetizing [ˈæpɪtaɪzɪŋ] adj. 开胃的，促进食欲的

dip [dɪp] v. 浸，蘸

soybean [ˈsɔɪˌbiːn] n. 大豆

stalk [stɔːk] n. 秆，（植物的）茎，（花）梗，（叶或果实）柄　vt.（非法）跟踪，潜近，趾高气扬地走

pancake [ˈpænkeɪk] n. 烙饼，薄饼，（化妆品的）粉饼

shallot [ʃəˈlɒt] n. 葱

as a result 结果

be supposed to 被认为

Exercises

1. Read and recite the following special terms

(1) cocktail party 鸡尾酒会

(2) welcome banquet 欢迎宴会

(3) farewell banquet 告别宴会

(4) buffet dinner 自助餐会

(5) continental breakfast 欧陆式早餐

(6) British breakfast (meat breakfast) 英国式早餐

(7) American (full) breakfast 美国式早餐

(8) table d'hote 包餐（客餐、和餐）

(9) a la carte 点餐（散餐）

(10) rare 三分熟

(11) medium 五分熟

(12) well-done 七分熟

(13) sweet and sour pork 咕噜肉（古老肉）

(14) twice-cooked pork 回锅肉

(15) steamed pork with salted dried mustard cabbage 梅干菜扣肉

(16) steamed pork with rice flour 米粉蒸肉

(17) fried spareribs with spiced salt 椒盐排骨

(18) diced chicken in chilli sauce 宫保鸡丁

(19) beggars chicken 叫花鸡

(20) mandarin fish in the shape of a squirrel 松鼠桂鱼

2. Complete the following dialogues

(The tour guide Wang Ming shows the tourist Mr. Smith to a restaurant and recommend some food to him.)

G＝Tour Guide　T＝Tourist

G：Oh, it is really a nice place to dine. ＿＿＿＿＿（1）＿＿＿＿＿（在你点菜之前要不要来杯开胃酒）?

T：No, I think I'd like to order straight away.

G：What would you like to have?

T：I'd like to try some Chinese food.

G：＿＿＿＿＿（2）＿＿＿＿＿（你以前吃过中国菜吗）?

T：No, I haven't. Back home, my friends talk about Chinese food all the time.

G：They serve different styles of Chinese food here. ＿＿＿＿＿（3）＿＿＿＿＿（但是我不知道你喜欢哪类菜）.

T: I have no idea about it. I'm in your hands.

G: Well, Cantonese food is rather light, Beijing food is heavy, and _____(4)_____ (川菜通常很辣).

T: Oh, I see. I'd rather have something hot.

G: _____(5)_____ (你可能想吃川菜). Most Sichuan dishes are very spicy and very hot. But they taste nice and different.

T: Really? So, what do you recommend?

G: I think _____(6)_____ (麻婆豆腐很特别).

T: All right. I'll have that.

G: Would you like to have some rice to go with this dish?

T: Yes. Please.

3. Translate the following sentences into English

(1) 中国菜的主要烹调方法有煎、炒、炖、蒸、煨。

(2) 在北方，人们早餐喝豆浆；而在南方人们喝大米粥。大米粥是用大米制作的流质食物，要长时间熬制。

(3) 中国的烹调历史比法国烹调更悠久。它是在高度文明中发展起来的一种艺术。

(4) 谈到广州人的饮食习惯，人们经常幽默地说，除了桌子以外，凡是四条腿的，广州人都用来当食品。

(5) 饺子的形式多种多样，水煮的叫水饺，蒸着吃的叫蒸饺，油煎的叫锅贴。

Unit 3 Keys

Unit 4
Transportation

Section 1 Situational Conversations

➤ Conversation 1 Asking the Way

(The tourist Peter wants to go to the Art Gallery, the tour guide Wang Gang is helping him how to get there and get back.)

G=Tour Guide   T=Tourist

G: Hello! Peter. You are going out alone?

T: Yes, I want to rub shoulders with locals this afternoon. I wonder if you could tell me where the bus station is.

G: Sure. But could I know where you'd like to go?

T: To the Art Gallery. Then, I shall take a walk at Wangfujing Shopping Center.

G: You don't have to take a bus. It's no distance at all, only about 10 minutes' walk.

T: Really?

G: Yes. Walk across the street at next traffic lights, go straight ahead, and the Art Gallery will be in front of you. You can't miss it.

T: Thanks a lot.

G: It's my pleasure. Well, let me write for you some slips of paper with some Chinese characters on them in case you get lost.

T: Oh, that's very considerate of you.

G: Look here, this one says: "I want to go back to Wangfu Hotel. Please tell me how to get there." Here is another one: "I want to go to the toilet. Please tell me how to get there."

T: What a wonderful idea!

G: See you, and have a good day!

扫码听听力

Questions:

(1) Why is the tourist Peter going out?

(2) What does Peter want the guide to tell him?

(3) Where would Peter like to go?

(4) How does the guide tell Peter to go to the Art Gallery?

(5) Why does the guide write some slips of paper with some Chinese characters on them for Peter?

Notes

(1) Art Gallery 美术馆

(2) rub shoulders with 与……有来往

(3) walk across the street 横穿街道

(4) traffic lights 红绿灯

(5) go straight ahead 笔直走

(6) in case 万一

(7) some slips of paper 一些纸条

➢ Conversation 2 Booking Tickets

(The tourist Miss Harring comes to the booking office of China Southern. The tour guide Li Ming shows her to the booking office. The booking office clerk greets her.)

C＝Booking Office Clerk   T＝Tourist

C: Can I help you, miss?

T: Yes, I'd like to book a flight ticket to Shanghai for the first of October.

C: Just a moment, please... There are two flights to Shanghai on the first of October. One departs at 7:05, arriving at 8:15. The other departs at 19:10, arriving at 20:30. Which do you prefer to take?

T: I'd like to take the evening one.

C: First class or economy class?

T: Economy class, of course.

C: OK, one moment, please. I'll check with the booking record to see if there's a vacancy left.

T: Sure.

C: You are lucky, miss. We have some tickets left. Would you like to book one now?

T: Yes. How much is the fare?

C: One way trip or round trip?

T: One way trip.

C: Economy fare for one way trip is 1200 yuan.

T: OK. Here you are.

C: May I see your passport, please?

T: Here it is.

C: Thank you... Keep your change. Here's your passport and your ticket. If there's any change in the flight schedule, we'll contact you.

T: Thank you very much.

Questions:

(1) What flight ticket would the tourist like to book?

(2) How many flights to Shanghai are there on the first of October? What are they?

(3) Which flight does the tourist prefer to take?

(4) Does the tourist want to take one way trip or round trip?

(5) If there's any change in the flight schedule, what will the booking office do?

Notes

(1) the booking office of China Southern 中国南方航空公司售票处

(2) first class 头等舱

(3) economy class 经济舱

(4) vacancy 空位

(5) one way trip 单程

(6) round trip 双程

➤ Conversation 3　Leading a Tour Group to Take the Train

(A tour guide is leading a tour group to the railway station. They want to take a train from Beijing to Guangzhou.)

G＝Tour Guide　　I＝Ticket Inspector　　T＝Tourist　　C＝Conductor

G: Ladies and gentlemen, this is the railway station. Please be in a line. Today we will take Train 15 to Guangzhou. The departure time is seven o'clock. It will arrive in Guangzhou at eight o'clock tomorrow morning. The train will leave from Platform 7, please take care of your tickets, we will have to hand our tickets to the ticket inspector. Now please follow me.

I: Your tickets, please.

G: These are our tickets.

I: Please come in.

G: This is Train 15, is everybody here?

T: Yes.

G: Our car is Car 14. Follow me, please. Here we are, Car 14.

C: Your tickets, please.

G: Here you are, altogether 10 people.

C: Please get on.

扫码听听力

G: Ladies and gentlemen, please put your suitcases on the rack. Can I help you with your luggage, Mrs. Smith?

T: Thank you.

T: Where is my berth, please?

G: It is over there. Let me show you.

(All the guests are seated.)

T: What program is being broadcast? The passengers are laughing.

G: It is called "cross talk", it is a type of comic show.

T: Oh, I see. Oh, look outside, it is green everywhere. It is different from Beijing.

G: Yes, due to the weather conditions, it is much more beautiful in the South in winter. Thus it is better to tour in the South at this time of the year.

T: Ah, you're right. By the way, where can I find the dining car? I feel like eating something.

G: It is Car 9.

T: Thank you. (The train stops at a station. The tourist finds that there is much food in the trolleys.) Oh, I think I can buy some food there.

G: Please be quick. The train will leave for the next stop within 5 minutes.

T: Don't worry.

(The train arrives at the railway station.)

G: Ladies and gentlemen, here we are in Guangzhou. Please get off the train. There will be a bus waiting for us outside the station. Are you ready?

T: Yes, indeed.

G: OK, let's go.

Questions:

(1) Which train will the tour group take to Guangzhou?

(2) When will the train depart? When will the train arrive in Guangzhou?

(3) How many people are there altogether in the tour group?

(4) What program is being broadcast?

(5) Which car is the dining car?

Notes

(1) Please be in a line. 请排队。

(2) ticket inspector 售票员，查票员

(3) Car 14 14号车厢

(4) Please put your suitcases on the rack. 请把手提箱放在行李架上。

(5) berth（船、列车等的）卧铺

(6) cross talk 相声

(7) a type of comic show 一种喜剧

(8) the dining car 餐车

New Words & Expressions

gallery ['gæləri] n. 画廊，美术馆，楼座，长廊

get back 回来

rub shoulders with locals 与当地人接触

character ['kærəktə] n. 特性，性质，字符，性格，特征，人物 vt. 刻，印，使具有特征

considerate [kən'sɪdərət] adj. 考虑周到的

toilet ['tɔɪlɪt] n. 盥洗室，厕所

depart [dɪ'pɑːt] vi. 离开，起程

economy [ɪ'kɒnəmi] n. 经济，节约，节省，经济状况

vacancy ['veɪkənsi] n.（职位）空缺，（旅馆等的）空房，空虚

fare [feə] n. 票价，费用，出租车乘客，饭菜

round trip 双程

change [tʃeɪndʒ] n. 改变，变化，转变，找回的零钱 vt. 改变，兑换

departure [dɪ'pɑːtʃə] n. 离开，出发

platform ['plætfɔːm] n.（车站）月台，讲台，讲坛，平台

produce [prə'djuːs] n. 产品，农产品 vt. 生产，制造，结（果实），引起

inspector [ɪn'spektə] n. 检查员，巡视员

conductor [kən'dʌktə] n.（乐队）指挥，售票员，列车长，导体

suitcase ['sjuːtkeɪs] n. 手提箱

trolley ['trɒli] n. 手推车，（运送食品、饮料的）小推车，电车

berth [bɜːθ] n. 泊位，舱位，卧铺 v. 使停泊

broadcast ['brɔːdkɑːst] n. 广播，播音，广播节目 v. 广播，播送

comic ['kɒmɪk] n. 喜剧演员 adj. 滑稽的，喜剧的

due to 由于

Section 2 Text

Public Transportation of Beijing

Beijing is so called the "Kingdom of bicycles", almost everybody has one. Bicycle is a convenient means of transportation, especially in the crowded city like Beijing. In recent years, private cars are rapidly increasing.

We also have the convenient subways in Beijing, which can provide the best choice for the citizens, especially during the rush hour. The subway in Beijing was the first one built in China. The construction of the first section started in 1965, and was completed in 1969. It starts from Beijing Railway Station in the east to Pingguoyuan Station in the west, with a total length of 23.6 kilometers long and 17 stations. The second phase was built in 1987, which runs around the city underneath the Second Ring road of Beijing. It is 16.1 kilometers long with 12 stops. The third line starts from Fuxingmen in the west to Bawangfen in the east with a total length of 13.5 kilometers and 11 stations. It was open to traffic in 1999. Upon completion, line1 subway runs from Pingguoyuan in the western part of Beijing directly to Bawangfen in the east of Beijing under Chang'an Avenue, with the interchange station at Fuxingmen and Jianguomen in the loop line while the loop line is considered as line2. In addition, Beijing's first complete light rail line, also known as No. 13 subway line, began operation on January 28, 2003. While the western half of the light rail line has been put to use since September 28 in 2002, people feel even more convenient for going in and out of the city by taking the light train. By the end of 2019, 21 subways has been built and put into operation. Thereby, the subway has greatly reduced the pressures of the evergrowing traffic on the street.

The public transportation in Beijing has witnessed rapid changes. In 1949, there were only 5 buses and 49 tramcars for the whole city of Beijing. But now the situation has been greatly improved, we have over 28000 public buses and 69000 taxies and the number is still growing. Now the public buses on the street are made in China, mainly in green with some yellow and red colors. The green color symbolizes the environmental protection; the yellow stands for the ancient imperial capital while the red represents the public transportation.

Before 1949 there were only 8 highways in the city of Beijing and 96% of them were muddy roads. After the founding of the People's Republic of China in 1949, construction of the road started. Up to now, we have more and more expressways and national level-A highways to different provinces. We also have many boulevards in the city, such as Chang'an Avenue (Everlasting Peace Avenue), the main boulevard runs from east to west in front of Tian'anmen Square through the center of the city. It is 40 kilometers long and 50 meters wide on average from Tongzhou District in the east to the Shijingshan District in the west; Ping'an Avenue starts from Dongsishitiao in the east to Guanyuan Bridge in the west. It is 7026 meters long and 28-33 meters wide. It was open to traffic in 1999; Guang'an Boulevard is 8 kilometers' long and 70 meters' wide that runs from Guangqumen in the east to Guang'anmen in the west. It was put to use in July 2001.

Apart from that, more and more beautiful overpasses have been built on the main roads in Beijing. These flyovers are playing a very important role in mitigating the heavy traffic of Beijing. The first flyover is Fuxingmen Flyover, built in 1974. Moreover, the smart transportation of Beijing is developing very fast and make people's travel more convenient.

PART I ENGLISH FOR INBOUND TOUR GUIDES

Notes

(1) kingdom of bicycles 自行车王国
(2) means of transportation 交通工具
(3) provide the best choice for the citizens 为市民提供最佳选择
(4) total length 全长
(5) the interchange station 联运车辆交接站
(6) loop line 环线
(7) going in and out of the city 进出城市
(8) tramcar 电车
(9) the environmental protection 环保
(10) light rail 轻轨
(11) overpass 天桥
(12) flyover 立交桥，天桥，高架公路

New Words & Expressions

vehicle ['viːɪkl] n. 交通工具，车辆，媒介物，传达手段
means [miːnz] n. 手段，方法 v. 意味，想要
subway ['sʌbweɪ] n. 地铁
convenient [kən'viːnjənt] adj. 方便的，便利的，合适的，附近的，近便的
provide [prə'vaɪd] vt. & vi. 提供，供给，供应 vt. 规定
construction [kən'strʌkʃən] n. 建造，建设，建筑业，建造物，建筑物，解释，意思
phase [feɪz] n. 阶段，状态，相，相位 v. 定相
loop [luːp] n. 圈，环，环状物，回路，循环 vt. & vi. （使）成环，（使）成圈
underneath [ˌʌndə'niːθ] adv. 在下面 prep. 在……的下面
completion [kəm'pliːʃən] n. 完成，结束
avenue ['ævɪnjuː] n. 林荫道，大街，方法，途径，路
interchange [ˌɪntə'tʃeɪndʒ] vt.（指两人等）交换事物，互换 vt. & vi.（使某事物）交替变化
underway [ˌʌndə'weɪ] adj. 在进行中的
boulevard ['buːləvɑːd] n. 大街，林荫道
pressure ['preʃə] n. 压，压力，电压
witness ['wɪtnɪs] n. 证人，证据，证明，证词 vt. 目击，为……作证 vi. 作证，成为证据
tramcar ['træmkɑː] n. 电车，矿车
environmental [ɪnˌvaɪərən'mentl] adj. 个人环境的，由个人环境产生的，环境的
stand for 代表
represent [ˌreprɪ'zent] vt. 表现，描绘，代表，象征，表示，作为……的代表

highway ['haɪweɪ] n. 公路，交通要道，（空中，水上或陆上的）直接航线或路线，最好的途径

average ['ævərɪdʒ] adj. 平均的，平常的，普通的 n. 平均；平均数 vt. 求……的平均数

symbolize ['sɪmbəˌlaɪz] vt. 象征，用符号表现 vi. 作为……的象征

mitigate ['mɪtɪgeɪt] vt. 减轻，缓和

Exercises

1. Read and recite the following special terms

(1)（hotel）shuttle bus（车站与旅馆间的）接送车

(2) one-way traffic 单行线

(3) car rental desk 租车服务台

(4) flyover 立交桥

(5) underpass 交叉道下道、地下通道

(6) car park 停车场

(7) monorail 轻轨

(8) lower berth 下铺

(9) mother-and-child room 母婴候车室

(10) cruise departure 游船出发港

(11) port of call 停靠港、（飞机）中间停留站

(12) port entry 入境口岸

(13) shore excursion 上岸旅行参观

(14) gangway (passageway, ramp, jetway) 跳板

(15) scheduled flight 定期航班

(16) automated ticket machine (ATM) 自动电子售票机

(17) safety inspection 安全检查

(18) boarding card 登机牌

(19) passenger coupon 旅客联

(20) baggage claim area 行李领取处

2. Complete the following dialogues

(Mr. White, a tourist, wants to see a friend working in China. After talking to the tour leader and the tour guide, he takes a taxi to see his friend.)

G＝Tour Guide　L＝Tour Leader　T＝Tourist　D＝Driver

T: Good evening, Mr. Smith, I have an American friend working as a visiting scholar in Zhongshan University. Can I go to see her?

L: Well, can you be back at the hotel tonight? ＿＿＿＿＿＿(1)＿＿＿＿＿＿（我们明天早上将去另外一座城市）.

T: I'll be back in two hours. My friend says it won't take long from Ramada

PART I ENGLISH FOR INBOUND TOUR GUIDES

Pearl Hotel to Zhongshan University.

L: Well, _____(2)_____ (我们最好让导游知道这件事).

T: All right.

T: Can I go to see a friend? She works in Zhongshan University.

G: _____(3)_____ (你告诉领队了吗)?

L: Yes, he promised me to be back in two hours.

G: Yes, of course.

T: Can you get a taxi for me?

G: Sure. _____(4)_____ (你想什么时间去)?

T: 10 minutes later.

G: _____(5)_____ (能告诉我你的房间号吗)?

T: Yes, it's 1736.

G: _____(6)_____ (我叫好了出租车就通知你).

T: Thank you.

G: (10 minutes later) Mr. White, _____(7)_____ (出租车准备好了).

T: Thank you, you've been so helpful.

G: You're welcome. (Mr. White is in the taxi)

D: Where do you want to go?

T: Zhongshan University. _____(8)_____ (你们怎样计费)?

D: We figure out the fare by meter. The first 3 kilometers are 8 yuan. Then every extra kilometer costs one yuan. _____(9)_____ (看计费器就可知道车费).

T: Oh, I see. How long will it take to get to the place?

D: Well, _____(10)_____ (那要看交通状况). It's not heavy this evening. We shall be there in 10 minutes.

T: Can you make a stop in front of a flower shop? I want to buy some flowers for my friend.

D: All right. There is a flower shop over there. _____(11)_____ (我们在下一个拐角处往右拐).

T: Thank you.

D: How beautiful these flowers!

T: Thank you!

D: Here we are. This is Zhongshan University.

T: How much do I owe you?

D: 23 yuan.

T: _____(12)_____ (这是车费,零钱不用找了).

D: Thank you.

3. Translate the following sentences into English

(1) 以里程计算,3千米之内6元钱,然后每超过1千米加收1元钱。

(2) 你是要单程票还是双程票?

（3）我们的游轮今天晚上 8 点离开始发港武汉，明天早上 7 点停靠岳阳，在那里我们将上岸游览两个半小时。

（4）武汉长江大桥是万里长江第一桥，1957 年建成，全长 1670 千米，由上下两层构成，上面是公路，下面是铁路。

（5）我要一张软卧票。请问去昆明的火车从哪一个站台出发？

Unit 4　Keys

Unit 5
Sightseeing

Section 1 Situational Conversations

➢ Conversation 1 Conducting a Sightseeing Tour in Hangzhou

(Wang Gang, a tour guide, is conducting a sightseeing tour in Hangzhou.)

G=Tour Guide   T=Tourist

G: OK, here we are in Hangzhou. There is an old saying in China which goes, "Up above there is paradise, down here there are Suzhou and Hangzhou." This shows the beauty of these two cities. The beauty of Hangzhou is associated with West Lake.

T1: I hear West Lake offers 10 scenic spots. Are we going to see all of them today, Mr. Wang?

G: No, not all of them. But we will see most of them.

T2: Here's the lake!

T3: It's such a lovely lake!

G: The lake has a water surface of 5.6 square kilometers.

T1: No wonder it looks so huge.

G: We are now walking on what is in fact an island. Here we get to one of the 10 scenic spots of West Lake—Autumn Moon over the Calm Lake.

T2: Why is it called "Autumn Moon over the Calm Lake"?

G: It's so named because in the pavilion over there the great poet Bai Juyi of the Tang Dynasty took a rest after drinking a little too much, and watched the moon over the lake.

T2: Very romantic.

G: Now let's board the boat and have a tour on the lake.

T2: Sure.

(They get on the boat.)

T3: Mr. Wang, what's that building over there? It looks like a huge pavilion.

G: You are right. That's the Heart of Lake Pavilion, situated on an islet. It was

扫码听听力

built in 1552 and is the largest pavilion on West Lake. Oh, here we are at the little Yingzhou Island. Let's get off the boat. Please watch your step.

T3: Oh, another world unveils itself to us.

T4: This is a paradise on the earth.

(After some time.)

G: Let's get moving. We've got to see one more place before heading back to the hotel.

Questions:

(1) What's the old saying about Hangzhou in China?

(2) What's the water surface of West Lake?

(3) Why is it called "Autumn Moon over the Calm Lake"?

(4) When was the Heart of Lake Pavilion built?

(5) Why does the guide ask the tourists to get moving?

Notes

(1) Up above there is paradise, down here there are Suzhou and Hangzhou. 上有天堂，下有苏杭。

(2) water surface 水面

(3) scenic spot 景点

(4) no wonder 难怪，怪不得

(5) Autumn Moon over the Calm Lake 平湖秋月

(6) board the boat 登船

(7) the Heart of Lake Pavilion 湖心亭

(8) the little Yingzhou Island 小瀛洲

(9) get moving 赶快，动起来，行动起来，动身

➢ Conversation 2　Taking a Natural Scenery Tour in China

(A tourist wants to take a natural scenery tour in China. The travel clerk suggests him going to Zhangjiajie.)

C＝Travel Clerk　T＝Tourist　G＝Tour Guide

C: Good afternoon! Can I help you?

T: I will have some holidays next week. I'd like to go to some scenic spots to enjoy the natural beauty, I don't know where to go. Can you give me some suggestions?

C: How about Guilin? The rivers and hills there are considered to be the best under heaven.

T: Yes, it is, but I have been there before.

C: Why don't you go to Hangzhou?

PART I ENGLISH FOR INBOUND TOUR GUIDES

T: Well, I have been there, too.

C: Then, have you ever been to Zhangjiajie?

T: No, never.

C: We have a four-day package tour to Zhangjiajie. It is in the mountains of a nature reserve in Hunan Province. It is worth seeing.

T: That's fine. I'll take the trip.

(The tourist is in the scenic spot now. He is with a tour group whose tour guide is Li Jun.)

G: Let's get off the bus, ladies and gentlemen. This is Zhangjiajie. We can take some time to look around. Please go back to the bus at four o'clock.

T: What a beautiful scenery!

G: Yes. It's really a nice place. The mountains have gradually eroded to form a peculiarly spectacular landscape of peaks and huge rock columns rising out of the forest. There are waterfalls, caves and streams everywhere.

T: This place is unique.

G: This is Jiangjun Cliff. On the right, it is Yuanyang Waterfall.

T: Oh, look at the people there! They are dressed differently.

G: Oh, they are people of the minority group—Tujia. This area is the home to three of the province's minority peoples—Tujia, Miao and Bai. These minority groups continue to speak their dialects and maintain their traditional culture.

T: Ah, I see.

G: On the way up, it is the Jumping Fish Pool.

T: It is so beautiful.

G: Did you enjoy yourself?

T: Yes, a great day I have!

G: It is nearly four o'clock now. We'd better go back to the bus.

T: All right, let's go.

Questions:

(1) Where does the tourist tell the travel clerk to like to go?

(2) How does the travel clerk describe the rivers and hills of Zhangjiajie?

(3) Where is Zhangjiajie?

(4) What are the characteristics of Zhangjiajie?

(5) How many minority peoples are there in Zhangjiajie? What are they?

Notes

(1) the best under heaven 甲天下

(2) a four-day package tour 四天的包价游

(3) nature reserve 自然保护区

(4) It is worth seeing. 值得一看。

(5) The mountains have gradually eroded to form a peculiarly spectacular landscape of peaks and huge rock columns rising out of the forest. 山岳受侵蚀，逐渐形成了"山峦跌宕，巨石林立"的奇观。

(6) Jiangjun Cliff 将军岩

(7) Yuanyang Waterfall 鸳鸯瀑布

(8) minority peoples 少数民族

(9) the Jumping Fish Pool 跳鱼潭

➢ Conversation 3　Visiting the Jade Buddha Temple

(A tour group visits the Jade Buddha Temple, the tour guide Wang Hui is giving an explanation to them.)

G＝Tour Guide　T＝Tourist

G：Ladies and gentlemen, your attention, please. Next we'll visit Jade Buddha Temple.

T：That's good. Could you give us some information about it?

G：Yes, of course. The temple is a monastery of great fame in the south of the Yangtze River, it was firstly built in 1882. Later the temple was partly destroyed by fire in 1918, it was rebuilt based on the architectural style of the Song Dynasty on the present site. There are five main buildings which are the Heavenly King Hall, the Grand Hall, the Hall of Reclining Buddha, the Jade Buddha Chamber and the Abbot's Room.

T：Well, considering the name of the temple, does the temple really house the jade Buddha?

G：Yes, there are two white jade statues of Sakyamuni enshrined in the temple. During the reign of Emperor Guangxu of the Qing Dynasty, a monk named Hui Gen from Mount Putuo went on a pilgrimage to India, Burma and brought back five jade statues of Sakyamuni. On his way back to Mount Putuo via Shanghai, he left two jade statues and had a temple especially built as a shrine for these two statues, hence the name Jade Buddha Temple.

T：Oh, I see. Thank you for your explanation.

G：It's my pleasure. Now, let's go inside to have a look.

(Entering the temple)

G：The first hall is the Heavenly King Hall which enshrines and worships Maitreya, the Laughing Buddha.

T：What is that big hall?

G：That's the Grand Hall. Its total construction area is nearly 3000 square meters, and from the ground up to the roof it is about 30 feet high.

T：It looks magnificent.

G: The Jade Buddha Chamber is on the second floor. Let's go upstairs.

T: How beautiful it is! It is carved of pure jade, isn't it?

G: Yes, the statue is carved out of a single piece of white jade. It is 1.92 meters tall and 1.34 meters wide. This Buddha is in sitting posture, the other one in reclining posture is enshrined in Reclining Buddha Chamber in the west of the monastery. Both statues are considered as precious relics of Buddhist art.

T: It's marvelous! No wonder the temple enjoys a good reputation.

Questions:

(1) When was the Jade Buddha Temple built firstly?

(2) What are the five main buildings of the Jade Buddha Temple?

(3) How did the Jade Buddha Temple get its name?

(4) What is the total construction area of the Grand Hall?

(5) How tall and wide is the Jade Buddha statue?

Notes

(1) the Jade Buddha Temple 玉佛寺

(2) a monastery of great fame south of the Yangtze River 长江以南的一座举世闻名的寺庙

(3) architectural style 建筑风格

(4) the Heavenly King Hall, the Grand Hall, the Hall of Reclining Buddha, the Jade Buddha Chamber and the Abbot's Room 天王殿、大雄宝殿、卧佛堂、玉佛楼和方丈室

(5) Sakyamuni 释迦牟尼

(6) went on a pilgrimage 朝圣

(7) Maitreya 弥勒佛

(8) It looks magnificent. 它看起来很宏伟。

(9) in sitting posture 呈坐姿

(10) in reclining posture 呈卧姿

(11) No wonder the temple enjoys a good reputation. 难怪这座寺庙享有如此高的声誉。

New Words & Expressions

scenery [ˈsiːnərɪ] n. 风景,景色

be associated with 与……有联系(有关)

calm [kɑːm] adj. (水面)平静的,沉着的,宁静的,心平气和的 vt. & vi. (使)平静,(使)镇定

pavilion [pəˈvɪljən] n. 亭,阁

unveil [ʌnˈveɪl] vt. 使公之于众,揭开,揭幕,除去……的面纱 vi. 显露,除去面纱

head back 返回

package ['pækɪdʒ] vt. 把……包装好，包装成　n. 包，包裹，盒，装，包装好的东西

reserve [rɪ'zə:v] vt. 保留（储备）某物，预订或保留（座位、住处等）

paradise ['pærədaɪs] n. 天堂

erode [ɪ'rəud] vt. 侵蚀，腐蚀，使变化　vi. 受腐蚀，逐渐侵蚀掉

peculiarly [pɪ'kju:lɪəlɪ] adv. 特有地，特别地

spectacular [spek'tækjʊlə] adj. 引人入胜的，壮观的

landscape ['lændskeɪp] n. 风景，山水画，地形

minority [maɪ'nɒrətɪ] n. 少数，少数民族

column ['kɒləm] n. 柱，圆柱，纵队，直行，栏，专栏（文章）

rise out of 拔……而出

dialect ['daɪəlekt] n. 方言，土语

monastery ['mɒnəstərɪ] n. 修道院

architectural [,ɑ:kɪ'tektʃərəl] adj. 建筑上的，建筑学的

recline [rɪ'klaɪn] vi. 斜倚，躺卧　vt. 斜倚，倚靠

Buddha ['budə] n. 佛

chamber ['tʃeɪmbə] n. 房间，（作特殊用途的）房间，会议厅，会所

abbot ['æbət] n. 男修道院院长，神父

Sakyamuni ['sɑ:kjəmuni] n. 释迦牟尼

pilgrimage ['pɪlgrɪmɪdʒ] n. 朝圣　vi. 朝拜，朝圣

enshrine [ɪn'ʃraɪn] vt. 入庙祀奉，铭记

be considered as 被认为

Burma ['bə:mə] n. 缅甸（东南亚国家）

hence [hens] adv. 从此时起，从此处，因此，所以

posture ['pɒstʃə] n. 姿势，姿态，看法；态度　vt. 做出某种姿势

marvelous ['mɑrvələs] adj. 引起惊异的，不可思议的，非凡的

Section 2　Text

The Yangtze Three Gorges

　　The Yangtze River is quite famous for its Three Gorges. The Three Gorges are a world-renowned tourist attraction. Beginning in the west at the White King City in Fengjie, Chongqing Municipality, and ending in the east at the Nanjin Pass in Yichang City, Hubei Province. It's 192 kilometers long and consists of the Qutang Gorge, Wu Gorge and Xiling Gorge.

　　The first gorge is the Qutang Gorge, just eight kilometers long, known for its majestic and overhanging precipices. In the gorge there are a lot of scenic spots such as the White King City, Kui Gate, Ancient Towing Path, Mengliang Staircase, Bellows Gorge and Daxi Town. Sighing over the marvelous sight of the Qutang Gorge, a famous poet of the Qing Dynasty ever wrote, "even ten thousand fluent pens, cannot describe the peaks along the Qutang Gorge."

The Wu gorge, the middle section of the Three Gorges, extends continuously for forty-four kilometers. It's famous for its secluded beauty. Its scenic spots are the Valley of the Golden Helmet and Silver Armour, Goddess Peak, Kongming Tablet and Beishi Town. The Goddess Peak is one of the twelve famous Wushan Mountain Peaks. According to legend, Yaoji, the youngest daughter of the mother of the western sky was very clever and smart, she once descended to the earth and passed by the Wushan Mountains. While there, she killed some trouble-making dragons with a thunderbolt, and helped Great Yu tame the Yangtze River. She finally felt so in love with the Wushan Mountains that she decided to remain. As time went by, her body gradually turned into the Goddess Peak. At some points of the Wu Gorge, the river seems to be blocked by a vertical cliff right in front, but a sudden turn of the boat brings it to another section of fine scenery. The twelve peaks of the Wushan Mountains have been well known since ancient times, they stand on the southern and northern sides of the Yangtze River, vying one another for beauty in their unique shapes.

The Xiling Gorge is seventy-six kilometers long, noted for its many rapids and dangerous shoals. It has a lot of scenic spots such as the Quyuan Temple, Huangling Temple, the Three-Gorge Project's dam site, the Fragrant Stream, the Gorge of Precious Sword and Book on the Art of War, the Blue Shoal and Kongling Shoal, the Gorge of Ox's Liver and Horse's Lung, the Three Travellers' Cave, Nanjin Pass and Gezhou Dam. In the Xiling Gorge, the swift current, boiling whirlpools and soaring waves made this section of the Yangtze River the graveyard of many a boat in the past. Since 1949, the navigation channel has been cleared of a lot of obstructions and the situation has changed greatly, ending the history that "the Three Gorges could not be navigated at night since remote past."

How were the Three Gorges formed? According to geologists and archaeologists, about seventy million years ago, the area of the present Three Gorges was a vast expanse of water. Later a crustal movement called the Yanshan Crustal Movement took place, resulting in the gradual rising of the earth's crust here. After many years' water erosion, the gorges gradually appeared.

Warm humid central Asian tropical climate dominates the area. The annual temperature averages 18.4 ℃. January is the coldest month with an average temperature of 7.1 ℃. July is the hottest month with the average temperature of 29.3 ℃. Annual precipitation averages 1000 to 1400 mm, most of rain falls in July and August when this area becomes one of the storm centers of China.

Local people are primarily engaged in manual agriculture operations. Agricultural products are rice, maize, sweet potatoes, oranges, tangerines and shaddocks. Medicinal herbs and raw lacquer are very abundant too.

In short, the beauty of the Three Gorges lies in their majesty, perilousness, singularity and seclusion, this applies respectively to every peak, shoal, cave and canyon in the Three Gorges. After visiting the Three Gorges, an eighty-year-old woman painter from the United States ever said: "I've been to over one hundred countries, the beautiful Yangtze and wonderful Three Gorges in China are the peak of my travels!"

Notes

(1) a world-renowned tourist attraction 一个世界闻名的游览胜地

(2) the Nanjin Pass 南津关

(3) the Qutang Gorge, Wu Gorge and Xiling Gorge 瞿塘峡、巫峡和西陵峡

(4) overhanging precipices 悬崖峭壁

(5) the White King City, Kui Gate, Ancient Towing Path, Mengliang Staircase, Bellows Gorge and Daxi Town 白帝城、夔门、古代的纤夫路、孟良梯、风箱峡和大溪镇

(6) Even ten thousand fluent pens, cannot describe the peaks along Qutang Gorge. 便将万管玲珑笔，难写瞿塘两岸山。

(7) secluded beauty 幽深秀丽

(8) the Valley of the Golden Helmet and Silver Armour, Goddess Peak, Kongming Tablet and Beishi Town 金盔银甲峡、神女峰、孔明碑和碚石镇

(9) thunderbolt 霹雳、雷电

(10) rapids and dangerous shoals 急流险滩

(11) the Quyuan Temple, Huangling Temple, the Three-Gorge Project's dam site, the Fragrant Stream, the Gorge of Precious Sword and Book on the Art of War, the Blue Shoal and Kongling Shoal, the Gorge of Ox's Liver and Horse's Lung, the Three Travellers' Cave, Nanjin Pass and Gezhou Dam. 屈原庙、黄陵庙、三峡工程坝址、香溪、兵书宝剑峡、青滩、崆岭滩、牛肝马肺峡、三游洞、南津关和葛洲坝

(12) The Three Gorges could not be navigated at night since remote past. 自古三峡不夜航。

(13) the Crustal Movement 地壳运动

(14) the Yanshan Crustal Movement 燕山运动

(15) warm humid central Asian tropical climate 温暖湿润的亚热带气候

(16) annual precipitation 年降水量

(17) In short, the beauty of the Three Gorges lies in their majesty, perilousness, singularity and seclusion, this applies respectively to every peak, shoal, cave and canyon in the Three Gorges. 总之，三峡之美在于它的雄、险、奇、幽，这里无峰不雄、无滩不险、无洞不奇、无壑不幽。

PART I ENGLISH FOR INBOUND TOUR GUIDES

New Words & Expressions

gorge [gɔːdʒ] n.（山）峡，峡谷，咽喉　vt. 阻塞，使扩张（+with）　vi. 狼吞虎咽（+on）
world-renowned [wɜː(r)ld-rɪˈnaʊnd] adj. 世界闻名的
municipality [mjuːˌnɪsɪˈpælɪtɪ] n. 自治市，市政当局
majestic [məˈdʒestɪk] adj. 雄伟的，威严的，崇高的
overhang [ˌəʊvəˈhæŋ] vt. 悬于……之上，突出于……之上　vi. 伸出，突出
precipice [ˈpresəpɪs] n. 断崖，绝壁，危急的处境，灾难的边缘
ancient [ˈeɪnʃənt] adj. 古代的，古老的　n. 老人，年高德劭者，古代人
marvelous [ˈmɑːvələs] adj. 令人惊叹的，非凡的，不可思议的
poet [ˈpəʊɪt] n. 诗人
section [ˈsekʃən] n. 片，块，部分，（文章等的）节，（条文等的）款，项　vt. 把……分成段（或组等）
extend [ɪksˈtend] vt. 延长，延伸，扩大，扩展
secluded [sɪˈkluːdɪd] adj. 与世隔绝的，隐退的，隐居的，僻静的
descend [dɪˈsend] vi. 下来，下降，下倾，传下来，来自　vt. 走下，沿……向下
thunderbolt [ˈθʌndəˌbəʊlt] n. 雷电，霹雳
tame [teɪm] adj.（动物）经驯养的，驯服的　vt. 驯化，驯养　vi. 变得驯服（或温顺）
block [blɒk] n. 块（+of），积木，街区，阻塞（物），障碍　adj. 大块的，成批的　vt. 阻塞，堵住
vertical [ˈvɜːtɪkəl] adj. 垂直的，竖的，立式的　n. 垂直线，垂直面，垂直位置
vying [ˈvaɪɪŋ] adj. 竞争的，竞赛的
rapid [ˈræpɪd] adj. 快的，迅速的，动作快的，陡的，险峻的　n. 急流，急湍
shoal [ʃəʊl] n. 浅水处，浅滩，沙洲　vi. 变浅　vt. 使变浅，驶入（浅水等）
dam [dæm] n. 水坝，水堤　vt. 筑坝于，筑坝拦（水），控制，抑制
graveyard [ˈgreɪvjɑːd] n. 墓地
liberation [ˌlɪbəˈreɪʃən] n. 解放（+from）；解放运动
navigation [ˌnævɪˈgeɪʃən] n. 航海，航空，航行航海术，航行学，领航，导航
channel [ˈtʃænl] n. 水道，航道，海峡，沟渠，手段，频道　vt. 在……开水道
obstruction [əbˈstrʌkʃən] n. 阻碍，妨碍，阻塞，阻塞物，障碍
geologist [dʒɪˈɒlədʒɪst] n. 地质学家，地质学者
archaeologist [ˌɑːkɪˈɒlədʒɪst] n. 考古学家
gradual [ˈgrædjʊəl] adj. 逐渐的，逐步的，（斜坡）平缓的
erosion [ɪˈrəʊʒən] n. 侵蚀，腐蚀
humid [ˈhjuːmɪd] adj. 潮湿的
dominate [ˈdɒmɪneɪt] vt. 支配，统治，控制，高耸于，俯视　vi. 处于支配地位（+over），高耸

average [ˈævərɪdʒ] n. 平均,平均数,普通,平均分 adj. 平均的,中等的 vt. 算出……的平均数
centigrade [ˈsentɪɡreɪd] adj. 摄氏度的,百分度的
manual [ˈmænjʊəl] adj. 手的,手工的,用手操作的 n. 手册,简介
tangerine [ˌtændʒəˈriːn] n. 橘子,柑橘,柑子,橘红色,橘子
herb [hɜːb] n. 草本植物,药草
lacquer [ˈlækə] n. 亮漆,漆,漆器 vt. 涂亮漆(或漆)于,使表面光洁
majesty [ˈmædʒɪstɪ] n. 雄伟,壮丽,庄严,权威,君权,(大写)陛下
perilous [ˈperələs] adj. 危险的,冒险的
singularity [ˌsɪŋɡjʊˈlærəti] n. 奇点,奇特
seclusion [sɪˈkluːʒən] n. 隔绝,孤立,隐居,隐退,隐蔽的地方,僻静之地

Exercises

1. Read and recite the following special terms

(1) The Palace Museum (The Forbidden City) 故宫(紫禁城)
(2) Sun Yat-sen Memorial Hall 孙中山纪念堂
(3) The Grand Mosque 大清真寺
(4) Shanghai Botanical Garden 上海植物园
(5) Seaside Pavillion 望海亭
(6) Outer Eight Temples 外八庙
(7) Resonant Sand Gorge 响沙湾
(8) Harbin Ice-Lantern Show 哈尔滨冰灯游园会
(9) Du Fu Thatched Cottage 杜甫草堂
(10) Songhua Ski Area 松花湖滑雪场
(11) Jinan Hot Springs 济南温泉
(12) Marine Products Museum and Aquarium 海产博物馆和水族馆
(13) The Tomb of Confucius (The Kong Family Graveyard) 孔林
(14) Suzhou Silk Printing Mill 苏州丝绸花印厂
(15) Zijin Mountain Observatory 紫金山天文台
(16) Mt. Huangshan Scenic Area 黄山风景区
(17) Longmen Grottoes 龙门石窟
(18) Yellow Crane Tower 黄鹤楼
(19) Zhangjiajie Nature Reserve 张家界自然保护区
(20) The Terra Cotta Warriors and Horses of Qin 秦始皇兵马俑

2. Complete the following dialogues

(A group of tourists is visiting the Great Wall. Li Ming serves as their tour guide.)

G＝Tour guide　T＝Tourist

G：_____(1)_____(我们正在靠近八达岭,过一会儿你们就可以看见长城了).

PART I ENGLISH FOR INBOUND TOUR GUIDES

T1: Wonderful! We've been waiting for it so long.

T2: What's the length of the Great Wall, Ming?

G: The Great Wall, ＿＿＿＿＿＿（2）＿＿＿＿＿＿（从东到西蜿蜒6000多千米或12000多米）. That's why we call it in Chinese "Wanli Changcheng".

T1: And it was built more than 2000 years ago?

G: Yes, ＿＿＿＿＿＿（3）＿＿＿＿＿＿（长城的兴建始于2500多年前的战国时期）. Small Kingdoms built huge walls hoping to protect their territories. When Qin Shihuang or the First Emperor unified China in 221 BC, ＿＿＿＿＿＿（4）＿＿＿＿＿＿（他决定把各段不同的城墙连起来加以延伸）. From that we got the Great Wall.

T2: And that's what we're going to see, right?

G: No, not really. ＿＿＿＿＿＿（5）＿＿＿＿＿＿（我们将在八达岭看见的这段长城建于明代）. Oh, here we are. Please remember the number of our bus and come back here before eleven o'clock.

3. Translate the following sentences into English

（1）大雁塔7层，高64米。虽然整个塔是灰砖砌成，风格古朴，但看上去与众不同，是典型的唐代建筑。

（2）西湖由两条古堤分成三部分。这两条堤用来控制山上流下的水，防止海风袭来时形成风暴。

（3）桂林的喀斯特风景最著名，很多画家和诗人都以此为题。桂林最引人注目的是奇特的山峰、地下河道和溶洞。

（4）巫峡西起巫山县的大宁河，东至巴东县的官渡口，全长44千米，以其幽深秀丽的风光而闻名。

（5）保和殿建于1420年，是举行"殿试"的考场。及第的考生还要在这里接受皇帝的最后考试。

Unit 5 Keys

Unit 6
Shopping

Section 1 Situational Conversations

➤ Conversation 1 At the Arts and Craft Store

(The tourists would like to buy pearl products, they asks the tour guide Wang Gang some information about pearl.)

G=Tour Guide T=Tourist

T: Mr. Wang, how many kinds of pearls in China?

G: There are two kinds of pearls, seawater pearl and freshwater pearl.

T: What is the difference between these two kinds of pearls?

G: There is a kernel in ocean pearls. First a grain of sand or a small plastic ball is placed in an oyster, then, cultivate it for five years in seawater, pearls will then form. Freshwater pearls have no kernel. The whole pearl is made of the same substance. At first, cut an oyster shell into tiny pieces. Put those tiny pieces in another oyster, after being cultivated for 3-5 years in freshwater, the freshwater pearls can form inside the oyster.

T: How can we tell the genuine pearl from the fake one?

G: If you snap a genuine pearl, you can hear a "sha-sha" sound, and see some powder. If you grind a pearl on glass, pearl powder will be left. Fake pearls have no powder.

T: How about the shape of a freshwater pearl?

G: The shapes of freshwater pearls vary from long ones, round ones to oblate ones. The round ones are more valuable.

T: How many different colors do freshwater pearls have? Which color is better?

G: The freshwater pearl has three different natural colors: white, golden yellow and purple. Purple pearls are very rare.

T: How are these natural colors formed?

G: The oysters absorb the metal trace elements from a river or lake. Golden yellow is formed by absorbing iron elements, white by silver elements, and black by copper elements.

T: Why do some people say freshwater pearls are also good curative products?

G: Freshwater pearls are not only a good ornament, but are also considered as a Chinese medicine. Pearl powder is good for the skin and has a curative effect on some heart diseases and hypertension. We can also use pearls to make pearl cream, which can make the skin smooth.

T: Thank you for your explanation, now I would like to buy some.

G: You are welcome.

Questions:

(1) How many kinds of pearls in China? What are they?
(2) How can we tell the genuine pearl from the fake one?
(3) How about the shape of a freshwater pearl?
(4) How are these natural colors formed?
(5) Why do some people say freshwater pearls are also good curative products?

Notes

(1) seawater pearl and freshwater pearl 海水珍珠和淡水珍珠

(2) a grain of sand 一粒沙子

(3) oyster 牡蛎

(4) the same substance 同种物质

(5) the genuine pearl and the fake one 真珍珠和假珍珠

(6) snap 咬

(7) grind 磨、碾、磨碎

(8) oblate 扁圆形的、扁球形的

(9) golden yellow 金黄色

(10) the metal trace element 金属微量元素

(11) good curative products 疗效好的产品

(12) Chinese medicine 中药

(13) pearl powder 珍珠粉

(14) heart diseases and hypertension 心脏病和高血压

➢ Conversation 2   At the Department Store

(A tour guide, Miss Li, and her tourist go to a department store. The tourist buys a dress at the store.)

G=Tour Guide   T=Tourist   C=Store Clerk

T: Are there any department stores near our hotel, Miss Li? I want to do a little shopping.

扫码听听力

G: Yes, there is a big department store just a few blocks away.

T: Can you go with me?

G: Of course.

(At the department store)

T: Where are the women's clothes? You know, most ladies are interested in clothes. I am not an exception.

G: It is on the third floor. There are different kinds of new fashions there.

T: Then, let's go upstairs.

C: May I help you?

G: No, thanks, I'm just looking.

T: These silk dresses are traditional Chinese. It is hard for me to choose one. They are all beautiful.

G: Take your time to choose the one you like most.

C: Can I help you, ma'am?

T: Yes, I want to look at these silk dresses.

C: We have a very good selection of silk dresses here. What color do you like?

T: I prefer the blue ones.

C: What size do you wear?

T: About size 13.

C: Here you are. It's size 13.

T: Can I try this on?

C: Of course, the fitting-room is over there.

T: It is a bit too large. Do you have anything smaller?

C: How about this one?

T: Yes, this one fits me well. What do you think of this dress, Miss Li?

G: It looks very good on you. It fits you perfectly and the color matches you very well.

T: Ok, I'll take this one. How much is it?

C: 500 yuan.

T: Well. It is too much. Can you give me a discount?

C: I'm afraid I can't. Our prices are all set in this department.

T: Ok, I'll take it. Here is 500 yuan. Please wrap it up for me.

C: Thank you.

Questions:

(1) Are there any department stores near the hotel?

(2) Does the tour guide go with the tourist?

(3) What color does the tourist like?

(4) What size does the tourist wear?

PART I ENGLISH FOR INBOUND TOUR GUIDES

(5) Can the store clerk give the tourist a discount? Why?

Notes

(1) just a few blocks away 仅离几个街区

(2) the department store 百货公司

(3) I am not an exception. 我也不例外。

(4) new fashions 新的时尚款式

(5) traditional Chinese 传统的具有中国特色的

(6) fitting-room 试衣间

(7) This one fits me well. 这件很适合我。

(8) The color matches you very well. 颜色与你非常相配。

(9) It looks very good on you. 它看起来很适合你。

(10) Can you give me a discount? 你能给我打个折吗?

(11) wrap up 包装，打包

➢ Conversation 3 At the Souvenir Department

(At the souvenir department, the tourist Mr. Smith wants to buy a cloisonné vase, the shop assistant is offering service to him.)

A＝Shop Assistant   T＝Tourist

扫码听听力

A: Good morning. May I help you?

T: I'm just looking right now, thank you. Oh, may I see some cloisonné vases?

A: Sure. Over there.

T: You seem to have quite a range here!

A: Yes. As a matter of fact, we are the biggest dealers in cloisonné in this area. Every day, we get hundreds of tourists coming in for different sizes.

T: Please show me that one on the second shelf.

A: Here you are. This one is bright-colored, and from Beijing.

T: I would like a medium-sized vase, and preferably something with a light blue background.

A: How about this one? The background is pale blue with Chinese traditional paintings of flowers and birds.

T: It seems to me that the Chinese paint flowers and birds everywhere.

A: In a way, the Chinese are naturalists, and flowers and birds are their favorite subjects.

T: Oh, this one is nice. I love it. It is distinctively Chinese. How much does it cost?

A: Two hundred and sixty yuan.

T: All right. Wrap it up for me.

A: Will you pay at the cashier's window over there, please?

T: All right. By the way, what do you accept here?
A: We accept cash, credit cards, cheques, and traveler's cheques.

Questions:

(1) What does the tourist want to see at the souvenir department?
(2) Which one would the tourist like to see?
(3) What kind of cloisonné vase would the tourist like?
(4) What are the favorite subjects of the Chinese?
(5) Where does the shop assistant ask the tourist to pay?

Notes

(1) cloisonné vase 景泰蓝花瓶
(2) a range 一系列
(3) as a matter of fact 事实上
(4) the biggest dealers in cloisonné 最大的景泰蓝经销商
(5) on the second shelf 在第二层架子上
(6) a light blue background 淡蓝色的底色
(7) favorite subjects 喜爱的主题
(8) the cashier's window 收银窗口
(9) We accept cash, credit cards, cheques, and traveler's cheques. 我们收现金、信用卡、支票和旅行支票。

New Words & Expressions

craft [krɑːft] n. 工艺，手艺，诡计，手腕
seawater [ˈsiːˌwɒːtə] n. 海水
freshwater [ˈfreʃwɔːtə] adj. 淡水的
kernel [ˈkɜːnəl] n. (硬壳果) 仁, 内核
substance [ˈsʌbstəns] n. 物质, 主旨, 实质
oyster [ˈɒɪstə] n. 牡蛎, 蚝
cultivate [ˈkʌltɪveɪt] vt. 培养, 耕作
genuine [ˈdʒenjʊɪn] adj. 真正的, 真诚的
fake [feɪk] n. 假货, 赝品, 冒充者 adj. 伪造的, 假的, 冒充的 v. 伪造, 冒充, 假装
powder [ˈpaʊdə] n. 粉, 粉末, 粉状物质 vt. 在……搽粉
grind [graɪnd] v. 磨(碎), 碾(碎)
oblate [ˈɒbleɪt] n. 献身教会工作的人 adj. 扁球形的, 椭圆的
absorb [əbˈsɔːb] vt. 吸收, 吸引
curative [ˈkjʊərətɪv] adj. 能治病的, 治愈的 n. 治疗物(法)
hypertension [ˌhaɪpəˈtenʃən] n. 高血压

exception [ɪkˈsepʃən] n. 例外
fashion [ˈfæʃən] n. 时尚，流行款式，时装
selection [sɪˈlekʃən] n. 选择，挑选，可供选择的东西
cloisonné [klwɑːˈzɒneɪ] 或 [klɒɪzəˈneɪ] n. 景泰蓝 adj. 景泰蓝的
vase [vɑːz] n. 花瓶
ornament [ˈɔːnəmənt] n. 装饰物 vt. 装饰
discount [ˈdɪskaʊnt] n. 折扣
souvenir [ˈsuːvənɪə] n. 纪念品
dealer [ˈdiːlə] n. 经销商，商人
shelf [ʃelf] n. 架子，搁板，暗礁
naturalist [ˈnætʃərəlɪst] n. 自然主义者
distinctive [dɪˈstɪŋktɪv] adj. 独特的，有特色的
cheque [tʃek] n. 支票

Section 2   Text

Shanghai Carpet Factory

The Shanghai Carpet Factory mainly produces hand-woven woolen carpets and a small amount of artistic tapestries. Most of its products are for export. The production process of hand-woven woolen carpets consists of three major procedures: preparation, formation and beautification. The six major workshops in the factory are those of wood spinning, dyeing, weaving, clipping, finishing and washing. Besides, there is a designing office. Today, we are going to see the three workshops of weaving, clipping, finishing and the showroom.

扫码听短文

Chinese carpets and tapestries have a long history. They are the traditional arts and crafts of China. Carpets in the ancient time were referred to as woolen "mats". The earliest ever produced was found in the cold and mountainous pastoral area in northwest China. That area abounds in sheep's wool, which is favorable for the development of the carpet industry. In the Han Dynasty, rugs were introduced into the Central Plains. The Yellow River valley is the cradle of ancient Chinese civilization. After the rugs from the northwest took root in the Central Plains, they absorbed the cream of the ancient Chinese culture and rendered the national color even richer. With the switchover of dynasties and the change of life styles, carpet production has gone through several ups and downs. But the carpet weaving technique has been developing all the time.

The Chinese carpets, varied in design, bright in color, exquisite in workmanship and durable, give a full expression of a unique national style. They not only embody the rich heritage of ancient Chinese art, but also integrate the cream of occidental culture in the patterns, bringing the carpets more to perfection, sorting out from a great amount of old designs and continually developing new ones by the artisans of various dynasties, four major patterns have been established. They are the Beijing design, the aesthetic design, the floral design and the plain antique embossed design.

As early as in 1903, Chinese carpets already won their reputation at the St. Louis World Fair for their unique beauty. They were accorded a gold medal at the 1965 Leipzig International Fair. In recent years, along with the development of foreign trade, new patterns have been created and developed. By taking the Chinese ancient art as a reference and "weeding through the old to bring forth the new", the Shanghai Carpet Factory has created over 100 and more classic patterns with silk rugs of high quality. These new patterns are closely related to the bronze art of the Warring States Period, the portraits and stone carvings of the Western Han and Eastern Han Dynasties, the paintings of plants and flowers of the Tang Dynasty and those of birds and flowers of the Song Dynasty.

In addition to the above mentioned four major types of carpets, the Shanghai Carpet Factory also produces artistic tapestry. It is the highest form of expression of the rug weaving art, an exquisite handicraft of superb artistry and typical national style. It is an embodiment of the talent and the wisdom of the rug weavers and it manifests an exclusive effect of the weaving art. The subjects of the artistic tapestry are based on famous paintings (including the traditional Chinese painting, water color, and oil painting) and photographs depicting the famous mountains and rivers of our motherland, historical sites, tourist resorts and works of famous painters both domestic and foreign, such as, the world famous Great Wall and the Temple of Heaven in Beijing, the Yellow Crane Tower, scenery of Huangshan Mountain and the Landscapes in Guilin, the "Galloping Horse" by Xu Beihong, a well-known Chinese painter, "Mona Lisa" by famous Italian Painter Leonardo da Vinci, etc. The finely-woven artistic tapestries, new and original in subject, rich in color and three-dimensional in appearance, are much appreciated by overseas customers.

Chinese carpets are world-famous for their carefully selected raw material and especially for the high standard of weaving technique, which greatly appeals to the customers. Seven types of fine wool from northwest China are selected for weaving the Chinese carpets. Such wool is characterized by its long fibre, high tensibility, elasticity and good lustre. They claim to be a high-quality raw material for weaving rugs.

The rug-making process is very complicated. Firstly, the sheep's wool needs to be carefully corded and spun into wooden yarn specially for rug weaving. Secondly, the woolen yarn is dyed with fine quality dyes into the right color phase. The dyed woolen yarn is treated acid-proof, alkali-proof and chloride-proof. The colors are fast and stand long wear, even after chemical cleaning and long use. The artistic effect of carpets finds its expression in the design. The process is complete through the stages of pattern designing, stencil drawing, color matching, weaving, trimming, clipping, washing and finishing.

The Weaving Workshop

Weaving is a major process. It is the decisive step in determining the internal quality, the external appearance, the artistic value and the practicality of the carpet. Rug weaving involves a high technique and a complicated operation. A weaver with woolen yarn in the left hand and a cutter in the right hand, dexterously ties with his fingers the woolen yarn 8-shape knots in the cotton warps. This is what we call knot-making. The knot is made so tightly that the back of the rug is strong while the front is soft and elastic. Rug weaving consists of making knots, packing the two edges, threading through the warp and cutting off the surplus wool. The pattern on a large-size carpet is made of thousands of such knots. Life-size patterns produce a superb and exquisite artistic effect through knots of different colors.

The Clipping Workshop

The clipping process is derived from ancient sculpture. The workers are engraving with electric scissors the patterns on the carpets to produce an embossed pattern resembling a bas-relief. The lines once embossed by scissors appear clear-cut and stream-lined. After washing there may appear around the patterns some naps affecting the appearance. In order to maintain clear-cut lines and different shades, it is necessary to give a finishing touch to the carpets by clipping off those naps. The clipping technique originated in Tianjin and was later introduced to Shanghai.

Chinese carpets are both high-class consumer goods and precious works of art. They should be well taken care of. When not in use, carpets should be rolled up in the direction of the adverse wool with edges neatly packed and kept in a cool, shady and dry place. When the carpets are in use, some measures should be taken to protect the spots that people often tread on and the parts that have somewhat worn out. The carpets should be turned around from time to time so as to reduce the constant pressure on the same spot. Besides, carpets should be dusted and gently swept in the direction of the wool. Cleaning tools should not be teethed or rough-edged devices lest the carpets be damaged. In case the carpets are stained with oil, you may rub it off with a fine-quality detergent. If a mark is left through pressure or adverse wool appears, you can first rub it with a wet towel soaked in hot water, and then comb the wool back to its original course, then place a wet cloth on the rug and press the spot to iron out the mark and adverse wool.

In a word, customers are advised to pay attention to the display and the upkeep of Chinese rugs, which would provide you an imposing, elegant and excellent art enjoyment. The carpets produced in this factory are available in the showroom. Cash, travelers' checks or credit cards are acceptable. Shipment can be arranged right on the spot.

Notes

(1) hand-woven woolen carpet 手工编织毛毯

(2) a small amount of artistic tapestries 少量艺术挂毯

(3) arts and crafts 工艺

(4) pastoral area 牧区

(5) That area abounds in sheep's wool. 那个地区盛产羊毛。

(6) the Central Plains 中原

(7) ups and downs 沉浮起落

(8) give a full expression of a unique national style 充分表达了其独特的民族风格

(9) occidental culture 西方文化

(10) They are the Beijing design, the aesthetic design, the floral design and the plain antique embossed design. 它们是北京式、美术式、采花式和素凸式。

(11) the St. Louis World Fair（美国）圣路易斯世博会

(12) the 1965 Leipzig International Fair 1965 莱比锡国际博览会

(13) weeding through the old to bring forth the new 推陈出新

(14) an exclusive effect 一个独特的效果

(15) three-dimensional in appearance 看起来呈立体状的

(16) long fibre, high tensibility, elasticity and good luster 长纤维、伸缩性强、弹性好和光泽明亮

(17) the right color phase 合适的色型

(18) The dyed woolen yarn is treated acid-proof, alkali-proof and chloride-proof. 染好的毛线经过防酸、防碱及防氯化物处理。

(19) The Weaving Workshop 编织车间

(20) knot-making 打结

(21) The Clipping Workshop 裁剪车间

(22) a bas-relief 一个浮雕

(23) clear-cut and stream-lined 轮廓分明和呈流线状的

(24) teethed or rough-edged devices 锯齿状和边缘粗糙的设施

(25) iron out 熨平

(26) the display and the upkeep of Chinese rugs 中国地毯的存放与保养

New Words & Expressions

woolen ['wʊlɪn] adj. 毛纺的

artistic [ɑːˈtɪstɪk] adj. 艺术的，有美感的，风雅的

tapestry [ˈtæpɪstrɪ] n. 挂毯，宴会厅的墙上挂有壁毯，绣帷，织锦

preparation [ˌprepəˈreɪʃən] n. 准备，预备，安排，筹备

beautification [ˌbjuːtifiˈkeiʃən] n. 美化
spin [spɪn] vt. & vi. 使……旋转　vt. 纺，杜撰
dyeing [ˈdaɪɪŋ] n. 染色，染色工艺
clip [klɪp] n. 夹子，回纹针，别针，剪，修剪，剪报，电影或电视片段
showroom [ˈʃəʊrʊm] n.（商品样品的）陈列室
mountainous [ˈmaʊntɪnəs] adj. 多山的，巨大的
pastoral [ˈpæstərəl] n. 牧歌，田园文学，田园诗　adj. 牧人的，田园生活的，牧师的
abound [əˈbaʊnd] vi. 大量存在，充满，富于
cradle [ˈkreɪdl] n. 摇篮，发源地，支船架　vt. 将……放在摇篮内
rug [rʌɡ] n. 小块地毯
render [ˈrendə] vt. 回报，归还，给予，呈递，提供
switchover [ˈswɪtʃəʊvə] n. 替换，转换
exquisite [ˈekskwɪzɪt] adj. 精致的，精美的，敏感的，细致的
workmanship [ˈwɜːkmənˌʃɪp] n. 手艺，技艺，技巧
embody [ɪmˈbɒdɪ] vt. 具体表达，使具体化，包含，收录
durable [ˈdjʊərəbl] adj. 持久的，耐用的
heritage [ˈherɪtɪdʒ] n. 遗产，继承权
integrate [ˈɪntɪɡreɪt] vt. 使结合成为整体　vt. & vi.（使）融入
occidental [ˌɒksɪˈdentl] adj. 西方的，西洋的
perfection [pəˈfekʃən] n. 完美，完善
sort out 整理，分类
artisan [ˌɑːtɪˈzæn] n. 技工，工匠
aesthetic [iːsˈθetɪk] adj. 有关美的，美学的，审美的，悦目的，雅致的
emboss [ɪmˈbɒs] vt. 装饰，浮雕（图案）
Leipzig [ˈlaɪpzɪɡ] 莱比锡（德国城市）
reference [ˈrefrəns] n. 提及，涉及，参考，参考书目，证明书，推荐信，推荐人
portrait [ˈpɔːtrɪt] n. 肖像，画像，生动的描写
embodiment [ɪmˈbɒdɪmənt] n. 体现，化身
originality [əˌrɪdʒəˈnælətɪ] n. 创意，新奇
brocade [brəˈkeɪd] n. 织有金银丝浮花的，织锦，锦缎
dazzling [ˈdæzlɪŋ] adj. 眼花缭乱的，耀眼的
manifest [ˈmænɪfest] vt. 清楚表示，显露　adj. 明白的，明显的
exclusive [ɪksˈkluːsɪv] adj. 高级的，奢华的，专用的，独家的　n. 独家新闻，独家报道
photograph [ˈfəʊtəɡrɑːf] n. 照片，相片　vt. & vi.（给……）拍照
depict [dɪˈpɪkt] vt. 描绘，描画，描述
gallop [ˈɡæləp] n.（马等）奔驰，骑马奔驰，（使马）飞奔，奔驰　vi. 快速做（说）某事
dimensional [dɪˈmenʃənəl] adj. 空间的

tensibility [ˌtensə'bɪləti] n. 伸长性

elasticity [ˌiːlæ'stɪsəti] n. 弹力，弹性

luster ['lʌstə] n. 光彩，光泽　vi. 有光泽，发亮　vt. 使有光泽

cord [kɔːd] n. (细) 绳，灯芯绒裤

yarn [jɑːn] n. 纱，纱线，纺线，奇闻漫谈，旅行轶事

acid-proof 抗酸性，耐酸性

alkali ['ælkəlaɪ] n. 碱　adj. 碱性的

chloride ['klɔːraɪd] n. 氯化物

stencil ['stensɪl] n. (有图案或文字的) 模板，刻字蜡纸，用模板印出的文字或图案

practicality [ˌpræktɪ'kæləti] n. 实例，实用性

dexterously ['dekstərəsli] adv. 巧妙地，敏捷地

warp [wɔːp] n. 弯曲，歪斜　vt. & vi. 弄弯，变歪

surplus ['sɜːpləs] adj. 过剩的，多余的　n. 过剩

derive from 来自

resemble [rɪ'zembl] vt. 像……，类似于

scissors ['sɪzəz] n. 剪刀

soak [səʊk] vt. & vi. 浸，泡，浸透，湿透　vi. 酗酒

detergent [di'tɜːdʒənt] n. 洗涤剂

adverse ['ædvɜːs] adj. 相反的，敌对的

upkeep ['ʌpkiːp] n. 保养，维修，维持

clip off 剪除

in a word 总之

shipment ['ʃɪpmənt] n. 船运，水运，(从海路、陆路或空运的) 一批货物

imposing [ɪm'pəʊzɪŋ] adj. 庄严的，仪表堂堂的，令人印象深刻的

Exercises

1. Read and recite the following special terms

(1) cornelian 红玉髓

(2) hand embroidery 刺绣

(3) clay figure modelling 泥塑

(4) Jingdezhen porcelain wares 景德镇瓷

(5) Tri-coloured glazed pottery of the Tang Dynasty 唐三彩

(6) Sichuan porcelain-bodied bamboo ware 四川瓷胎竹编

(7) Suzhou rosewood furniture 苏州红木家具

(8) the four treasures of the study (brush, inkstick, paper and inkstone) 文房四宝 (笔、墨、纸、砚)

(9) cloisonné 景泰蓝

(10) Suzhou sandal wood fan 苏州檀香扇

PART I ENGLISH FOR INBOUND TOUR GUIDES

(11) snuff bottle 鼻烟壶

(12) Beijing inner painted snuff bottle 北京内画壶

(13) batik 蜡染

(14) gemstone pendant 宝石坠子

(15) diamond bracelet 钻镯

(16) amethyst 紫水晶

(17) amber 琥珀

(18) turquoise 绿松石

(19) true jade (jadeite) 翡翠

(20) ink painting (black and white painting) 水墨画

2. Complete the following dialogues

(The salesgirl Yao Jun is serving the tourist Mrs. Smith to buy some local products.)

S＝Salesgirl　T＝Tourist

S：Good evening, Madam. What can I show you?

T：I'd like some silk figures.

S：We have several kinds. ＿＿＿＿(1)＿＿＿＿ (这些是中国古典小说中的人物,那些是传说中的人物).

T：This one is lovely, how much is it?

S：＿＿＿＿(2)＿＿＿＿ (不算玻璃框一百五十元).

T：Then how much with the glass case?

S：The case costs fifty-five yuan.

T：Can you pack the silk figure and send it to the United States for me?

S：Yes, we can. ＿＿＿＿(3)＿＿＿＿ (另收二十元的邮寄费). ＿＿＿＿(4)＿＿＿＿ (还要另收十五元的包装费), because we will have to make a special wooden box.

T：All right. I'll take this silk figure. Please ship it to this address. By the way, I'd like to buy a souvenir for a friend. He is a painter. Can you suggest something?

S：Sure. ＿＿＿＿(5)＿＿＿＿ (他很可能喜欢剪纸).

T：Good idea. They are beautiful and artistic, and easy to carry.

S：Yes, indeed. ＿＿＿＿(6)＿＿＿＿ (我们出售来自全国许多地方的剪纸). This one is from Shanghai, and that's from Guangzhou.

T：How much is one set?

S：This one is four yuan and seventy cents, and ＿＿＿＿(7)＿＿＿＿ (那一套三元五角).

T：I'll take five sets of this kind.

S：＿＿＿＿(8)＿＿＿＿ (还要点什么吗)?

T：No, thank you. Let's see what is the cost.

S：Two hundred and sixty-three yuan and fifty cents.

3. Translate the following sentences into English

(1) 这些壶是黏土做成的，叫作宜兴紫砂壶，这种茶具在中国非常有名。

(2) 这是复制品，但它充分保留了原件生动的气韵，以至于你很难判别真伪。

(3) 售货员说橱窗里陈列的那条珍珠项链现在没货。

(4) 中国茶分为绿茶、白茶、乌龙茶、红茶、黑茶 、花茶。你喜欢哪一种？

(5) 这幅画是真品，不是仿制品，所以价格较高。如果你想买，可以试着请售货员给你打个折。

Unit 6　Keys

Unit 7
Entertainment

Section 1 Situational Conversations

➤ Conversation 1 Talking about the Recreation and Fitness Center

(The tour guide Wang Gang tells the tourist Mr. Smith some information about the recreation and fitness center of the hotel.)

G=Tour Guide   T=Tourist

扫码听听力

G: Anything particular you'd like to do this evening?

T: I don't know. Is there anything interesting to do in the hotel?

G: Sure. There is a musical fountain performance in the discotheque near the lobby. People can enjoy the beautiful fountains while listening to the wonderful music.

T: Mm, sounds interesting.

G: There are various computer games in the recreation center.

T: And do they have a fitness center here?

G: Yes, they have one. It's on the second floor.

T: What service do they have?

G: Massage and sauna. Apart from that, they also have facilities like a very big swimming pool, a gym, a billiards room, a bowling room...

T: That's great! Bowling is my favorite. I must go and enjoy myself. Is it open now?

G: It's 19:10. Yes, it's open now.

T: Super! Thank you for your information.

Questions:

(1) What does the tour guide ask the tourist?

(2) What does the tourist ask the tour guide?

(3) Where is the discotheque?

(4) What are there in the Recreation Center?

(5) Where can the tourist get massage and sauna services?

Notes

(1) There is a musical fountain performance in the discotheque near the lobby. 在大厅附近的迪斯科舞厅里有一个音乐喷泉表演。

(2) computer games 电脑游戏

(3) recreation center 娱乐中心

(4) musical fountain performance 音乐喷泉

(5) fitness center 健身中心

(6) massage and sauna 按摩和桑拿

(7) apart from 除……之外

(8) billiards room 台球室

(9) bowling room 保龄球馆

▶ Conversation 2　Booking Tickets for Beijing Opera

(The tourist Mrs. Freeman asks the tour guide Li Ming to book tickets for Beijing Opera.)

G＝Tour Guide　T＝Tourist

G：Good evening, Mrs. Freeman, thinking of doing anything interesting?

T：My husband and I would like to go to a Beijing Opera. What theater would you recommend?

G：How about the Capital Theater?

T：What's on this evening?

G：The program includes "The Monkey King" and "The Autumn River". Would you like to go?

T：Yes. Can you get me some tickets?

G：How many tickets would you like to have?

T：Two.

G：One moment, please. Let me contact them for you... I'm sorry, there aren't any tickets left for this evening. Is tomorrow evening all right?

T：Tomorrow evening will also be fine.

G：Please pick up the tickets here tomorrow afternoon at your convenience.

T：Thank you very much.

G：There is a football match on TV channel 8, if you care to watch that.

T：Oh, no. Don't tell my husband about that. He gets totally involved whenever there is a football match on the TV.

G：OK, then I'll keep quiet about it.

Questions:

(1) What would the tourists like to do?

(2) Which theater does the tour guide recommend to the tourists?

(3) What's on this evening?

(4) Has the tour guide bought this evening's tickets? Why?

(5) Why does Mrs. Freeman ask the tour guide not to tell her husband there is a football match on TV channel 8?

Notes

(1) Beijing Opera 京剧

(2) the Capital Theater 首都剧场

(3) pick up the tickets 取票

(4) at your convenience 在你方便的时候

➢ Conversation 3　Making Appointment

(The tourist Mr. Smith asks the tour guide Yang Hui how to get the massage service.)

扫码听听力

G＝Tour Guide　T＝Tourist

T: Mr. Yang, where can I get the massage service?

G: Massage is provided in the massage room on the third deck. Here is the appointment form. When would you want to take massage?

T: Right now.

G: Sorry. The masseur is engaged at this time. But he is available at these times. Would you like to choose another time?

T: Is 7:00 p.m. OK?

G: I don't think this is a good time, because at this time, there is a crew's show and I do not think you want to miss the show.

T: Then is it 9:30 p.m. all right?

G: 9:30 p.m. is OK. May I put down your name and cabin number?

T: My name is Black Smith and my room number is 315.

G: OK, the appointment has been made. The masseur will be in the massage room and wait for you at that time. Enjoy the massage.

Questions:

(1) Where can the tourist get the massage service?

(2) What does the tour guide give the tourist?

(3) Why doesn't the tour guide think 7:00 p.m. is a good time?

(4) What time has the tourist chosen finally?

(5) What's the room number of the tourist?

Notes

(1) the third deck 第三层甲板

(2) Here is the appointment form. 这是预约表。

(3) masseur 男按摩师

(4) The masseur is engaged at this time. 按摩师现在没空。

(5) But he is available at these times. 但他这些时间有空。

(6) put down your name 记下你的名字

(7) cabin number 房间号

New Words & Expressions

recreation [ˌriːkrɪ'eɪʃn] n. 娱乐(方式)，消遣(方式)

fitness ['fɪtnɪs] n. 健康，适当，适切性

discotheque ['dɪskətek] n. 迪斯科舞厅

corridor ['kɒrɪdɔː] n. 走廊

apart from 除……之外

massage ['mæsɑːʒ] n. 按摩 v. 按摩

sauna ['sɔːnə] n. 桑拿浴

gym [dʒɪm] n. 健身房，体育馆

billiard ['bɪljəd] adj. 台球的

bowling ['bəʊlɪŋ] n. 保龄球

convenience [kən'viːnjəns] n. 方便，便利，便利的事物(或设施)，方便的用具

appointment [ə'pɔɪntmənt] n. 约会，约定，任命，委派

masseur [mæ'sɜː] n. 男按摩师

engaged [ɪn'geɪdʒd] adj. 已订婚的，从事于，忙于，被占用的

Section 2 Text

Peking Opera

Peking Opera has a history of over 200 years already. Originally Peking Opera was a form of local theater, but now it has become the national-opera of China. Like most Chinese local operas, it is truly a comprehensive art combining stylized acting with singing, acrobatics and colorful costumes.

Before Peking Opera, Kun Opera was a very popular opera in Beijing, especially in the Imperial Palace and among the upper classes in Beijing. About 200 years ago,

Emperor Qianlong of the Qing Dynasty toured in southern China and developed an interest in the local operas. On his 80th birthday, he had different local opera troupes come to Beijing to perform for him. After the birthday celebration, four famous troupes from Anhui Province remained in Beijing. Because of its vigorous clear tones, Anhui Opera gradually replaced Kun Opera, and gradually became very popular in the palace and among the upper classes. Later in 1828, another troupe from Hubei Province came to Beijing. They often performed together with Anhui troupes. The two types of singing blended on the same stage. They naturally learnt from each other, taking in the strong points from others to enrich their own skill and then by integrating the Beijing accent into their singing. Gradually it gave birth to a new opera—Peking Opera, which assimilated the best elements from operatic forms.

The singing in Peking Opera can greatly enable the performers to express the thoughts and emotions of different characters in different situations. You can learn any plot by movement or gesture, even without speaking. Acting in Peking Opera can show a vivid plot by movements and gestures, such as stroking a beard, swing a long sleeve or lifting a foot, etc. The performers use gestures and body movements to represent actions to suggest something that is non-existent on the stage, for instance: opening and closing a door, going up or down stairs or a mountain, and getting on or getting off or traveling by the boat, etc. Through hand gestures the performers can give the audience a sense of reality. Peking Opera combines stylized acting with singing, dancing, dialogue, colorful facial make-up, acrobatic fighting and fantastic costumes.

There are five main types in Peking Opera: Sheng (male roles), Dan (female roles), Jing (martial roles), Mo (male aged roles) and Chou (clown roles). Each type of role is recognizable by its costume and, in some cases, by its make-up. Each of the patterns and brilliant colors on the "painted faces" has a symbolic meaning: when red is the main color, it suggests loyalty, blue suggests cruelty, yellow suggests cunning, white suggests treachery.

Language in the Peking Opera is hard to understand because of the opera styled pronunciation and intonation as well as the archaic Chinese. But people can understand the plot through the performers' action. Everything the actor does— entrance, exits, hand gestures and movements, all according to a stylized routine: a decorated whip represents an actor riding a horse; riding a carriage is represented by an attendant holding two flags painted with a wheel design on either side of the performer; when an actor walks in a circle, it means he has gone on a long journey; four generals and four soldiers signify an army of thousands; two actors can portray groping and fighting in the dark through dance and acrobatics on a brightly lit stage, etc. The skillful techniques of the singing, dancing and acrobatics are really an art of

Peking Opera.

The musical instruments accompanying the Peking Opera are string and wind instruments as well as Chinese styled percussion instruments—gongs, drums and bamboo castanets. The most important one is a kind of two-stringed musical instrument—Erhu or Jinghu in Chinese.

The famous Dan actor Mr. Mei Lanfang was the first performer to introduce Peking Opera to Japan in 1919, to the United States in 1929 and to the Soviet Union in 1935. After 1949, Peking Opera troupes made frequent trips abroad, such as Europe, America, and Africa, etc. Today Peking Opera has won high praise around the world.

Notes

(1) the national-opera of China 中国的国剧

(2) different local opera troupes 不同的地方剧团

(3) taking in the strong points 吸收优点

(4) You can learn any plot by movement or gesture, even without speaking. 你可以通过动作或手势获知任何情节,甚至不用说话。

(5) stroking a beard, swing a long sleeve or lifting a foot 抚摸一下胡须,摆动一下长袖或抬一抬脚

(6) the archaic Chinese 古汉语

(7) a stylized routine 一个固定的程序

(8) string and wind instruments 弦乐器和管乐器

(9) Chinese styled percussion instruments 中国式打击乐器

(10) bamboo castanets 竹制响板

(11) Imperial Palace 皇城

(12) Sheng (male roles), Dan (female roles), Jing (martial roles), Mo (male aged roles) and Chou (clown roles) 生、旦、净、末、丑

(13) Erhu or Jinghu 二胡或京胡

New Words & Expressions

comprehensive [ˌkɒmprɪˈhensɪv] adj. 广泛的,综合的,有充分理解力的

combine [kəmˈbaɪn] vt. 使结合,使联合(+with) vi. 结合(+against),化合(+with)

stylize [ˈstaɪˌlaɪz] vt. 风格化,使格式化,使程序化

acrobatics [ˌækrəˈbætɪks] n. 杂技,杂技表演,技巧,特技飞行

costume [ˈkɒstjuːm] n. 服装,装束,戏装 vt. 给……穿上服装

upper [ˈʌpə] a. 较高的;上面的;上首的 n. 鞋帮;上铺;上齿

emperor [ˈempərə] n. 皇帝,帝王,君主

troupe [truːp] n. (演员等的)一团,一班(+of) vi. 巡回演出

vigorous ['vɪgərəs] adj. 精力充沛的，健壮的，强有力的
tone [təʊn] n. 音，音色 音调，腔调，语气　vt. 用某种调子说　vi. 颜色调和（＋with）
blend [blend] vt. 使混合，使混杂，使交融（＋with/into）vi. 混合（＋into/with）n. 混合物
stage [steɪdʒ] n. 舞台，戏剧，阶段　vt. 上演　vi.（剧本）适于上演
enrich [ɪn'rɪtʃ] vt. 使富裕，使丰富，使（土壤）肥沃，装饰，增进（食品的）营养价值
integrate ['ɪntɪgreɪt] vt. 使成一体，使结合，使完整，使完善　vi. 成为一体
accent ['æksənt] n. 重音，重音符号，口音，腔调，语调，声调　vt. 重读，强调，带……口音讲话
assimilate [ə'sɪməleɪt] vt. 消化吸收（食物），理解，使（民族、语音）同化　vi. 被同化
element ['elɪmənt] n. 元素，要素，成分，一点儿
operatic [ˌɒpə'rætɪk] adj. 歌剧的，似歌剧的
character ['kærɪktə] n.（人的）品质，性格，（事物的）性质，特性　vt. 描述，使具有特性
plot [plɒt] n.（小说，戏剧等的）情节，小块土地　vt. 标绘，测定（点，线）的位置
movement ['muːvmənt] n. 运动，活动，动作，姿态，倾向，动向
gesture ['dʒestʃə] n. 姿势，手势，姿态，表示　v. 做手势，用动作示意
vivid ['vɪvɪd] adj. 鲜明的，活泼的，生动的
represent [ˌreprɪ'zent] v. 代表，描绘，表现，象征，表示，表述
audience ['ɔːdjəns] n. 听众，观众，读者群
sense [sens] n. 感官，官能，感觉，意识，观念　vt. 感觉到，意识到
reality [rɪ'æləti] n. 现实，真实，事实，实际存在的事物
facial ['feɪʃəl] adj. 脸的，面部的　n. 脸部按摩，美容
fantastic [fæn'tæstɪk] adj. 奇异的，古怪的，很棒的，了不起的
recognizable ['rekəgnaɪzəbl] adj. 可辨认的，可识别的，可承认的
pattern ['pætən] n. 花样，图案，形态，样式，样品　vt. 以图案装饰，给……加上花样
symbolic [sɪm'bɒlɪk] adj. 象征的，象征性的，作为象征的（＋of）
loyalty ['lɔɪəlti] n. 忠诚，忠心（＋to）
cruelty ['kruːəlti] n. 残酷，残忍，残酷的行为
cunning ['kʌnɪŋ] adj. 狡猾的，奸诈的，精巧的，熟练的，灵巧的　n. 狡猾，奸诈，灵巧，熟练
treachery ['tretʃəri] n. 背叛，变节，背信
pronunciation [prəˌnʌnsɪ'eɪʃən] n. 发音，发音法，读法
intonation [ˌɪntə'neɪʃən] n. 语调，声调，抑扬之声，吟诵
routine [ruː'tiːn] n. 例行公事，日常工作，惯例　adj. 日常的，例行的，常规的

decorate ['dekəreɪt] vt. 装饰，点缀，粉刷　vi. 装饰，布置
whip [wɪp] n. 鞭子，抽打　vt. 鞭笞，抽打　vi. 抽打，拍击
carriage ['kærɪdʒ] n. 四轮马车，（火车）客车厢，婴儿车，运输，运费
circle ['sɜːkl] n. 圆，圆圈　vt. 画圆圈，圈出，围着　vi. 盘旋，旋转，环行
general ['dʒenərəl] n. 将军，上将，一般　adj. 一般的，普遍的，非专业性的，全体的，公众的
soldier ['səʊldʒə] n. 兵，士兵　vi. 当兵，服兵役
siginify ['sɪgnɪfaɪ] vt. 表示，表明，示意，意味着，预示　vi. 有重要性，要紧
portray [pɔːˈtreɪ] vt. 描写，描绘，扮演
instrument ['ɪnstrəmənt] n. 仪器，器具，器械，乐器，手段，工具
string [strɪŋ] n. 琴弦，弦乐，线，细绳，带子　vt. 缚，扎，挂　vi. 成线索状，连成一串
percussion [pəˈkʌʃən] n. 打，敲，冲击，振动，敲打乐器
gong [gɒŋ] n. 锣，铜锣
drum [drʌm] n. 鼓，圆桶　v. 打鼓
bamboo [bæmˈbuː] n. 竹，竹子

Exercises

1. Read and recite the following special terms

(1) recreation center 娱乐中心
(2) discotheque 迪斯科舞厅
(3) fitness center 健身中心
(4) mahjong 麻将
(5) billiards (snooker) 台球
(6) skating rink 滑冰场
(7) race court 跑马场
(8) member charges 会员收费标准
(9) beauty parlour (beauty shop) 美容室
(10) to have one's hair done (to have hair set) 做头发
(11) race apparatus 跑步机
(12) symphonic music 交响乐
(13) string instrument 弦乐器
(14) plucked instrument 弹拨乐器
(15) percussion instrument 打击乐器
(16) wind instrument 管乐器
(17) type of facial make-up (facial type) 脸谱
(18) shadow show 皮影戏
(19) girl poses as boy 女扮男装
(20) turning a somersault (loop the loop) 翻筋斗

PART I ENGLISH FOR INBOUND TOUR GUIDES

2. Complete the following dialogues

(The tour guide Huang Jun shows the tourists to watch a performance by Chinese Acrobatic Circus.)

G=Tour Guide　T=Tourist

T：What activities are we going to have tonight?

G：_____(1)_____ (我们将去看中国杂技团表演节目).

T：That's great!

G：The programs are marvelous, _____(2)_____ (其中一些节目赢得了各种知名的国际竞赛金奖), such as in France, Hungary, Russia and Italy.

T：What kind of things do they have?

G：All kinds. They have _____(3)_____ (魔术表演), flying trapeze acts, _____(4)_____ (走钢丝) and even the clowns. It is a combination of Chinese acrobatic art, Chinese kungfu, Chinese dance and Chinese music.

T：That's great! I am eager to go now. When and where is it on?

G：It is on in Poly Plaza International Theatre at seven o'clock.

T：It is already 6:30 now, Let's go.

(At the theatre)

T：Look at _____(5)_____ (空中飞人). They are scary! I am afraid that the acrobats might fell down to the ground.

G：Don't worry about them. _____(6)_____ (他们都是技术高超的杂技演员), and what is more, they have safety ropes fastened on them.

T：They are doing a very hard and dangerous job. It is really breathtaking.

G：Look at this program. _____(7)_____ (这个节目很滑稽轻松).

T：Ah, the clown is doing tightrope walking. _____(8)_____ (他正在同观众做鬼脸).

G：It is not an easy job, isn't it?

T：No, this would also take a lot of skill. What a special costume he has!

G：Now, look at the girl who is building a pagoda of bowls. This program won a gold medal in the international acrobatic contest in Italy.

T：Oh, this is incredible.

G：_____(9)_____ (你觉得今晚的节目怎么样)?

T：_____(10)_____ (这些节目很有中国特色). The dance, the music, the costume and the art are so wonderful. This circus gave me a touch of the Chinese culture.

G：I am glad to hear that.

3. Translate the following sentences into English

(1) 中国有几百种地方戏曲。每一种戏曲在曲调、音乐和方言上都不同。但在表演形式方面，大多数中国传统戏曲却有共同之处。

(2) 中国的每个民族都有本民族的乐器,总共有三百多种,分为四类。

（3）这个小提琴演奏叫《梁祝》。梁山伯与祝英台是中国古代的一对恋人，他们是中国的罗密欧和朱丽叶。因此这个演奏反映的是中国古代的一个爱情故事。

（4）这是你们观看杂技演出的门票，你们的座位是7号和8号，都在D排。

（5）这艘游船的健身房在第四层甲板上，里面有各种各样的健身器材，你们可以免费使用。

Unit 7　Keys

Unit 8
Farewell

Section 1 Situational Conversations

Conversation 1 Bidding Farewell to the Tourist

(The tour guide Li Fang is bidding farewell to the tourist Mr. Graham who is leaving for his country.)

G=Tour Guide   T=Tourist

扫码听听力

G: Good morning! Are you sure there is nothing left?

T: Yeah, I am sure. What is the departure time of my flight?

G: It is eleven o'clock this morning.

T: Then, we don't have to be in a hurry.

G: Well, I think we should start earlier. It may take some time on the way. There are always many traffic jams in this city. Besides, we should arrive at the airport one hour before the plane takes off so that we may have time to go through the customs.

T: In that case, let's go a little bit earlier.

G: It's a pity you are leaving. I hope you will come back to China again.

T: I will. Before I came, my knowledge about China mainly came from travel books and TV programs, many of which are quite stereotyped. After a trip in China, I've got a better understanding of China and Chinese culture, and I'm quite happy about the trip.

G: I'm glad you have enjoyed your stay in China.

T: You've been very considerate and helpful. I'd like to express my heartfelt gratitude to you.

G: It has been my pleasure to help you.

T: Everything I've seen here has left a deep impression on me. I'll never forget my stay here in China. Thank you again for all the trouble you've taken, you're a very good guide.

G: Thank you for your compliment. Have a pleasant journey home.

Questions:

(1) What is the departure time of the tourist's flight?

(2) How about the traffic in this city?

(3) Why should the tourist arrive at the airport one hour before the plane takes off?

(4) Before the tourist came to China, how did he understand China?

(5) What's the comment of the tourist on the tour guide?

Notes

(1) bid farewell 告别，辞行

(2) What is the departure time of my flight? 飞机几点启程？

(3) traffic jam 交通堵塞

(4) stereotyped 老一套的，有成见的

(5) heartfelt gratitude 衷心的感谢

(6) Thank you for your compliment. 谢谢你的赞美。

➢ Conversation 2　Checking in at the Airport

(The tourist Mr. William is leaving for his country, the tour guide Li Hua is helping him to check in at the airport.)

G=Tour Guide　T=Tourist　C=Airport Clerk

G: Here we are at the airport.

T: Where is the customs?

G: It is on the right.

T: Let's go in.

G: You'd better have your passport ready.

C1: Do you have anything to declare?

T: Yes.

C1: Here is a customs declaration form for you to fill in.

G: Do you need any help?

T: No, thanks. It's in English.

T: It's ready. Here you are.

C1: Please wait a minute. Let me examine your luggage and check it with your form. Yes, that's all.

T: Where can I get my boarding pass and have my luggage weighed?

C1: It is in the front.

T: Thank you.

C2: Ticket, please.

PART I ENGLISH FOR INBOUND TOUR GUIDES

T: Here you are.

C2: Which seat do you prefer, a window seat or an aisle seat?

T: A window seat, please.

C2: Please put your suitcase on the scale.

T: Is it overweight?

C2: No, It is not. Here is your luggage check. This is your boarding pass. You will have to show it on the way to board the plane.

T: Thank you. Well, that's everything, isn't it?

G: Yes. Now, are you going to board the plane?

T: Yes, I'm going to leave now. Thank you for all of your help.

G: Don't mention it. I hope you will be back sometime in the future.

T: I hope so. You've done a very good job. Thank you again for everything.

G: Goodbye. I wish you a pleasant journey.

T: Goodbye.

Questions:

(1) What does the tour guide suggest the tourist doing when the tourist gets into the airport?

(2) Does the tourist have anything to declare? What should he do?

(3) Why does the airport clerk ask the tourist to wait a minute?

(4) Which seat does the tourist prefer?

(5) Where will the tourist have to show the boarding pass?

Notes

(1) Do you have anything to declare? 你有没有什么东西要申报的？

(2) Let me examine your luggage and check it with your form. 照单检查你的行李。

(3) boarding pass 登机牌

(4) A window seat or an aisle seat? 靠窗还是靠走道的座位？

(5) Please put your suitcase on the scale. 请将你的行李过磅。

(6) Is it overweight? 超重了吗？

(7) board the plane 登机

(8) Don't mention it. 不足挂齿。

➢ Conversation 3　Seeing the Tourist off

(The tour guide Li Tao has come to the airport to see the tourist Mr. Abraham off.)

　　G＝Tour Guide　T＝Tourist

T: Time really flies! The time has come for us to say goodbye.

扫码听听力

G: I feel very sad to see you go.

T: I'll come again. I won't forget your kind help during my stay here.

G: But we've enjoyed your stay here, too. It's hard to leave an old friend, but I'm sure we will meet again.

T: You are welcome to come and visit us in the United States.

G: I hope so. Don't forget to e-mail me as soon as you are back home. You have my e-mail address and telephone number, don't you?

T: Sure. I'll keep in touch with you. You know, China is such a large country with such a long history and rich culture that I think my brief visit can hardly do it justice. There are still so many places I would like to visit and so many things I'd like to see. I'll definitely come back.

G: Good. Don't forget to say hello to your family and friends.

T: I won't. Thank you again for all the trouble you've taken. Now I have to say goodbye to you.

G: OK, see you again soon.

Questions:

(1) What does this sentence "Time really flies!" mean?

(2) Is the tourist satisfied with the service of the tour guide? What does he say?

(3) Where does the tourist come from?

(4) What does the tour guide ask the tourist don't forget to do as soon as he is back home?

(5) Can the tourist do China justice through this visit in China? Why?

Notes

(1) Time really flies! 时间过得真快！

(2) I'll keep in touch with you. 我会和你保持联系的。

(3) I think my brief visit can hardly do it justice. 我想我短暂的参观几乎不能对它做出公正的评价。

(4) Don't forget to say hello to your family and friends. 别忘了代我向您的家人和朋友问好。

New Words & Expressions

bid farewell to 告别

traffic jam 交通堵塞

knowledge ['nɒlɪdʒ] n. 了解，理解，个人的知识(学识，见闻)，学问

stereotyped ['steri:ətaɪpt] adj. 用铅版印刷的，套用老调的

heartfelt ['hɑːtfelt] adj. 衷心的，诚挚的

gratitude ['grætɪtjuːd] n. 感激，感谢

PART I ENGLISH FOR INBOUND TOUR GUIDES

impression [ɪmˈpreʃən] n. 印象，感想，盖印，压痕
compliment [ˈkɒmplɪmənt] n. 赞美（话），向……送礼以表示敬意 vt. 表扬，恭维
aisle [aɪl] n. 过道，通道
appreciation [əˌpriːʃɪˈeɪʃən] n. 感谢，感激，正确评价，欣赏，增值，赞扬
overweight [ˌəʊvəˈweɪt] n. 超重
versatile [ˈvɜːsətaɪl] adj. 多功能的，有多种用途的，有多种技能的，多才多艺的，多面手的
definitely [ˈdefɪnɪtli] adv. 明确地，干脆地
to keep in touch with sb. 与某人保持联系

Section 2 Text

A Farewell Speech

扫码听短文

Ladies and gentlemen, may I have your attention, please? I would like to say something about tomorrow's departure arrangement. We will do the checked luggage count after this briefing. Please place your checked bags in front of your rooms by 7:30 tomorrow morning. The bellman will collect them. The bus will leave for the airport at 8:15 tomorrow morning, and I hope everyone will be in the bus before that time. The airport departure tax for the international flight is RMB 90 yuan per person. If you have any RMB yuan left, you can convert it back into either Hong Kong dollars or U. S. dollars at the bank at the airport. Since we are leaving early tomorrow morning, please check out for your incidentals tonight. If your checked luggage is overweight, please be prepared to pay for the overweight as the airline is quite strict on overweight luggage. You do not need to fill in any customs declaration forms if you have nothing to declare. The last but not least, please make sure that you have your passport and air ticket with you at hand.

Ladies and gentlemen, the 15-day journey in the inland of China is drawing to a close. In this period, I have accompanied you on sightseeing around China from the south to the north and from the east to the west and you got a general impression on China. Fifteen days are not so long and not so short, however, living in harmony makes me forget that I am a guide. I have not only finished my work but also obtained happy experiences unconsciously. Until the moment when I'll see you off, I find that I'm so reluctant to part with you. I'll keep all of you firmly in mind and even the happiness and the hardship for the 15 days. An old saying goes in China, "there is no banquet without ending and no friends stay together forever." But I believe that in the near future, we'll get together on this special piece of land and review the sweetness and pleasure of friendship. Finally, many thanks for your all-round cooperation again and wish you good health and happiness!

Notes

(1) do the checked luggage count 清点托运的行李
(2) The bellman will collect them. 行李员会来收行李。
(3) the airport departure tax 离开时的机场税
(4) convert it back into either Hong Kong dollars or U. S. dollars 将其换回港币或美元
(5) check out for your incidentals 结清你的各项杂费
(6) overweight luggage 超重行李
(7) The last but not least, please make sure that you have your passport and air ticket with you at hand. 最后也是最重要的,请一定将你们的护照和机票放在手头。
(8) draw to a close 渐近结束
(9) living in harmony 和谐共处
(10) unconsciously 不知不觉地
(11) keep all of you firmly in mind 牢牢记住你们
(12) to part with you 与你们分别
(13) there is no banquet without ending 天下无不散的筵席
(14) all-round cooperation 全面合作

New Words & Expressions

farewell [ˌfeəˈwel] n. 告别,送别 adj. 告别的 int. 再会!
departure [dɪˈpɑːtʃə] n. 离开,出发,起程(+for)
arrangement [əˈreɪndʒmənt] n. 安排,准备工作(+for),约定
bellman [ˈbelmən] n. 行李员
convert [kənˈvɜːt] v. 转变,变换(+to/into)
incidental [ˌɪnsɪˈdentl] n. 附带事件,偶然事件 adj. 附带的,伴随的
custom [ˈkʌstəm] n. 习俗,惯例,海关
declaration [ˌdekləˈreɪʃən] n. 宣告,声明,申诉,申报,报单
passport [ˈpɑːspɔːt] n. 护照,通行证,执照
inland [ˈɪnlənd] n. 内地,内陆 adj. 内地的,内陆的 adv. 在内陆,向内陆
accompany [əˈkʌmpəni] v. 陪同,伴随
harmony [ˈhɑːməni] n. 和睦,融洽,一致,和谐
obtain [əbˈteɪn] v. 得到,获得
unconsciously [ʌnˈkɒnʃəsli] adv. 未意识到地,不知道地,无意识地
reluctant [rɪˈlʌktənt] adj. 不情愿的,勉强的
hardship [ˈhɑːdʃɪp] n. 艰难,困苦
banquet [ˈbæŋkwɪt] n. 宴会,盛宴 vt. 宴请 vi. 参加宴会
sweetness [ˈswiːtnəs] n. 愉快,乐趣,甜美,芳香
cooperation [kəʊˌɒpəˈreɪʃən] n. 合作,协力

PART I ENGLISH FOR INBOUND TOUR GUIDES

Exercises

1. Read and recite the following special terms

(1) on behalf of 代表……
(2) to propose a toast to 提议为……干杯
(3) to join me in a toast to 和我一起为……干杯
(4) in the name of 以……名义
(5) Let's drink to 让我们为……干杯
(6) on one's own behalf 以……个人名义
(7) common aspiration 共同愿望
(8) mutual understanding 相互理解
(9) substantial support 大力支持
(10) on the initiative of 由……发起
(11) cooperative efforts 共同努力
(12) to exchange experience (compare notes) 交流经验
(13) farewell speech 欢送词
(14) exit visa 出境签证
(15) make apologies for 为……而道歉
(16) look forward to doing sth 期待做某事
(17) free baggage allowance 免费行李限额
(18) see off 送别
(19) departure time 离开时间
(20) sincere (heartfelt) thanks 衷心的感谢

2. Complete the following dialogues

(Mr. Masson and his wife, Jennifer, have stayed in China for two weeks. They are now leaving. Mr. Wang, the tour guide, is seeing them off.)

G＝Tour Guide   T＝Tourist

G：_____(1)_____(你们可以肯定没有什么东西忘了拿吧)?

T1：Yeah, I'm sure.

G：_____(2)_____(时间过得真快)! You've been in China for half a month. _____(3)_____(仿佛就在昨天) when I went to meet you at airport. And now you're leaving.

T1：Yeah, it has been a most wonderful experience for us.

G：What's your impression of China now?

T2：Well. _____(4)_____(和我们来之前听到的完全不一样). You know, before we came, our knowledge about China mainly came from books and TV programs, many of which were quite stereotyped. I think I have a much better understanding of China and Chinese culture now.

T1：The more I know about China, the more I want to learn.

G：_____(5)_____（你们在中国玩得很愉快我很高兴）.

T2：_____(6)_____（一路上你给了我们很大帮助），Mr. Wang. We'd like to express our heartfelt gratitude to you.

T1：Yes. Your companionship and consideration have made our trip the most fruitful.

T2：Here, this is for you, as a going-away token.

G：Wow! So lovely! Thank you very much. _____(7)_____（作为你们的导游我感到非常荣幸）.

T1：Well, it's time to board the plane. Thank you for everything.

G：Goodbye and _____(8)_____（一路平安）.

3. Translate the following sentences into English

（1）你喜欢什么样的座位，是靠窗的还是靠通道的？

（2）我们要在飞机起飞前一个小时抵达机场，以便有足够的时间办理海关手续及其他手续。

（3）我诚恳地希望你们对我及我们旅行社的服务提出宝贵的意见和建议。

（4）请允许我代表我们旅行社及以我个人的名义向你们表示衷心的感谢。感谢你们的大力支持与合作。

（5）我确信，今后的合作和不断的交往，能使我们两国人民更亲近，并促进世界和平。

Unit 8　Keys

PART II
ENGLISH FOR OUTBOUND TOUR LEADERS

Unit 9 Practicalities at the Airport and the Duty of a Tour Leader

Section 1 Situational Conversations

➢ Conversation 1 At the Information Desk

(At the airport, the tour leader from China Travel Service asks airport clerk some questions at the information desk.)

L＝Tour Leader C＝Airport Clerk

扫码听听力

L: Good afternoon.

C: Good afternoon, sir. May I help you?

L: Could you tell me where I can check in for the flight CA 112 to Seoul?

C: Down to the far end of the lounge and you'll see the counter for flights to Seoul.

L: Do you know when they begin to check in?

C: What is the departure time of your flight?

L: 3:20 p. m..

C: Let's see. It's 11:50 now. So they will start in about an hour.

L: Thank you very much. By the way, where can I make a phone call?

C: You'll find phone booths upstairs, sir.

L: Thank you. Bye.

C: Bye.

Questions:

(1) Where will the tour group fly?

(2) What's the flight number of the tour group?

(3) Where should the tour group check in?

(4) What's the departure time of the tour group?

(5) Where can the tour leader make a phone call?

Notes

(1) the information desk 问讯处

(2) airport clerk 机场工作人员

(3) China Travel Service 中国旅行社

(4) Seoul 首尔

(5) lounge 休息厅

(6) check in 办理登机手续

(7) phone booth 电话亭

➤ Conversation 2   At the Check-in Counter

(At the airport, the tour leader from China Travel Service is checking in for his tour group at the check-in counter.)

L＝Tour Leader   C＝Airport Clerk

L：Miss. Is this the counter for CA 114 to Singapore?

C1：Yes, sir. Are you a group?

L：Yes, we are.

C1：Please go to the next counter for group check-in.

L：Hello, we are a group of 25 people going to Singapore by CA 114.

C2：Can I have your tickets and passports, please?

L：Sure, here you are.

C2：How many pieces of luggage would you like to check in?

L：Twenty-five pieces in all.

C2：Here are your tickets, passports and boarding passes. Your luggage claim tags are attached to the tickets cover.

L：Thank you.

C2：You're welcome.

Questions：

(1) What does the tour leader want to do at the airport?

(2) Where will the tour group fly?

(3) What's their flight number?

(4) How many pieces of luggage would they like to check in?

(5) Where are their luggage claim tags attached?

Notes

(1) check-in counter 乘机登记处

(2) ticket and passport 机票和护照

(3) boarding pass 登机牌

(4) luggage claim tag 行李牌

(5) are attached to the tickets cover 贴在机票的封皮上

➤ Conversation 3　Going Through Security Check

(At the airport, the tour leader from China International Travel Service is leading his tour group to go through security check.)

扫码听听力

L＝Tour Leader　O＝Security Officer

O: Will you please put your bag on the conveyer belt?

L: Sure.

O: Would you please put your watch, keys and other metal articles into this tray? Now, please walk through the gate, collect your bag and other personal belongings at this other side over there.

L: Thanks.

O: Could you tell me what's in your bag, please?

L: Now let me see, some clothes, my shaving kit, a couple of books and some souvenirs.

O: Anything else?

L: No, I can't think of anything else.

O: Would you mind opening it, please?

L: Just a minute. It's locked. Now where are my keys? Ah. I've got it. Here you are.

O: Well, you are in the clear now. Sorry to have bothered you.

L: That's all right.

Questions:

(1) Where does the security officer ask the tour leader to put his bag?

(2) Where does the security officer ask the tour leader to put his watch, keys and other metal articles?

(3) How does the tour leader collect his bag and other personal belongings?

(4) What's in the tour leader's bag?

(5) Has the tour leader found his keys?

Notes

(1) security officer (机场) 安检员

(2) the conveyer belt 传送带

(3) metal articles 金属物品

(4) personal belongings 个人财物

(5) shaving kit 刮胡工具

(6) in the clear 不再有危险

Conversation 4 At the Transfer Desk

(At the airport, the tour leader from China Travel Service is handling transfer procedures for his tour group at the transfer desk.)

L=Tour Leader   C=Airport Clerk

L: Excuse me. We are to transfer to flight JL458 to Tokyo. Can you help me?

C: Yes. May I have your tickets?

L: Here are 10 tickets. Can we have our seats as close to each other as possible?

C: Let me see. The aircraft is quite full now. I can hardly give you 10 seats together. Do you want smoking seats?

L: We need three smoking seats and seven non-smoking seats.

C: Here are your tickets, and boarding passes. I have given you seats as close together as possible. Departure time is 11:15, Gate 28.

L: Could you tell me the way to Departure Gate 28?

C: Take the escalator down to the next floor, get on the travelator to the departure area, and then you will easily find Gate 28. You may wait in the departure lounge for boarding as there is not much time left.

L: Thank you.

C: Not at all. Goodbye.

L: Goodbye.

Questions:

(1) Which flight will the tour group transfer to?

(2) How does the tour leader ask the airport clerk to arrange their seats?

(3) Why can't the airport clerk give the tour leader 10 seats together?

(4) What's the departure time?

(5) How to get to Departure Gate 28?

Notes

(1) the transfer desk 中转处

(2) aircraft 飞机，航空器，飞行器

(3) non-smoking seats 非吸烟座位

(4) departure time 登机时间

(5) departure gate 登机口

(6) escalator 自动扶梯

(7) travelator 自动人行道

(8) the departure lounge 候机室

PART II ENGLISH FOR OUTBOUND TOUR LEADERS

➤ Conversation 5　Flight is Delayed

（According to the airport announcer, Flight BL 123 to Berlin has been delayed due to engine trouble.）

　　L＝Tour Leader　C＝Airport Clerk

　　L: Excuse me, Sir. I just heard an announcement that our flight has been delayed.

　　C: What's your flight number?

　　L: Flight BL 123 to Berlin.

　　C: Oh, yes, the delay is due to engine trouble.

　　L: Engine trouble? Is it serious? If so, it would be very dangerous to take this flight.

　　C: Don't worry about that. It is not serious at all. So it is not dangerous to fly it, either. You see, the plane is Boeing 747, the first class aircraft in the world.

　　L: Oh, I see.

　　C: By the way, the pilot flying your plane is very skilled and experienced.

　　L: All right, when will our flight depart then?

　　C: I'm sorry, I don't know either. Anyway, you'll be informed when the trouble is overcomed.

　　L: I'm the tour leader of a tour group. There are some aged people and children in my group.

　　C: Our airline will provide free meal and drinks for passengers. Please take your group to the coffee bar next to the departure lounge. You can have some food and take a rest there with your boarding passes. I'm really sorry for the inconvenience.

　　L: Thank you very much for your help, sir.

　　C: You are welcome.

Questions:

（1）What's the announcement the tour leader heard?

（2）What's the flight number?

（3）Why has the flight been delayed?

（4）When will the flight depart then?

（5）What will the airline provide for passengers?

Notes

（1）airport announcer 机场播音员

（2）engine trouble 引擎故障

（3）the first class aircraft in the world 世界上一流的飞机

（4）I'm really sorry for the inconvenience. 给你们带来了不便，我感到非常抱歉。

➢ Conversation 6   Luggage Claim

(At the airport, the tour leader from China Travel Service is inquiring of the airport clerk about their luggage.)

L＝Tour Leader   C＝Airport Clerk

L：Excuse me. I came from Beijing by CA458. Where can I get my luggage?

C1：The luggage claim area is downstairs.

L：Which carousel is for the luggage from Beijing?

C1：The one in the middle, about No. 5.

L：Excuse me, sir. The handle of suitcase is broken. Where can I go to report it?

C1：Please go to the Luggage Service over there. They will help you.

(The tour leader has come to the Luggage Service with his group.)

L：Excuse me. One tourist of our group couldn't find his luggage. Can you help me?

C2：Certainly. Show me your ticket and luggage check, please.

L：Here you are.

C2：Thank you. Would you please look at this chart and indicate the type of suitcase, which is similar to yours?

L：He says that his suitcase is a black, big one made of leather. It looks like this one, type 5.

C2：Fine. What articles were in his suitcase?

L：There are one camera, three shirts, four pairs of gray trousers, one black overcoat and other things.

C2：Yes, I see. As soon as I find his luggage, I'll call you. May I have your address and telephone number?

L：I am not sure the hotel we will stay in at this moment, but you can contact with the travel agency. Here is the address and telephone number.

C2：Yes, we will notice you as soon as possible.

L：I'm sorry for having given you so much trouble.

C2：No trouble at all. It's our responsibility.

Questions：

(1) Where can the tour leader get his luggage?
(2) Which carousel is for the luggage from Beijing?
(3) Which is similar to the lost luggage?
(4) What articles are in the lost suitcase?
(5) What should the airport clerk do as soon as he finds the luggage?

Notes

(1) luggage claim 行李提取

PART II ENGLISH FOR OUTBOUND TOUR LEADERS

(2) carousel 行李转盘

(3) the handle of suitcase 行李箱的把手

(4) the Luggage Service 行李服务处

(5) Would you please look at this chart and indicate the type of suitcase, which is similar to yours? 请你看看这张表，描述一下，哪种型号的箱子与你的相似？

(6) What articles were in his suitcase? 他的行李箱里有什么物品？

(7) I'm sorry for having given you so much trouble. 很抱歉给你添了这么多麻烦。

(8) It's our responsibility. 这是我们的职责。

➤ Conversation 7 Handling the Immigration Procedures

(At the airport, the tour leader from China Travel Service is handling the immigration procedures for his tour group at the immigration office.)

L＝Tour Leader   O＝Immigration Officer

O: Please show your passport and arrival card.

L: I'm the leader of the tour group. We have the visa for group tourist.

O: Please pass me it.

L: Certainly, here you are.

O: And all passengers' passports.

L: OK, just a moment, I'll collect them.

O: Leader, please come here, this passenger's date of birth is different from his passport's, why?

L: Let me have a look. Oh, I had made a mistake when I filled in the visa form. Sorry, would you please correct it for me?

O: Sure, please let me have the address, telephone number and name of linkman of the local travel agency.

L: No problem.

O: Please let your passengers keep their arrival cards in passports, and go through one by one according to the order of the name list.

L: Yes, can I be the last one to pass?

O: Sure, you can.

Questions:

(1) What does the immigration officer ask the tour leader to show?

(2) What kind of visa does the tour leader tell the immigration officer?

(3) Who will collect all passengers' passports?

(4) Why is one passenger's date of birth on the group visa different from his passport's?

(5) What does the immigration officer ask the tour leader to tell his passengers to do?

扫码听听力

Notes

(1) the immigration procedures 入境手续

(2) the immigration office 出入境管理处

(3) arrival card 入境卡

(4) the visa for group tourist 团体旅游签证

(5) the visa form 签证表

(6) linkman 联系人

(7) Please let your passengers keep their arrival cards in passports, and go through one by one according to the order of the name list. 请你的客人按名单表上的顺序,把入境卡夹在护照里,依次通过。

➢ Conversation 8　　Handling the Emigration Procedures

(At the airport, the tour leader from China Travel Service is handling the emigration procedures for his tour group at the immigration office.)

L＝Tour Leader　　O＝Immigration Officer　　I＝Customs Inspector

O：May I have your passport and exit card, please?

L：Certainly, officer. Here you are.

O：It's all right. Please go to the customs.

I：Please show me your customs declaration form, sir. Do you have anything to declare?

L：No, I don't think so.

I：Well, would you mind opening this bag?

L：I guess not.

I：Let me examine your luggage and check it with your declaration form. Please show me the valuable articles you brought in.

L：Certainly, officer.

I：Do you still have this article?

L：I'm sorry. It has been lost.

I：Do you have a certificate for the loss?

L：Yes. This is the certificate for the loss.

I：All right. Everything is fine. Your luggage is passed.

Questions：

(1) What does the immigration officer ask the tour leader to show?

(2) What does the customs inspector ask the tour leader to show?

(3) Does the tour leader have anything to declare?

(4) Why does the customs inspector ask the tour leader to open his bag?

(5) Does the tour leader has a certificate for the loss?

PART II ENGLISH FOR OUTBOUND TOUR LEADERS

Notes

(1) handling the emigration procedures 办理出境手续

(2) exit card 离境卡

(3) Please show me the valuable articles you brought in. 让我看看你带进来的贵重物品。

(4) the certificate for the loss 遗失证明

New Words & Expressions

practicality [ˌpræktɪˈkæləti] n. 实用性，可行性
lounge [laʊndʒ] n. 休息厅，休息室 vi. 懒散地斜倚（靠坐）
counter [ˈkaʊntə] n. 柜台，计数器 v. 反对，反驳
booth [buːθ] n. 售货棚，摊位，小房间
Singapore [ˌsɪŋɡəˈpɔː] n. 新加坡（东南亚国家）
claim [kleɪm] v. 声称，断言，索取 n. 宣称，断言
attach [əˈtætʃ] v. 贴上，系，附上
security check 安全检查
belonging [bɪˈlɒŋɪŋ] n. 所有物，行李，附件
kit [kɪt] n. 衣物和装备，成套用品，配套元件
transfer [trænsˈfɜː] v. 转移，迁移，转让 n. 转移，转让
Tokyo [ˈtəʊkjəʊ] n. 东京（日本首都）
escalator [ˈeskəleɪtə] n. 自动扶梯
travelator [ˈtrævəˌleɪtə] n. 自动人行道
announcer [əˈnaʊnsə] n. 广播员
pilot [ˈpaɪlət] n. 飞行员，驾驶员，领航员 vt. 驾驶
boarding pass 登机牌
carousel [ˌkærəˈsel] n. 旋转木马，（机场的）行李传送带
address [əˈdres] n. 演说，演讲，住址 vt. 向……讲话，向……发表演说，写信给……
the immigration office 出入境管理处
linkman [ˈlɪŋkmæn] n. 联系人，中间人，（广播或电视的）节目主持人
emigration [ˌemɪˈɡreɪʃən] n. 移民出境，侨居，移民
exit [ˈeksɪt] n. 出口，通道，太平门，退出，退场 v. 离开，退场
certificate [səˈtɪfɪkɪt] n. 证明书，证明，合格证书

Section 2 Text

The Duty of a Tour Leader

The tour leader is one of the most attractive and challenging positions in the travel industry. A good tour leader should entertain and manage travelers in ways that are fascinating, remarkable and exciting. He is the primary point of contact and an adviser to the tour group that he manages. In general the tour leader should be passionate about the destinations and view tour leader as the ultimate job, he should possess the following qualities matching the tour leader needs in any destinations.

Destination knowledge

This requires a deep knowledge of the destination's culture and natural history, a true and natural affinity for its local people, a consummate familiarity with its geography, and a fine understanding of its logistical demands.

Language

As experts on a particular culture, the tour leader is expected to be conversant, if not fluent, in the destination's language.

Concern for health and safety

Whenever and wherever, the safety of our travelers must be first and foremost in the mind of the tour leader. The tour leader is in a unique position to foresee many dangers not immediately apparent to the first-time visitor, and is required to have a fine sense for the safety and well-being of our travelers. He must be able to respond quickly and compassionately in the event of client accident or illness, demonstrating sincere concern for clients' health needs.

Communication skills

Perhaps the foundation of good tour leader is the ability to communicate one's love of a culture in a clear and inspiring way. The ability to communicate a positive outlook in the face of a setback is essential as well. Further, it is important that the tour leader elicits the best dynamic within a group.

Keen response abilities

The tour leader must possess the ability to respond competently to unforeseen circumstances, such as client illness, rerouted planes, loss of baggage, or worse.

Formal education

The travelers are sophisticated and in general highly educated. The tour leader must be at ease dealing with a variety of people on a range of subjects. The tour leader's responsibilities include leading trips for some of most demanding institutions, including the universities, high schools, government offices, to name a few. The tour leader must move in these circles with a knowledgeable grace.

Environmental Awareness

As the representative of travel services in the host country, the tour leader is expected to demonstrate respect and care for the local environment. This may include simply ensuring that a "leave no trace" ethic prevails throughout the trip, but may also manifest in a more profound stewardship, such as educating travelers or even locals on the importance of promoting environmental health and respect for the Earth.

PART II ENGLISH FOR OUTBOUND TOUR LEADERS

Intangibles

The tour leader should possess some amazing skills that are impossible to calculate. He should have a superb sense of humor and a delightful sense of the impromptu gesture, like ordering a special local cake for a traveler's birthday celebration. He should enjoy a cherished relationship and affinity with locals of tourist destinations.

Notes

(1) A good tour leader should entertain and manage travelers in ways that are fascinating, remarkable and exciting. 一位好的领队应该以一种有吸引力的、引人注目的和令人兴奋的方式来招待和管理游客。

(2) the ultimate job 首要工作

(3) He should possess the following qualities matching the tour leader needs in any destinations. 在任何目的地，他应该具备下列与旅游团领队相适应的品质。

(4) a true and natural affinity for its local people 对当地人真实、自然的喜爱

(5) a consummate familiarity with its geography 全面了解它的地理状况

(6) to be conversant 熟悉、了解

(7) well-being 健康、幸福、福祉

(8) in a clear and inspiring way 以一种清楚而又鼓舞人的方式

(9) to communicate a positive outlook in the face of a setback 面对挫折时传达一种积极的观点

(10) Further, it is important that the tour leader elicits the best dynamic within a group. 另外，领队激发旅行团内的活力也是很重要的。

(11) unforeseen circumstances 意料之外的情况

(12) rerouted planes 变更了行程的飞机

(13) The travelers are sophisticated and in general highly educated. 旅游者是见多识广的，通常受过高等教育。

(14) most demanding institutions 要求最严格的机构

(15) to name a few 仅举几例

(16) ensuring that a "leave no trace" ethic prevails throughout the trip, but may also manifest in a more profound stewardship 确保在整个旅行中不要"留下任何痕迹"，也可以表现在更深、更细的工作方面

(17) intangibles 无形的东西

(18) that are impossible to calculate 数不胜数

(19) a superb sense of humor 极好的幽默感

(20) a delightful sense of the impromptu gesture 即兴动作的愉悦感

New Words & Expressions

attractive [əˈtræktɪv] adj. 吸引的，有吸引力的，诱人的

entertain [ˌentə'teɪn] v. 款待，招待，使欢乐，娱乐
fascinating ['fæsɪneɪtɪŋ] adj. 迷人的，有极大吸引力的
remarkable [rɪ'mɑːkəbl] adj. 异常的，引人注目的，不寻常的
in general 一般地，大体上，通常
passionate ['pæʃənət] adj. 充满激情的，激昂的，热切的，强烈的
ultimate ['ʌltɪmɪt] adj. 最后的，最终的，终极的，根本的，极限程度的
affinity [ə'fɪnɪti] n. 喜爱
consummate ['kɒnsəmeɪt] vt. 使完整，使完美　[kən'sʌmət] adj. 技艺高超的，完美的
familiarity [fəˌmɪli'ærəti] n. 熟悉，通晓，认识，友好随和，亲近
logistical [lə'dʒɪstɪkəl] adj. 后勤的，物流的
conversant [kən'vɜːsənt] adj. 熟悉的，通晓的
foresee [fɔː'siː] vt. 预知，预见
well-being [ˌwel'biːɪŋ] n. 健康，幸福，福祉
compassionately [kəm'pæʃənətli] adv. 表示怜悯地，有同情心地
inspiring [ɪn'spaɪərɪŋ] adj. 鼓舞人的，启发灵感的
outlook ['aʊtlʊk] n. 景色，景致，观点，见解，展望，前景
in the face of 面对
setback ['setbæk] n. 挫折，阻碍
essential [ɪ'senʃəl] adj. 非常重要的，本质的，基本的　n. 要素，要点
elicit [i'lɪsɪt] vt. 引出，探出
dynamic [daɪ'næmɪk] adj. 有活力的，强有力的，不断变化的，动力的，动态的
sophisticated [sə'fɪstɪkeɪtɪd] adj. 老练的，精密的，高雅的，有教养的
at ease 放心
to name a few 仅举几例
knowledgeable ['nɒlɪdʒəbl] adj. 博学的，有见识的，知识渊博的
prevail [prɪ'veɪl] vi. 盛行，流行，（思想、观点等）战胜
manifest ['mænɪfest] vt. 显示，显现，表明　adj. 明显的
profound [prə'faʊnd] adj. 深远的，知识渊博的，见解深刻的，深奥的
intangible [ɪn'tændʒəbl] adj. 难以形容的，难以理解的，（指企业资产）无形的
impromptu [ɪm'prɒmptjuː] adj. 事先无准备的，即兴的　n. 即兴曲
cherish ['tʃerɪʃ] vt. 珍爱，珍惜，爱护，怀有（好感），抱有（信念、希望）

Exercises

1. Read and recite the following special terms

（1）date passport issued 护照签发日期
（2）date passport expires (date of expiry) 护照有效截止日期
（3）disembarkation card/landing card/arrival card/incoming passenger card）入境卡
（4）embarkation card/departure card/outgoing passenger card）出境卡

PART II ENGLISH FOR OUTBOUND TOUR LEADERS

(5) place of residence 居住地

(6) in block (capital) letter 用大写字母

(7) duration of stay (length of stay) 停留时间

(8) purpose of your trip 旅行目的

(9) purpose of entry 入境目的

(10) company paid holiday 公司带薪假期

(11) marital status 婚姻状况

(12) port of entry 入境口岸(城市)

(13) customs inspector 海关检查员

(14) transit visa 过境签证

(15) entry visa 入境签证

(16) through passenger 直达旅客

(17) passenger coupon 旅客联

(18) international airport 国际机场

(19) international departure 国际航班出港

(20) international terminal 国际航班候机楼

2. Complete the following dialogues

Tax Refund

(At the Customs, the tour leader from China Travel Service wants to get his tax refund.)

O＝Customs Officer   L＝Tour Leader

O1: Good morning, sir. ＿＿＿＿＿(1)＿＿＿＿＿(我能帮您做点什么吗)?

L: Yes. Is this the place where I can draw back the tax paid for the necklace I bought in Austria? ＿＿＿＿＿(2)＿＿＿＿＿(我想将我的退税单盖章).

O1: Certainly, sir. May I have your passport, boarding pass, tax refund form and ＿＿＿＿＿(3)＿＿＿＿＿(您购买的商品), please?

L: Here you are.

O1: All right. Here is your tax refund form. Please go to get your tax refund at the Cash Refund Counter at the Emigration.

L: I see. Thank you, officer.

L: Excuse me, Miss. May I get my tax refund here?

O2: Certainly, sir. ＿＿＿＿＿(4)＿＿＿＿＿(请把盖了章的退税单给我), please?

L: Here you are, and my passport and boarding pass.

O2: Thank you. ＿＿＿＿＿(5)＿＿＿＿＿(您买这条项链付了480欧元). The tax is 17%. So you'll get a refund of 81.6 Euros. How would you like to have it, ＿＿＿＿＿(6)＿＿＿＿＿(是直接付现金给您还是打到您的账户上)?

L: Cash, please.

O2: All right. ＿＿＿＿＿(7)＿＿＿＿＿(这些是您的护照、登机牌和所退的81.6欧元).

L: Thank you very much.

3. Translate the following sentences into English

（1）出境时，须将出境卡及护照一同交给出入境管理处检查。

（2）如果你滞留的时间超过90天，你就必须向出入境管理处通报你的住处，每90天你都需要办理此手续。

（3）如果你有应缴纳关税的、禁止或受限制的物品，请在"报关"一栏打√，并选择红色通道通关。

（4）你是否曾违反美国签证的有关规定？是否曾非法进入美国或曾被美国递解出境？

（5）领队必须具备这样的能力，即对顾客生病、飞机更改线路、丢失行李或更糟糕的一些意外情况做出恰当的反应。

Unit 9　Keys

Unit 10 Practicalities on Board the Plane & Air Travel Tips

Section 1 Situational Conversations

➢ Conversation 1 Asking for Drinks

(On the plane, the tour leader from China International Travel Service is asking for some drinks from the stewardess.)

扫码听听力

L＝Tour Leader   S＝Stewardess

S: What would you like to drink, sir?

L: What sort of drinks do you have?

S: Orange juice, seven-up, coke and Pepsi, and also mineral water.

L: A coke would be nice. Thank you.

(The stewardess is serving drinks for the second time.)

S: Tea or coffee?

L: Coffee, please.

S: With milk?

L: Yes, please.

S: More coffee?

L: No more, thanks. But I want to take tablets. Would you bring me a glass of water?

S: Yes, sir. I'll be back in a minute.

L: Thank you.

Questions:

(1) What sort of drinks does the stewardess have?

(2) What would the tour leader like to drink?

(3) What would the tour leader like to drink, coffee or tea?

(4) What would the tour leader like to drink black coffee or coffee with milk?

(5) Why does the tour leader want to have a glass of water?

Notes

(1) on board 在飞机(船或车)上

(2) China International Travel Service (CITS) 中国国际旅行社

(3) stewardess (air-hostess) (飞机上的)女乘务员

(4) seven-up 七喜

(5) Pepsi 百事可乐

(6) mineral water 矿泉水

(7) to take tablets 吃药片

(8) a glass of water 一杯水

➢ Conversation 2 Meals on Board

(On the plane, the tour leader from China International Travel Service has meals on board.)

L＝Tour Leader S＝Stewardess

S: Excuse me. It is time for supper. Would you please put down the tray?

L: Sure.

S: We have Chicken with Steamed Rice and Beef Steak Curried with Noodle. Which one do you prefer?

L: Chicken with Steamed Rice, please.

S: Would you like something to drink? We've got whisky, wine, beer, juice and soda.

L: Some red wine, please.

S: OK. Anything else?

L: Can I have some coffee, please?

S: We will serve coffee and tea later.

L: Thank you.

Questions:

(1) Why does the stewardess ask the tour leader to put down the tray?

(2) What kind of food does the stewardess have?

(3) Which kind of food does the tour leader prefer?

(4) What kind of drinks does the stewardess have?

(5) What kind of drinks would the tour leader like to have?

Notes

(1) put down the tray 把小桌板放下来

(2) Chicken with Steamed Rice 鸡肉米饭

(3) Beef Steak Curried with Noodle 咖喱牛排面

(4) whisky 威士忌酒

(5) soda 苏打水，汽水

➢ Conversation 3　Airsickness

(On the plane, a tourist is suffering from airsickness, the tour leader from China International Travel Service asks the stewardess to help her.)

L＝Tour Leader　S＝Stewardess

L：Excuse me, madam, a tourist of our group feels like vomiting. Can I bother you for some ice water, please?

S：Certainly, sir. But can I suggest a glass of warm water instead? I think it may help settle her stomach down.

L：Yes, please.

S：She can find an airsick bag in the seat pocket in front of her, if she needs it.

L：Thank you very much for your kindness.

S：No problem, I'll be back with the warm water in a minute.

L：Thanks.

Questions：

(1) What's wrong with the tourist?

(2) What does the tour leader ask for?

(3) Does the stewardess give him any ice water? Why?

(4) What's the function of a cup of warm water?

(5) Where can the sick find an airsick bag?

Notes

(1) airsickness 晕机

(2) suffer from 遭受

(3) vomit 呕吐

(4) settle her stomach down 让她的胃舒服一点

(5) airsick bag 呕吐袋

(6) She can find an airsick bag in the seat pocket in front of her. 在她前座的椅背袋里有个呕吐袋。

➢ Conversation 4　Feeling a Little Cold

(On the plane, some tourists feel a little bit cold, the tour leader from China International Travel Service is asking for some blankets from the stewardess.)

L＝Tour Leader　S＝Stewardess

L：Excuse me, Miss. Would you please give us some blankets? Some tourists of our group feel a little cold.

扫码听听力

扫码听听力

S: Sure. I will get some for you. By the way, did you turn off the air conditioning overhead?

L: Yes, we did. But we still feel cold.

S: I will be back with the blankets shortly.

L: Thanks a lot.

Questions:

(1) What does the tour leader ask for?

(2) Why does the tour leader ask for something from the stewardess?

(3) Did the tourists turn off the air conditioning overhead?

Notes

(1) feel a little cold 感觉有点冷

(2) some blankets 几条毛毯(或毯子)

(3) Did you turn off the air conditioning overhead? 你们把头顶上的冷气关了没有？

➤ Conversation 5 Asking for Entry Cards & Customs Declarations

(On the plane, the tour leader from China International Travel Service is asking for some entry cards & Customs declarations from the stewardess.)

L＝Tour Leader　S＝Stewardess

L: May I have some entry cards & Customs declarations?

S: Yes. We will be handing out entry cards and customs declarations for passengers to fill out.

L: There are 16 members in our tour group. Please give me 16 forms. I will fill them out.

S: Here are 16 forms. Tell your passengers that they don't need any more, please.

L: Thank you.

S: Please fill them out before your arrival. If there is anything you don't understand, I'll be glad to help you.

L: Thank you.

Questions:

(1) What is the tour leader asking for?

(2) How many members are there in the tour group led by the tour leader?

(3) How many forms does the tour leader need?

(4) Who will fill out the forms?

(5) What does the stewardess ask the tour leader to tell his passengers?

PART II ENGLISH FOR OUTBOUND TOUR LEADERS

Notes

(1) entry cards 入境卡

(2) Customs declarations 海关申报单

(3) hand out 分发

(4) fill out 填写，填好

(5) If there is anything you don't understand 如果有什么不明白的地方

➤ Conversation 6 Inquiry

(On the plane, the tour leader from China International Travel Service inquires of the stewardess about some information.)

L＝Tour Leader　S＝Stewardess

L: Excuse me, Miss.

S: Yes? What can I do for you, sir?

L: When do we arrive in Tokyo?

S: We're due in Tokyo at 11:30 a.m., Tokyo time. Our flight has delayed about an hour and 40 minutes to take off because of the bad weather.

L: What time are we going to arrive?

S: About 13:10, Tokyo time.

L: What's the weather like in Tokyo?

S: It may be sunny. The temperature is 16-22 ℃. You can look at the flight information on the screen.

扫码听听力

Questions:

(1) When does the tour group arrive in Tokyo according to the original schedule?

(2) How long has the flight delayed to take off?

(3) Why has the flight delayed to take off?

(4) When will the tour group arrive in Tokyo now?

(5) What's the weather like in Tokyo?

Notes

(1) inquire 问询

(2) Tokyo 东京（日本首都）

(3) We're due in Tokyo at 11:30 a.m., Tokyo time. 我们原计划在东京时间11:30抵达。

(4) to take off 起飞

(5) the flight information on the screen 屏幕上的航班信息提示

New Words & Expressions

stewardess [ˌstjuːəˈdes] n.（飞机上的）女乘务员

coke [kəuk] n. 可乐
tablet ['tæblət] n. 药片,（固定于墙上作纪念的）牌, 碑匾
put down 放下
suffer from 遭受
overhead ['əuvəhed] adj. 地面以上的, 头上方的 adv. 在头上方, 在空中
entry ['entri] n. 进入, 参与, 加入（指权利、机会）, 条目, 词条
hand out 分发
declaration [ˌdeklə'reɪʃən] n. 宣布, 宣告, 声明, 申报（单）
inquire [ɪn'kwaɪə] v. 询问
due [djuː] adj. 应支付（给予）的, 应有的, 应得到的, 到期的, 预期的, 适当的, 由于
temperature ['temprətʃə] n. 温度, 气温

Section 2 Text

Air Travel Tips to Make Your Flight Easier

Taking an airplane is probably the fastest way to get to anywhere right now. It is also much faster than it is to drive. There are many people who love to fly. You get to see the great views and get where you are going in a hurry. Then there are those who absolutely hate to fly and would do anything to get out of it. Here are just a few good tips for you to make your flight much better. It can truly be the best way to travel.

What to pack?

The most difficult part of traveling by plane is to decide what to bring with you on the plane. You should always try to pack as light as you can to stop any possible problems from arising. You should only take what you absolutely need so that you can get through the lines as quick as possible. You have to remember that you are going to have to lug your bags around. You do not want to bring the jumbo hair dryer to hurt your back on every trip. Just tell your wife to leave the ten pairs of shoes at home in the closet. A very important thing to do is make sure that you take enough socks and underwear for the entire trip so that you don't have to try to find a store selling your size at 3:00 in the morning. You also want to take at least one outfit for everyday. You may want more than one pair depending on what the weather is going to be like and where you are going. There are a lot of places the weather changes drastically from hour to hour each day. Take the clothes that you will be most comfortable in and that you will not freeze in or boil alive in. Make sure to bring some kind of coat no matter where you go. If you are going on a business trip, then make sure that you bring clothes that are suitable for your business needs. It would also be

PART II ENGLISH FOR OUTBOUND TOUR LEADERS

a good idea to bring an umbrella if you wear clothes that could be wrecked by the weather.

Motion sickness!

If you get airsick easily while flying an airplane, then you may want to think about bringing some Dramamine to keep you feeling good. Dramamine has worked very well for everybody as I know. There are lots of other drugs that can also help you if you need something stronger. The most important thing to remember about this kind of medicine is to take your medicine before you are ready to fly. Most of the drugs used to help motion sickness are designed to stop it before it starts. You may be able to get some medicine in the airport store if you forget to get some or you run out. If you do have to buy it in the airport, take it as soon as you can. If you forget to take your medicine before you go, chew some mint gum, it normally seems to help. You always have airsick bags in the plane handy for a last resort if you are going to be sick.

Arrive at the airport early!

When you are taking a plane, the best advice I can give you is to get there at least a couple hours before your flight. There is so much security check at the airports and you will be slowed down a lot if there is any sort of problem. There is a huge chance that you may miss your flight if you do not give yourself enough time to get through all the checks. You will not get a refund in most cases if you miss your plane. You should allow lots of time for the delays. They will inevitably come up at the worst time possible and you will wish you showed up earlier.

Pack some fun.

Flights are very long and boring if you are traveling alone or with children. One way to pass the time is to bring along something for you to do while you are on your flight. Crossword puzzles, good books, hand held video games, magazines from the gift shops, or audio books, laptops to do a little work or watch a movie, are all great ideas to keep you busy. This will keep your mind occupied and the time will fly. If you have kids that need to be kept quiet or calm, coloring books, portable DVD players, video games, and portable board games are a huge help for them.

These are just a few great tips that you can find to help you have a great trip. It is the fastest and safest way to travel. Be safe and have a great trip or vacation.

Notes

(1) air travel tips 航空旅行常识

(2) Then there are those who absolutely hate to fly and would do anything to get out of it. 还有那些完全讨厌飞行，想方设法摆脱飞行的人。

(3) What to pack? 携带什么行李？

(4) You have to remember that you are going to have to lug your bags around. 你必须记住，你不得不拉着你的行李到处走。

(5) to take along at least one outfit 至少随身携带一套服装

(6) Take the clothes that you will be most comfortable in and that you will not freeze in or boil alive in. 携带一些穿着最舒适，穿着既不会很冷也不会很热的衣服。

(7) be wrecked by the weather 被天气毁坏

(8) motion sickness 晕车（机、船等）

(9) some Dramamine 一些茶苯海明

(10) chew some mint gum 嚼一些薄荷味的口香糖

(11) Most of the drugs used to help motion sickness are designed to stop it before it starts. 绝大多数治疗晕机的药在晕机发生之前就可以防止晕机的发生。

(12) You always have airsick bags in the plane handy for a last resort if you are going to be sick. 如果你晕机，你手边总有晕机袋作为最后一招。

(13) You should allow lots of time for the delays. 你应该准备足够的时间以防延误。

(14) They will inevitably come up at the worst time possible and you will wish you showed up earlier. 它们可能会不可避免地出现在最坏的时刻，那时你就会觉得你早点到就好了。

(15) crossword puzzles 填字游戏

(16) hand held video games 手持视屏游戏

(17) music or audio books 音乐或有声读物

(18) laptop 便携式电脑

(19) coloring books 彩色书

(20) portable DVD players 便携式 DVD 播放机

(21) portable board games 便携式棋盘游戏

New Words & Expressions

absolutely [ˈæbsəluːtli] adv. 完全地，绝对地

to get out of 摆脱

pack [pæk] n. 包裹，背包，小纸盒，一群，（纸牌的）一副　vt. & vi.（把……）打包，收拾行李，塞进

stop from 阻止，防止

line [laɪn] n. 线，线路

as quick as possible 尽可能快

lug [lʌg] vt. 用力拖（拉）　n. 手柄，耳朵

jumbo [ˈdʒʌmbəʊ] adj. 巨型的，巨大的

underwear [ˈʌndəweə] n. 内衣

outfit [ˈaʊtfɪt] n. 全套装备，全套工具，全套服装，团队，小组

drastically [ˈdræstɪkəli] adv. 激烈地，彻底地
from hour to hour 时不时地
alive [əˈlaɪv] adj. 活着的，在世的，有活力的
wreck [rek] vt. 毁坏（毁灭）某物 n. 沉船
motion [ˈməʊʃən] n. 运动，动作，提议，动议 vt.（以手或手）做动作，示意
Dramamine [ˈdræməmiːn] n. 茶苯海明（抗组织胺药）
chew [tʃuː] v. 咀嚼，咬
mint [mɪnt] n. 铸币厂，大量的钱，薄荷，薄荷糖 v. 铸造
gum [gʌm] n. 牙龈，口香糖，树胶 vt. 在……上涂胶
handy [ˈhændi] adj. 方便的，手边的，手巧的
resort [rɪˈzɔːt] n. 求助，诉诸，采取，旅游胜地 v. 诉诸，求助于
slow down 减缓
inevitably [ɪnˈevɪtəbli] adv. 不可避免地，必然地
come up 发生，出现，想出，走近
crossword [ˈkrɒsˌwɜːd] n. 纵横填字游戏
laptop [ˈlæptɒp] n. 便携式电脑

Exercises

1. Read and recite the following special terms

(1) emergency exit 紧急出口
(2) aisle seat 靠通道座位
(3) window seat 靠窗口座位
(4) occupied （厕所）有人
(5) vacant （厕所）无人
(6) fasten seat belt 系好安全带
(7) oxygen mask 氧气罩
(8) life vest under your seat 救生衣在座椅下
(9) air (flight, cabin) crew 空勤人员
(10) ground crew 地勤人员
(11) seat reclining button 调节椅背按钮
(12) hat rack (storage box) 行李架
(13) window shade 遮光罩
(14) air-sickness bag 清洁袋
(15) smoking seat 吸烟座位
(16) ground speed 飞行速度
(17) outside air temperature 外面的气温
(18) lavatories in rear 后部的盥洗室
(19) in-flight 飞行中
(20) transit stop 过境停留

2. Complete the following dialogues

Handling the Flight Facilities Problems

(On the plane, the tour leader from China Travel Service asks the air stewardess to handle the flight facilities problems.)

S＝Air Stewardess　　L＝Tour Leader　　T＝Tourist

L: Excuse me, Miss. ＿＿＿＿＿＿(1)＿＿＿＿＿＿（我不知道怎样调节气流）. It is blowing right to the old lady. Could you help me?

S: Sure. You just turn the knob here above you in whichever direction you like, ＿＿＿＿＿＿(2)＿＿＿＿＿＿（或你将调节器向左旋转将其关掉）.

L: Oh, I see. And I want to see a film. ＿＿＿＿＿＿(3)＿＿＿＿＿＿（请你给我一副耳机，好吗）?

S: Certainly. Here you are.

L: Thank you. But how should I do with it?

S: Oh, it's very easy. ＿＿＿＿＿＿(4)＿＿＿＿＿＿（现在将插头插进插座里，拧这个调节器）. Have you got it now?

L: Yes, thank you.

S: Is there anything else I can do for you, Sir?

L: Oh, ＿＿＿＿＿＿(5)＿＿＿＿＿＿（这位女士的耳机出了故障）.

S: Let me check them, madam. Can you hear anything now?

T: Yes, but it's too loud.

S: Please adjust the volume. ＿＿＿＿＿＿(6)＿＿＿＿＿＿（音量调节器就在这里）.

T: I see, Miss. Which one is the music channel?

S: Channel 2.

L: Thank you for your help, Miss.

S: You are welcome. ＿＿＿＿＿＿(7)＿＿＿＿＿＿（在飞机上照顾好旅客是我们应尽的职责）.

3. Translate the following sentences into English

(1) 打扰一下，请您把我带到我的座位上，好吗？
(2) 请您帮我把行李放到上面的行李柜里，好吗？
(3) 抱歉，先生。飞机现在正遇到一股气流，请系紧您座位上的安全带，好吗？
(4) 需要在本站转乘飞机到其他地方的旅客请到候机室中转柜台办理中转手续。
(5) 我是领队，现在我们旅游团有位客人生病了。

Unit 10　Keys

Unit 11 Practicalities at the Hotel and Classifications of Hotel

Section 1 Situational Conversations

➢ Conversation 1 Check in

(After having arrived at the hotel, the tour leader from China International Travel Service checks in for his group.)

L＝Tour Leader   R＝Receptionist

扫码听听力

R: Good afternoon, sir. What can I do for you?

L: We are the tour group from China International Travel Service. My name is Wu Min. Our company booked 8 double rooms for our group three weeks ago.

R: Just a moment, please, Mr. Wu. I'll check our reservation records. China International Travel Service. Yes, you have reserved 8 double rooms from today to June 7.

L: Yes, exactly.

R: Can I see your passport, please?

L: Sure, here are the name list of our tour group and passports.

R: Thank you, sir. And would you please fill in the registration form?

L: OK.

R: How are you going to pay, in cash or by credit card?

L: Do you take traveler's checks?

R: Certainly. Here are the keys to your rooms. Please make sure that you have them with you all the time. You need to show them when you sign for your meals and drink in the restaurant and bars. The bellman will show you up.

L: Thanks a lot.

Questions:

(1) Where is the tour group from?

(2) How many rooms did the tour company book for this tour group?

(3) When did the tour company book for this tour group?

(4) How does the tour leader pay for his group?

(5) What should the tourists do when they sign for their meals and drink in the restaurant and bars?

Notes

(1) double rooms 双人间

(2) reservation records 预订记录

(3) the name list of our tour group 我们旅行团的名单

(4) fill in the registration form 填写登记表

(5) in cash or by credit card? 用现金还是用信用卡(结账)?

(6) traveler's checks 旅行支票

(7) Please make sure that you have them with you all the time. 请一定要随身携带它们(钥匙)。

▷ Conversation 2　Room Service

(Living in the hotel, the tour leader from China International Travel Service asks for room service.)

L＝Tour Leader　A＝Room Service Attendant

L: I'd like to have breakfast in our room tomorrow morning. Could you bring it here? I'm in Room 528.

A: Yes, of course. We can offer very good room service. What would you like to order, American breakfast or continental breakfast?

L: Just American breakfast, please.

A: With coffee or tea, sir?

L: Black coffee, please.

A: Orange juice or grapefruit juice?

L: Orange juice.

A: Would you like toast with butter or jam?

L: With butter, please.

A: How would you like the eggs done, easy over or sunny-side up?

L: Easy over.

A: With ham or bacon?

L: With ham.

A: OK. You need American breakfast with black coffee, orange juice, butter, easy over eggs and ham. Is that all?

L: Yes. By the way, is there any other way to have room service?

A: Yes, sir. Just check the items you would like for breakfast in your doorknob menu, mark down the time, and hang it outside your door before you go to bed.

PART II ENGLISH FOR OUTBOUND TOUR LEADERS

L: Thanks. Then what should we do with the dishes when we finish eating?

A: Please leave them outside your room.

L: Oh, I see. Thank you.

Questions:

(1) What kind of breakfast would the tour leader like to order?

(2) Which kind of drinks would the tour leader like?

(3) How would the tour leader like the eggs done?

(4) Is there any other way to have room service in the hotel?

(5) What should the tour leader do with the dishes when he finishes eating?

Notes

(1) American breakfast or continental breakfast? 美式早餐还是欧陆式早餐?

(2) black coffee 黑咖啡

(3) grapefruit juice 葡萄柚汁

(4) easy over 双面煎蛋

(5) sunny-side up 单面煎(蛋)

(6) bacon 熏猪肉，培根

(7) doorknob menu 门把菜单

(8) mark down 记下，标出

(9) hang it outside your door 挂在门的外边

➢ Conversation 3 Wake-up Call Service

(The tour leader from China International Travel Service is making a phone to the operator and requests a wake-up call service for his group.)

扫码听听力

L＝Tour Leader   O＝Operator

L: Operator?

O: Yes, can I help you, sir?

L: I'm Wang Gang, the leader of tour group. We are going to the airport early tomorrow morning. I'd like to request a wake-up call.

O: Yes, please tell us your room number.

L: Room 1006, 1102-1108, and room 1209, 9 rooms in all.

O: I repeat the room numbers: 1006, 1102-1108, 1209.

L: That's right, you've got it.

O: Mr. Wang. What time would you like us to call you tomorrow morning?

L: I'm not sure. But we have to be at the airport to check in by 7:30.

O: Let me see. It will take you about half an hour to get there by bus.

L: In that case. I'd like you to call me at 6:00.

O: OK. We will wake you up at 6:00 tomorrow morning.

L: Thank you very much.

O: You are welcome.

Questions:

(1) Why does the tour leader request a wake-up call service for his tour group?

(2) What are the room numbers of the tour group?

(3) By what time does the tour group have to be at the airport to check in?

(4) How long will it take to get to the airport by bus?

(5) When will the tour leader request to be woken up?

Notes

(1) wake-up call service 叫醒服务

(2) operator 电话接线员

(3) to request a wake-up call 请求叫醒服务

(4) But we have to be at the airport to check in by 7:30. 但是我们必须 7:30 前到机场办理登机手续。

➢ Conversation 4　Laundry Service

(The tour leader from China International Travel Service is calling the Laundry Department and requests laundry service.)

L＝Tour Leader　C＝Laundry Clerk

C: What can I do for you?

L: Could you send someone up for my laundry, please? Room 808, Wang Gang.

C: Certainly, Mr. Wang. A valet will be up in a few minutes.

L: Fine. I have a silk shirt which I don't think is colorfast. Will the color run in the wash?

C: We'll dry-clean the shirt. Then the color won't run. But you must notify in the laundry list.

L: You're sure? Good! And the lining of my jacket has come unstitched. It might tear over further while being washed.

C: Don't worry, sir. We'll stitch it before washing.

L: That's fine. Now, when can I have my laundry back?

C: Usually it takes one day to have the laundry done. All deliveries will be made before 6:00 p.m.. And we also have express service.

L: What is the difference in price?

C: We charge 50 percent more for express, but it only takes 3 hours.

L: I'll have express then. Oh, I think your valet is at the door.

C: Please feel free to ask him anything. Also, please refer to your laundry list for further information. Thank you for calling and have a nice day!

PART II ENGLISH FOR OUTBOUND TOUR LEADERS

Questions:

(1) Who will be up in a few minutes?

(2) Will the color of the tour leader's silk shirt run in the wash? Why?

(3) What's wrong with the jacket of the tour leader?

(4) When can the laundry be returned to the tour leader?

(5) What's the difference between common laundry service and express laundry service?

Notes

(1) laundry clerk 洗衣房员工

(2) valet（旅馆中）为顾客洗衣服的服务员

(3) I don't think is colorfast. 我想会褪色。

(4) Will the color run in the wash? 在洗涤过程中会褪色吗?

(5) dry-clean 干洗

(6) And the lining of my jacket has come unstitched. It might tear over further while being washed. 我的夹克衬里脱线了，在洗涤过程中可能扯得更开。

(7) All deliveries will be made before 6:00 p.m.. 所有衣物将在下午6点以前送还。

(8) express service 快洗服务

➢ Conversation 5 Check Out

(The tour leader from China International Travel Service is checking out at the cashier's desk.)

扫码听听力

L＝Tour Leader　C＝Cashier

C: Good morning, sir. May I help you?

L: Yes. I'd like to pay our tour group's bill now.

C: Your name and room number?

L: Li Gang. Room 6111, 6112, 6113, 6114, 6115 and 6116.

C: Just a moment, please, Mr. Li. Let me prepare your bill for you.

(The cashier makes up the bill and gives it to Mr. Li.)

Here you are, Mr. Li. It totals 3450 U.S. dollars, including 15 percent service charge. Please check it.

L: Mm. No problem. But I paid 4000 U.S. dollars deposit when I checked in. This is the deposit receipt.

C: Thank you. We'll refund you 550 U.S. dollars. Please check it and keep the invoice. The telephone charge for room 6116 has not been paid yet.

L: (After checking) Yes. Telephone charge will be paid individually. Maybe she forgot it. Please wait for a moment, I'll let her pay for it. One more thing, I'd like to get our valuables back from safe-deposit box. This is the receipt you gave me 3 days ago.

C: Here you are. Please check if they are all right.

L: Right. Thank you.

C: You are welcome. I hope you enjoyed your stay with us here and that you'll have a pleasant trip home.

Questions:

(1) What would the tour leader like to do?

(2) How much does the bill total?

(3) How much deposit has the tour leader paid when he checked in?

(4) Has the tour leader paid the telephone charge for room 6116? Why?

(5) When did the tour leader deposit their valuables in the safe-deposit box?

Notes

(1) make up the bill 整理账单，总计账单

(2) including 15 percent service charge 包括15％的服务费

(3) This is the deposit receipt. 这是押金收据

(4) refund 退还

(5) keep the invoice 保留好发票

(6) One more thing... 还有一件事……

(7) valuables 贵重物品

(8) safe-deposit box 保险箱

➢ Conversation 6 Reservation

(The tour leader from China International Travel Service is reserving some rooms for his group.)

L＝Tour Leader   R＝Reservationist

R: Reservations, may I help you?

L: Yes. I'd like to reserve several rooms for my group.

R: What kinds of room would you like, sir?

L: Double rooms. Do you have any vacancies? I'd like 3 double rooms from May 7 for 2 nights.

R: Let me see. Yes, we do. May I have your name, please?

L: My name is Li Ming. I'm from China. How much is it for each per night?

R: A hundred dollars for each per night.

L: I reserve for our travel agency. Could you give me a discount?

R: For which travel agency?

L: China International Travel Service. We have contract with your hotel.

PART II ENGLISH FOR OUTBOUND TOUR LEADERS

R: I'll check it. Yes. According to the contract, less than 3 rooms 80 dollars a night, 4 or more than 4 rooms 60 dollars a night. You want to reserve 3 rooms, so each room for 80 dollars a night.

L: That's fine. I'll take it. Do I have to leave a deposit?

R: Yes, sir. Will you be paying in cash or by a credit card?

L: By a credit card. You're in Archer Plaza, aren't you?

R: No, sir. We're on the corner of Hill Street. It's very easy to find.

L: That's downtown, isn't it?

R: That's right, sir. We're expecting your coming.

Questions:

(1) What would the tour leader like to do?

(2) What kinds of room would the tour leader like?

(3) When would the tour leader like to have the rooms?

(4) According to the contract, how much should the tour leader pay for each room a night?

(5) Where is the hotel?

Notes

(1) reservationist 预订员

(2) Do you have any vacancies? 你们有没有一些空房间？

(3) Could you give me a discount? 你能给我一个折扣吗？

(4) We have contract with your hotel. 我们与你们酒店有协议。

(5) 4 or more than 4 rooms 60 dollars a night. 4 个或 4 个以上的房间每天 60 美元。

(6) Do I have to leave a deposit? 我必须交定金吗？

New Words & Expressions

show up 露面

grapefruit ['greɪpfruːt] n. 葡萄柚，西柚

bacon ['beɪkən] n. 培根，咸猪肉

doorknob ['dɔːnɒb] n. 门把手

wake up 叫醒，醒来

send up 把……往上送，呈递

notify ['nəʊtɪfaɪ] vt. 通知，告知

unstitched [ʌnˈstɪtʃt] adj. 未缝合的

tear over 撕开

delivery [dɪˈlɪvəri] n. 传送，交付，分娩

valet ['vælɪt] n.（照管男子衣、食等的）贴身仆人，（旅馆中）为顾客洗衣服的服务员 v. 服侍

make up 弥补

deposit [dɪˈpɒzɪt] vt. 放置，存放，将（钱）存入银行，付定金　n. 定金，押金，沉积物

refund [ˈriːfʌnd] n. 退款，返还额　vt. 退（款），退还

vacancy [ˈveɪkənsɪ] n. 空房间，（职位）空缺

contract [ˈkɒntrækt] n. 契约，合同　[kənˈtrækt] vt. 与……订立合同（契约），收缩

downtown [ˈdaʊnˈtaʊn] n. 市中心　adv. 在市中心　adj. 闹市区的

Section 2　Text

Classifications of Hotel

There are four major classifications of American hotels today：①the commercial or transient hotel；②the resort hotel；③the residential hotel；④the motel or motor hotel. Among the 22000 hotels approximately 75 percent are commercial，16 percent are resort，and 9 percent are residential. There are approximately 61500 motels.

The commercial hotel directs its appeal primarily to the individual traveling for business reasons, although most commercial hotels do have some permanent guests. Commercial hotels now typically rely on executives and engineers and more and more on the individual traveling for pleasure. The past few years have even seen a very active commercial hotel campaign for family business.

The commercial hotel guest can expect a room with a private bath, a telephone, a radio, and a television set at no added cost. The hotel will usually have a coffee shop serving popular-priced menus and a dining room for those desiring a more formal atmosphere, featuring the classical cuisine and a high standard of service. For the guest traveling by automobile, parking and garage facilities are available, although possibly not directly under the control of the hotel.

For many years the majority of resort hotels were seasonally operated and thus open for either the summer or the winter season. Today, however, the trend is for resorts to operate year-round. Many resorts have found the expense of remaining open during the "off season" to be lower than the cost of closing down, maintenance, reopening, and often, recruiting many new staff members.

The resort hotel caters to vacationers and recreation-minded people. Usually located at the shore, in the mountains, or at a spa, a resort is free of the large city clamor but is still easily accessible by plane, train, or automobile. Both summer and winter resorts offer the usual hotel service, but because their clientele is made up principally of vacationers, they must provide guest entertainment. The resort guest, however, expects to be treated as a member of the family and to be completely entertained right on the premises.

PART II　ENGLISH FOR OUTBOUND TOUR LEADERS

　　The residential hotel is found principally in the United States. Many Americans early developed the habit of living permanently in hotels, and this branch of the industry evolved primarily to provide for these individuals. Essentially, a residential hotel is an apartment building offering maid service, a dining room, room meal service, and possibly a cocktail lounge. The food and beverage department is usually small and exists more as a convenience for the residents than as a true source of income, some residential hotels lease their food and beverage area to an outside catering organization. Residential hotels range from the luxurious, offering full suites for families, to the moderate, offering single rooms for either young men or young women. Although they represent only a segment of the industry, these hotels nevertheless perform an important function in the American way of life.

　　Motels or motor hotels actually fall into two categories, similar to those of hotels. A motel may be primarily commercial, or it may be a resort-type operation. Motel can generally be said to provide services very similar to those hotels. In fact, it is no longer possible to differentiate between a new motor hotel and a hotel. The one distinguishing aspect is free parking on the premises, few hotels can offer this feature to all guests. Though commercial travelers often patronize motels, the chief motel guest is the person traveling for pleasure with his family.

　　Another distinguishing feature of the modern motel is the swimming pool. It is doubtful that anyone would dare to build a new motel without a pool. While the guest may not use the pool—only a minority ever actually do—he will not stop at a motel that does not have one.

Notes

　　(1) the commercial or transient hotel 商务或暂住酒店

　　(2) directs its appeal 对准某一目标，定位

　　(3) Although most commercial hotels do have some permanent guests. 虽然大多数商务酒店确实拥有一些常客。

　　(4) at no added cost 不增加任何费用

　　(5) popular-priced menus 价格受欢迎的菜单

　　(6) the "off season" 淡季

　　(7) Usually located at the shore, in the mountains, or at a spa, a resort is free of the large city clamor but is still easily accessible by plane, train, or automobile. 度假胜地通常位于海滨、山区，或者温泉疗养地，远离大城市的喧嚣，乘飞机、火车或汽车很容易抵达。

　　(8) clientele（统称）顾客，客户

　　(9) on the premises 在现场

　　(10) Many Americans early developed the habit of living permanently in hotels. 许多美国人很早就养成长期住在旅店的习惯。

　　(11) maid service 女佣服务

(12) The food and beverage department is usually small and exists more as a convenience for the residents than as a true source of income. 餐饮部通常很小，它的存在是为了方便居民，而不是作为创收的真正来源。

(13) some residential hotels lease their food and beverage area to an outside catering organization 一些住宅酒店将他们的餐饮区出租给外面的餐饮机构

(14) a segment of the industry 该行业的一部分

(15) fall into two categories 分成两类

(16) In fact, it is no longer possible to differentiate between a new motor hotel and a hotel. 事实上，要区分新型的汽车旅馆和一般旅馆是不可能的了。

(17) patronize 光顾，惠顾

(18) another distinguishing feature 另一个显著特点

New Words & Expressions

  classification [ˌklæsɪfɪˈkeɪʃən] n. 分类，分级，类别，种类，门类
  transient [ˈtrænzɪənt] adj. 短暂的，片刻的，转瞬即逝的
  residential [ˌrezɪˈdenʃəl] adj. 住宅的，适合居住的
  appeal [əˈpiːl] n. 呼吁，恳求，感染力，上诉　vi. 呼吁，上诉，有吸引力
  permanent [ˈpɜːmənənt] adj. 永久(性)的，固定的
  executive [igˈzekjətiv] n. 主管，执行官，(政府的)行政部门　adj. 有执行权的，行政的
  automobile [ˈɔːtəməbiːl] n. 汽车
  garage [ˈgærɑːʒ] n. 车库，汽车修理厂
  seasonal [ˈsiːzənl] adj. 季节的，季节性的，随季节变化的
  recruit [rɪˈkruːt] v. 招聘，吸引(新成员)，招募　n. 新成员
  vacationer [vəˈkeɪʃənə] n. 度假者，休假者
  spa [spɑː] n. 矿泉疗养地
  clamor [ˈklæmə] n. 喧闹，叫嚷　v. 喧嚷，用吵吵嚷嚷的方法迫使
  clientele [ˌklaɪənˈtel] n. (统称)顾客，客户
  evolve [iˈvɒlv] v. 演变，进化
  lease [liːs] vt. 租，租借　n. 租约，租契，租赁
  luxurious [lʌgˈʒʊəriəs] adj. 奢侈的，豪华的
  segment [ˈsegmənt] n. 部分，片段
  nevertheless [ˌnevəðəˈles] adv. 然而，不过　conj. 尽管如此，然而
  fall into (可)分成，落入，注入
  differentiate [ˌdɪfəˈrenʃieɪt] v. 区分，区别，辨别
  patronize [ˈpætrənaɪz] vt. 摆出高人一等的派头，光顾，资助

Exercises

1. Read and recite the following special terms

(1) the star rating system 饭店星级评定制

PART II ENGLISH FOR OUTBOUND TOUR LEADERS

(2) commercial hotel 商务酒店

(3) chain hotel (hotel chain) 连锁饭店

(4) in-house guest 住店客人

(5) stand-by guest 候补客人

(6) group guests 团体客人

(7) bowling alley 保龄球场

(8) roof revolving restaurant 屋顶旋转餐厅

(9) trunk dock 行李装卸处

(10) golf course (golf links) 高尔夫球场

(11) resident manager 驻店经理

(12) duty manager 值班经理

(13) room rate 房价

(14) voucher 凭证,券

(15) massage parlor 按摩室

(16) fire exit 火警出口

(17) cafeteria 自助餐厅

(18) Pay-TV 收费电视

(19) television remote control 电视遥控开关

(20) fully booked 全被订满

2. Complete the following dialogues

Additional Bed

(The tour leader from China Youth Travel Service is helping the tourist of her group to add one extra bed at the reception.)

L＝Tour Leader   R＝Receptionist

R：Good evening. May I help you?

L：Good evening. I'm Wang Fang, the tour leader of China Youth Travel Service. The Australia Bound Travel ＿＿＿＿＿(1)＿＿＿＿＿（为我们做了预订）.

R：Just a moment, please. Let me check our list... Yes, you've made a reservation for 12 double rooms and 4 single rooms. ＿＿＿＿＿(2)＿＿＿＿＿（你们团队的人数有无变化啊）?

L：Yes. There are 29 persons in our group now. Mr. and Mrs. Li have brought their daughter with them. ＿＿＿＿＿(3)＿＿＿＿＿（所以我们需要增加一个单间）.

R：I'm sorry, Ms. Wang. We don't have any vacancy at the moment.

L：What should we do now?

R：Can the Lis have an extra bed in their double room for their daughter? ＿＿＿＿＿(4)＿＿＿＿＿（这样更方便他们照顾他们的女儿）.

L：That's a good idea. ＿＿＿＿＿(5)＿＿＿＿＿（加一张床的费用是多少）?

R：It costs 30 U.S. dollars per night.

L：That is all right. ＿＿＿＿＿(6)＿＿＿＿＿（我们公司来付加床费）. Thank you

very much.

R: With pleasure. ＿＿＿＿＿＿(7)＿＿＿＿＿＿（你们有没有团体签证）?

L: Yes. Here you are.

R: All right. I'll make a copy of your group visa. Please wait a moment.

3. Translate the following sentences into English

（1）请再查一下好吗？是为来自中国的旅行团预订的，时间是星期一。

（2）我想要一间 40 美元左右、有淋浴设备的单人房。

（3）请送一份牛排餐、一个海鲜盘、一瓶白葡萄酒和一桶冰块来，好吗？

（4）这个钥匙卡很难用。我可以换个新的吗？

（5）虽然大多数商务酒店确实拥有一些常客，但它们主要定位于商务旅行者。

Unit 11　Keys

Unit 12
Practicalities at the Restaurant & Bar and Western Table Etiquette

Section 1　Situational Conversations

➤ **Conversation 1　Arranging the Tour Group to Have Meal**

(In the western restaurant, the tour leader from CTS asks the hostess to seat his group.)

扫码听听力

L＝Tour Leader　H＝Hostess

H: Good evening! Welcome, may I help you?

L: Good evening! We are the tour group for dinner.

H: Have you made a reservation, sir?

L: Yes, we have. American Express Travel Related Services has already reserved for us. We have 18 guests, one driver and two guides.

H: May I have your name?

L: My name is Wang Gang, the tour leader of this group. Guide Li is coming soon. Would you please make an arrangement for us?

H: No problem. Your 18 tourists can use the front two rows, three of you can sit here.

L: By the way, how much do the guests pay for the drink?

H: There is a marked price on each table. You must pay cash for the drinks, but can't sign the bill.

L: Thank you.

Questions:

(1) Has the tour group made a reservation for dinner?

(2) Which travel service is receiving this tour group?

(3) How many tourists are there in the tour group?

(4) Where can the tourists sit?

(5) How do the guests pay for the drink?

Notes

(1) CTS (China Travel Service) 中国旅行社

(2) Have you made a reservation, sir? 先生，你们有预订吗？

(3) American Express Travel Related Services 美国运通旅游有关服务（世界较大的旅行社，在全球设有 1700 多个旅游办事处）

(4) the front two rows 前两排

(5) There is a marked price on each table. 每张餐桌上有标价。

Conversation 2　Ordering Dinner

(In the western restaurant, the tour leader from CTS orders his dinner.)

L＝Tour Leader　W＝Waitress

W：Would you like dinner a la carte or table d'hôte?

L：A la carte, please.

W：Here's the menu a la carte. Please take your time. I'll come to take your order in a while.

(A few minutes later, the waiter comes over.) Excuse me, sir. May I take your order?

L：Oh, Let's skip the appetizer and order straight away.

W：Yes, sir. What would you like to begin with?

L：I'd like a soup as the starter. What's your recommendation?

W：What about vichyssoise? It's a creamy soup made of leeks, onions, and potatoes, with cream.

L：OK. And a Caesar Salad, please.

W：Very well. And your entrée, sir?

L：What kind of beef steak do you serve?

W：We have T-bone, fillet steak, and sirloin steak.

L：A sirloin steak for the main dish.

W：Rare, medium, or well-done?

L：Rare, please.

W：Yes, sir. What side dish would you like to go with it?

L：Make it some peas and carrots and some French fries, please. Anything special about dessert?

W：Yes, we have Malakoff Pudding. It's a cold sweet. It consists of a mixture of fruit, ground almonds, egg yolks, and cream, with lady finger biscuits. It's flavored with rum.

L：That's good. (Returning the menu).

And a glass of Chateau Haut Lafite with the steak.

PART II ENGLISH FOR OUTBOUND TOUR LEADERS

Questions:

(1) Would the tour leader like dinner a la carte or table d'hôte?

(2) Has the tour leader ordered the appetizer?

(3) What is the vichyssoise made of?

(4) What's the main dish of the tour leader?

(5) What side dish would the tour leader like to go with it?

Notes

(1) a la carte（法语）按菜单点菜（与套餐相对）

(2) table d'hôte（法语）定餐的，套餐的

(3) appetizer 开胃品

(4) What about vichyssoise? 您认为维希奶油浓汤（用韭葱、土豆等烹制的奶油汤）怎样？

(5) Caesar Salad 凯撒沙拉

(6) And your entrée, sir? 先生，您的前菜呢？

(7) We have T-bone, fillet steak, and sirloin steak. 我们有丁骨牛排、里脊牛排和牛腰排。

(8) Rare, medium, or well-done? 三分熟，五分熟，还是七分熟？

(9) side dish 配菜

(10) Malakoff Pudding 马拉科夫布丁（用面粉经烘烤或蒸煮做成的甜品）

(11) ground almonds, egg yolks 杏仁、蛋黄

(12) lady finger biscuits 细长条饼干（如女士手指般，意指饼干为细条形）

(13) And a glass of Chateau Haut Lafite with the steak. 再来一杯拉菲酒庄的红酒（法国波尔多出产的拉菲古堡高级红酒）配牛排吧。

➤ Conversation 3 Bill Payment

(In the western restaurant, the tour leader from CTS is paying bill for his tour group.)

扫码听听力

L=Tour Leader W=Waiter

L: Waiter! Can I have the bill?

W: Yes, sir. (The waiter brings the bill.) Here it is, sir.

L: How much?

W: Your bill amounts to 1280 U.S. dollars, please.

L: I see, thanks. I'm afraid I haven't brought enough cash with me. Do you honor credit cards?

W: Yes. What kind have you got, sir?

L: American Express.

W: That will be fine. May I take a print of it?

L：Here you are.

W：Thank you, sir. Just a moment, please.

(On returning.) Thank you for waiting, sir. Would you please sign your name here on the print?

L：Yes, of course.

(The tour leader signs his name on the print.)

W：Thank you. Here is your credit card. Please keep it. And have a nice day!

Questions：

(1) How much does the bill amount to?

(2) Does the tour leader bring enough cash with him?

(3) How does the tour leader pay his bill?

(4) Where does the tour leader sign his name?

Notes

(1) Your bill amounts to 1280 U. S. dollars, please. 您的账单总计1280美元。

(2) Do you honor credit cards? 你们受理信用卡吗?

(3) American Express 美国运通卡

(4) Would you please sign your name here on the print? 请把您的名字签在复印件上，好吗?

➢ Conversation 4　At the Bar

(At the bar, the tour leader from CTS is ordering drinks for his group.)

L＝Tour Leader　B＝Bartender

B：Good evening, sir! What would you like to drink?

L：We'd like to take some wine.

B：We have a good selection of classified Bordeaux wines and Californian wine. Here is the wine list, sir. Please take your time.

(In a few minutes, the bartender comes back.) May I take your order now, sir?

L：There are so many wines here. We really don't know which one to have?

B：What about a bottle of Chateau Haut Lafite? It is very good. Many tourists give high comments on it.

L：Fine, a bottle of this wine then.

(The bartender takes the order.)

B：(Presenting the bottle to the guests.) This is the bottle of Chateau Haut Lafite 1964, sir.

L：Ah, it looks quite good.

B：May I open it now?

L：Open now, please.

PART II ENGLISH FOR OUTBOUND TOUR LEADERS

B:(Pouring a bit of wine into the wine glass of the tour leader.) Sir, would you please taste the wine?

L:(Tasting.) Excellent! Thank you for your recommendation.

Questions:

(1) What would the tour leader like to drink?

(2) What kinds of wine does the bar have?

(3) What kind of wine does the tour leader order?

(4) What's the comment of many tourists on this wine?

(5) What does the tour leader think of this wine?

Notes

(1) bartender 酒吧间销售酒精饮料的人,酒吧招待

(2) We have a good selection of classified Bordeaux wines and Californian wine. 我们有精选的上乘波尔多葡萄酒和加利福尼亚葡萄酒。

(3) Many tourists give high comments on it. 许多游客对它的评价很高。

(4) Thank you for your recommendation. 谢谢你的推荐。

New Words & Expressions

hostess [ˈhəustəs] n. 女主人,(餐馆的)女迎宾,女主持人

arrangement [əˈreɪndʒmənt] n. 安排,筹备,约定,整理好的东西,改编乐曲

a la carte [ɑːlɑːˈkɑːt] (法语)按菜单点菜(与套餐相对)

table d'hôte [tɑːblˈdəut] (法语)定餐的,套餐的

appetizer [ˈæpɪtaɪzə] n. 开胃菜

starter [ˈstɑːtə] n. (主菜之前的)开胃小吃,赛跑、赛马等起跑线上的人(马,汽车等),发令员,起动装置

vichyssoise [viːʃiːˈswɑːz] n. 维希奶油浓汤(用韭葱、土豆等烹制的奶油汤,通常冷食)

leek [liːk] n. 韭葱

Caesar [ˈsiːzə] n. 恺撒(公元前100—公元前44 古罗马杰出的军事统帅、政治家)

entrée [ˈɒntreɪ] n. 主菜,两道正菜(鱼和肉)之间的小菜

fillet [ˈfɪlɪt] n. 无骨的鱼或肉排

sirloin [ˈsɜːlɔɪn] n. 牛的上部腰肉

almond [ˈɑːmənd] n. 杏树,杏仁

yolk [jəuk] n. 蛋黄

rum [rʌm] n. (用甘蔗酿造的)酒,朗姆酒

Chateau [ˈʃætəu] n. (法国的)城堡,乡间别墅,大宅邸,庄园

haut [əu] adj. (法语)高级的,豪华的,上流社会的

Lafite [lɑˈfaɪt] n. 拉菲酒庄(出产知名的法国红酒，被誉为葡萄酒王国中的"皇后")
amount to 总共达，等于
bartender [ˈbɑːtendə] n. 酒吧间销售酒精饮料的人，酒吧招待
classified [ˈklæsɪfaɪd] adj. 机密的，分成类的，被归入一类的
Bordeaux [bɔːˈdəʊ] n. 波尔多
Californian [ˌkæləˈfɔːnjən] adj. 加利福尼亚的 n. 加利福尼亚人
give high comments on 给予高度评价

Section 2   Text

Western Table Etiquettes

There is a very famous saying: "The way to a man's heart is through his stomach." A girl should cook good meals if she wants to master her boyfriend's heart. Although it is a joke, to some extent, it has some reasonable factors, because people can not live without food and people attach importance to food whether in the West or in the East. And all people are proud of their culture of cuisine. Also, what is eaten and how we eat are important as well. Etiquette in each country is different. What is polite in China may not be polite in other countries. These rules will help you enjoy western food with your foreign friends.

Using a Napkin

You have been invited to a fancy dinner and you look at all the silverware, look at all the glasses, where do we start? Well, the first thing that we need to think about is your napkin. That is where you start; you need to place your napkin on your lap. Shaking your napkin as if it's a flag is a good example of what not to do. You should not put your napkin on your neck as a bib. What you should do is to unfold your napkin on your lap and you are ready.

Pick up Silverware

The fork is held in your left hand and the knife is held in your right. If you are left-handed and you prefer to switch, just do it at the time that you're going to eat. Do not switch all of the silverware when you first sit at the table because it does not look nice. This is how we are going to eat whether it is American or Continental: You would hold the food with the fork, keep your knife in your right hand and cut going one way, and then bring the food to your mouth with the tines down. That is how you eat continental style. Sometimes you need to push your food on to the fork; you would do it with your knife. Your knife and your fork will be in your hands at all times, so we continue to eat this way. It is important when you are eating that you do not spread out your arms, and always keep it close to your body.

Using Glasses

When sitting at a table and looking at so many glasses, you wonder which one you should pick up first. If you are invited to a fancy wedding or you go on a cruise, you do not need to worry about it because the servers know exactly what to do, but I will give you a rundown just in case. Your water glass will be very close to the knife. There is a small glass for your white wine, a bigger one for your red wine, and of course we have our champagne flute that will be served with your dessert. And the little glass is your sherry glass that you will use to drink your sherry when you have your soup.

Holding a Wine Glass

The correct way to hold the glasses when you are drinking wine: If you are drinking the white wine, you would be holding your glass by the stem because the white wine is served chilled and you do not want to change the temperature. On the other hand if you are drinking red wine, you can hold it by the stem if you wish or you may hold it partially by the bowl because red wine is usually served at room temperature and that will not affect your fingers on it. Champagne would be of course by the stem because champagne is cold when served. The water glass does not make a difference which way you hold it. And the sherry glass is usually slightly chilled and it is best to hold it by the stem.

Placing Silverware in the Inverted V Position

When you are eating in continental style, you know that you are holding your silverware in your hands at all times, but sometimes you need to get to your bread or to your drink. In that case you would place your silverware in almost an inverted 'V' position on the plate very wide open (with the blade inwards) which says that I am resting, I am not finished. Then you would go to your bread or your drink. If you must leave the table for a while, your silverware should be put in an inverted 'V' position, too. When you are finished with your dining, you would put your silverware together at six o'clock with your fork on the left (tines facing up) and knife on the right, with the knife blade facing in. This is your silent signal to the staff or to your host/hostess that you have finished.

Leaving the Table

It is impolite for a guest to leave the table during a meal, or before the hostess gives the signal at the end. When the hostess indicates that the dinner is over, she will place her silverware in the description above, her napkin on the table and rise from her seat and all guests rise from theirs at the same time. Well, the men will help the ladies with their chairs.

Notes

(1) etiquette 礼仪、礼节

(2) The way to a man's heart is through his stomach. 犹得君心，必先悦君腹。

(3) to some extent 在某种程度上

(4) attach importance to 注重

(5) to place your napkin on your lap 把餐巾放在大腿上

(6) You should not put your napkin on your neck as a bib. 你不应该将你的餐巾当作婴儿的围嘴围在你的颈部。

(7) cut going one way 从一个方向切

(8) bring the food to your mouth with the tines down 齿尖朝下送到你的口中

(9) spread out your arms 张开你的双臂

(10) But I will give you a rundown just in case. 但是我还是要向你简要说明一下，以防万一。

(11) champagne flute 香槟笛形杯

(12) sherry glass 雪利酒杯

(13) to hold it by the stem 握住酒杯的颈部

(14) In that case you would place your silverware in almost an inverted 'V' position on the plate very wide open (with the blade inwards) which says that I am resting, I am not finished. 在那种情况下，你就要把你的餐具呈倒"V"字形分开摆放在盘中，刀刃朝内，表明我停一下，还没吃完。

(15) It is impolite for a guest to leave the table during a meal, or before the hostess gives the signal at the end. 客人在用餐过程中离开或者在女主人发出结束用餐的信号之前离开都是不礼貌的。

New Words & Expressions

etiquette [ˈetɪket] n. 礼仪，礼节
attach importance to 重视
fancy [ˈfænsi] v. 想象，设想，喜欢，以为   n. 设想，空想，想象（力）
silverware [ˈsɪlvəweə] n. 银器，镀银器皿（尤指餐具），（体育比赛中的）银杯
lap [læp] n.（人坐着时）大腿部分   vt. 舔，舔食，轻拍，领先一圈
bib [bɪb] n.（小儿用的）围嘴，围兜
unfold [ʌnˈfəʊld] v. 展开，打开，显露，展现
continental [ˌkɒntɪˈnentəl] adj. 大陆的，大陆性的，欧洲大陆的
tine [taɪn] n. 尖头，尖齿，叉
spread out 散开
pick up 拾取
cruise [kruːz] vi. 乘船巡游，以快而平稳的速度长距离行驶   n. 乘船游览
server [ˈsɜːvə] n. 服务员，侍者，服务器
rundown [ˈrʌndaʊn] n.（尤指商业）削减，紧缩，描述
champagne [ʃæmˈpeɪn] n. 香槟酒
flute [fluːt] n. 笛形杯，笛形物，长笛

sherry [ˈʃeri] n. 雪利酒

stem [stem] n. 高酒杯的脚，（花草的）茎，（树木的）干，词干　vt. 遏制（阻止）（液体的流动等）

partially [ˈpɑːʃəli] adv. 部分地

inverted [inˈvɜːtid] adj. 反向的，倒转的

Exercises

1. Read and recite the following special terms

(1) barkeeper 酒吧老板，酒吧招待员

(2) paper napkin 餐巾纸

(3) chopstick rest 筷子架

(4) toothpick holder 牙签筒

(5) salt shaker 盐瓶

(6) appetizer 开胃小菜，开胃品

(7) vegetarian 素食者

(8) executive chef（chef de cuisine）厨师长

(9) grillroom（rotisserie）烤肉餐厅（烤肉馆，烤肉店）

(10) steak house 牛排餐馆

(11) hash house（美）廉价餐馆

(12) fast-food restaurant 快餐饭店

(13) theme restaurant 主题餐厅

(14) continental breakfast 欧陆式早餐

(15) American（full）breakfast 美式早餐

(16) curry paste 咖喱酱

(17) caviar 鱼子酱

(18) be done to a turn 烧得恰到好处

(19) beefsteak with onion 葱头牛肉扒

(20) savory pork chop 美味猪排

2. Complete the following dialogues

Asking for Service During the Meal

(At the restaurant, the tour leader from China Travel Service is asking for service during the meal.)

W＝Waiter　L＝Tour Leader

L：Waiter,　　　(1)　　　（你过来一会儿，好吗）？

W：Yes,　　　(2)　　　（我马上过来）.

　　　Yes, sir? What can I do for you?

L：　　　(3)　　　（恐怕这不是我点的菜）.

W：I'm sorry for that. What did you order?

L：Roast beef.

W: There must be a mistake. Those are fried oysters. _____(4)_____（您是想保留这道菜还是要更换呢）？

L: Roast beef, of course. That's what I ordered.

W: Just a moment and your order will be served right away, sir. _____(5)_____（对不起，给您带来了不便）.

(A few minutes later)

Sorry to have kept you waiting, sir. Your roast beef, please.

L: Thank you. _____(6)_____（我刚才把餐叉弄掉了）. Can I have another one?

W: Certainly, sir. Here you are. _____(7)_____（我可以把这个盘子拿走吗）？

L: Sure, go ahead.

W: _____(8)_____（您觉得我们的菜怎样）？

L: Very good. It is done just right. Thank you.

3. Translate the following sentences into English

（1）你能推荐一些价廉物美的酒水吗？

（2）您的鸡蛋要怎么做？炒、煎还是煮？

（3）我的鸡蛋不要单面煎，双面煎吧。

（4）我要一杯咖啡，但不要煮得太久了。

（5）每个国家的礼节是不一样的，在中国是礼貌的在其他国家可能不礼貌。

Unit 12　Keys

Unit 13 Practicalities on Shopping and Hong Kong—The Shopping Paradise

Section 1　Situational Conversations

➢ Conversation 1　Buying Cosmetics

(In the shop, the tour leader from CYTS helps her tourists to buy some cosmetics.)

扫码听听力

L＝Tour Leader　A＝Shop Assistant

A: Good afternoon, Miss. Can I help you?

L: Yes. I'm looking for souvenirs. Do you have anything for ladies?

A: We have several items. How about cosmetics?

L: All right. I'd like a lipstick.

A: Which brand do you want?

L: Christian Dior.

A: Which color do you like?

L: I like rose.

A: What about this one?

L: It's too dark.

A: Maybe you're right. Is this one better?

L: Yes, I'll take it. By the way, do you have a cream make-up?

A: Yes, this is a cream make-up with a sponge.

L: I also need powder.

A: How about this one?

L: OK, I'll take it.

A: Do you want eyelash curlers, too?

L: No, that's all. Thank you.

Questions:

(1) What is the tour leader looking for in the shop?

(2) Does the shop have anything for ladies?

(3) Which brand of lipstick does the tour leader want?

(4) Has the tour leader bought a cream make-up?

(5) Has the tour leader bought eyelash curlers?

Notes

(1) CYTS(China Youth Travel Service) 中国青年旅行社

(2) I'm looking for souvenirs. 我正在找纪念品。

(3) cosmetic 化妆品

(4) lipstick 口红，唇膏

(5) Christian Dior 克里斯汀·迪奥（法国知名化妆品品牌）

(6) a cream make-up with a sponge 附海绵的上妆底霜

(7) powder 香粉

(8) eyelash curler 睫毛夹

Conversation 2　Buying Watches

(In the shop, the tour leader from CYTS helps his tourists to buy some watches.)

L＝Tour Leader　A＝Shop Assistant

A：May I help you, sir?

L：May I just look around?

A：We have Swiss made watches, and we also have a wide range of Japanese watches.

L：Please show me this Swiss watch.

A：It is automatic and waterproof, with date, and the price is very reasonable. It's a fine watch.

L：Will you please show me that one?

A：That is a good, electronic, quartz watch with date and alarm. It loses just one second a month.

L：Where is it made?

A：Casio, a Japanese company. We sell a lot of these watches.

L：How much is it?

A：158 U.S. dollars.

L：Can you give me a better price?

A：We usually give 5% discount for one watch and 10% for two watches.

L：All right. I'll take this one. Do you have quality certification?

A：Of course we have. You can have your money back with the quality certification and receipt within one year if your watch has any problem.

L：Oh, I need the receipt.

PART II ENGLISH FOR OUTBOUND TOUR LEADERS

Questions:

(1) What watches does the shop have?

(2) What are the advantages of the Swiss watch?

(3) Where is the quartz watch made?

(4) How much is the quartz watch?

(5) What should the tour leader do if the watch has some problems?

Notes

(1) Swiss made watches 瑞士手表

(2) a wide range of Japanese watches 各种各样的日本手表

(3) waterproof 防水

(4) a good, electronic, quartz watch with date and alarm 一款好的电子石英表，有日期显示、闹铃的功能

(5) It loses just one second a month. 它一个月只相差一秒。

(6) 5% discount for one watch 一块手表有5%的折扣

(7) quality certification 质量保证书

➤ Conversation 3 Buying Some Fish Oil and Sheep Oil Skin Care Items

(In the shop, the tour leader from CYTS helps his tourists to buy some fish oil and sheep oil skin care items.)

L＝Tour Leader A＝Shop Assistant

A: Welcome. What can I do for you?

L: Oh, yes. A tourist of my tour group wants to buy some fish oil and sheep oil skin care items.

A: You can buy fish oil in the shop next door, please. We have all kinds of products of sheep oil including skin care items.

L: This guest wants to know the duty free limit.

A: It seems no limit, but I am not clear about Chinese Customs' regulations. Why don't you ask any other passenger who hasn't got such products to take some for him?

L: It sounds a good idea. He says that he'd like to buy 20 bottles as presents to his relatives and friends after he returns to China.

A: You can have 5% discount for more than 10 bottles.

L: Australian dollar or U.S. dollar?

A: Both. One U.S. dollar changes 1.2 Australian dollars here.

L: It seems to be reasonable to pay with Australian dollar.

扫码听听力

Questions:

(1) What does one of the tour group want to buy?

(2) Does the tourist can buy fish oil in the same shop?

(3) What's the duty free limit for fish oil and sheep oil skin care items?

(4) How many bottles does the tourist want to buy? Why?

(5) What's the rate between US dollar and Australian dollar?

Notes

(1) some fish oil and sheep oil skin care items 一些深海鱼油和绵羊油护肤品

(2) the duty free limit 免税限额

(3) Why don't you ask any other passenger who hasn't got such products to take some for him? 你为什么不请其他没有买这种产品的客人帮他带一些呢?

(4) You can have 5% discount for more than 10 bottles. 买 10 瓶以上可以给你 5%的折扣。

(5) It seems to be reasonable to pay with Australian dollar. 看起来付澳元比较划算。

➢ Conversation 4 Buying Fruits

(In the shop, the tour leader from CYTS helps his tourists to buy some fruits.)

L＝Tour Leader A＝Shop Assistant

A：Can I help you, sir?

L：Yes. I'd like some grapes.

A：All right. How many kilos do you want?

L：I want a kilo.

A：OK. We have some very fine oranges as well, sir. Do you want some?

L：It seems they aren't ripe enough.

A：Oh, yes, sir. They are, indeed. I don't mind if you try one.

L：Thanks. Well, it's not too bad. Give me half a kilo, please.

A：Thank you, sir. Do you want some watermelons? They are very sweet.

L：Are you sure they are very sweet? I don't like sour melons.

A：I can promise you, sir. They are as sweet as pure sugar. And they are seedless.

L：All right. I'll take one.

A：Is that all, sir?

L：Yes. How much together?

A：8 dollars in all.

L：Here you are.

A：Thank you, sir.

Questions：

(1) What would the tour leader want to buy?

PART II ENGLISH FOR OUTBOUND TOUR LEADERS

(2) How many kilos of grapes does the tour leader want?

(3) Has the tour leader bought some oranges?

(4) Has the tour leader bought any watermelons?

(5) How much should the tour leader pay together?

Notes

(1) I'd like some grapes. 我想要点葡萄。

(2) It seems they aren't ripe enough. 看样子好像不够熟。

(3) sour melon 酸的西瓜

(4) I can promise you, sir. 先生,我可以保证。

(5) And they are seedless. 并且它们是无籽西瓜。

➤ Conversation 5   Returning Goods for a Refund

(In the shop, the tour leader from CYTS helps the tourist of his last tour group to return goods for a refund.)

扫码听听力

L＝Tour Leader   A＝Shop Assistant

A: Welcome. Can I help you?

L: Yes, I'm the leader of tour group. One of my tourists bought a necklace here two months ago. However, she found there was quality problem with it after she returned to China. She requested our travel agency to send her money back. So I really hope you can return all her money.

A: Let me check it up, please.

L: Here it is.

A: Do you have the receipt?

L: Yes. I also have the quality certification.

A: The necklace is OK. Maybe she pulled it broken hard with her hand. Usually we can't return it in this case.

L: Your jewelry shop is our company's partner. I hope you can deal with this case properly. Otherwise, it's hard for us to explain to our passengers.

A: We'll change a new one, the same style. Is that OK?

L: I don't mind, but I'm afraid that the passenger can not receive it.

A: If the passenger disagrees, let your colleague bring it back next time, we will return the money.

L: That's a good idea. I agree. Thank you.

Questions:

(1) Why does one of his tourists want to return the necklace for a refund?

(2) Does the tourist have the receipt?

(3) What is the real problem with the necklace?

(4) Has the tour leader returned the necklace to the shop for a refund finally? How did the shop assistant deal with the problem?

(5) What should the tour leader do if the tourist disagrees and insists returning the necklace for a refund?

Notes

(1) return goods for a refund 退货退钱

(2) There was quality problem with it. 它质量有问题。

(3) quality certification 质量认证书

(4) Maybe she pulled it broken hard with her hand. 可能是她用力过猛给拉断了。

(5) Usually we can't return it in this case. 这种情况下我们一般不退货。

(6) jewelry shop 珠宝店

(7) Otherwise, it's hard for us to explain to our passengers. 否则，我们难以向客人交代。

Conversation 6　In the Duty Free Shop

(In the duty free shop, the tour leader from CYTS helps his tourists to buy some cigarettes and liquor.)

L＝Tour Leader　A＝Shop Assistant

A：What can I do for you?

L：I'd like to have some cigarettes and liquor. I am going back to China. Do you know the duty free limit?

A：You can bring in two hundred cigarettes and two bottles of liquor with you?

L：Thank you. Could you give me a carton of Hilton, a bottle of Red Label and a bottle of Scotch whisky, please?

A：Okay. Anything else?

L：That's it. How much?

A：That'll be 80 U.S. dollars.

L：I still have some local cash left. Can I pay with them? The rest will be paid in U.S. dollar.

A：Yes, you can. But the exchange rate will be a little higher.

L：No problem. Please give me a receipt.

Questions:

(1) What would the tour leader like to buy?

(2) What's the duty free limit for cigarettes and liquor?

(3) What has the tour leader bought?

(4) How much has the tour leader paid?

(5) What kinds of money does the tour leader pay with?

PART II ENGLISH FOR OUTBOUND TOUR LEADERS

Notes

(1) duty free shop 免税店

(2) I'd like to have some cigarettes and liquor. 我想买点烟和酒。

(3) a carton of Hilton, a bottle of Red Label and a bottle of Scotch whisky 一条希尔顿、一瓶红方酒和一瓶苏格兰威士忌。

(4) I still have some local cash left. 我还剩一些当地货币。

➢ Conversation 7 Inquiring about Tax Refund

(In the shop, the tour leader from CYTS asks about tax refund.)

L＝Tour Leader   A＝Shop Assistant

L：How can I get tax refund?

A：When you buy something in shops, you may ask the shop assistant for a duty-free list, which shows your name, price of goods and duty-free rate.

L：Is that all? Where can I get the refund?

A：You should keep this list handy. When you bring the goods out of the customs, the officer will seal the list, then you send the list back to the shop where you bought the goods, they will return you the tax money.

L：Can I get the refund of tax for all the goods I bought?

A：Yes, but please remember the rate of tax refund is about 10％ and you will be charged for the customs seal.

扫码听听力

Questions：

(1) How can the tour leader get tax refund?

(2) Where can the tour leader get the refund?

(3) Can he get the refund of tax for all the goods he bought?

(4) What's the rate of tax refund?

(5) Will he be charged for the customs seal?

Notes

(1) tax refund form 退税单

(2) a duty-free list 退税单

(3) duty-free rate 退税税率

(4) You should keep this list handy. 您要把退税单放在手边。

(5) The officer will seal the list. 海关官员在税单上盖章。

New Words & Expressions

cosmetic [kɒzˈmetɪk] n. 化妆品   adj. 装点门面的，整容的

lipstick [ˈlɪpstɪk] n. 口红，唇膏

Christian [ˈkrɪstʃən] n. 基督教徒　adj. 信基督教的，基督教的，基督教徒的
make-up [ˈmeɪkʌp] n. 化妆品，组成成分，性格，补考
sponge [spʌndʒ] n. 海绵　vt.（用海绵或海绵状物）擦拭
powder [ˈpaʊdə] n. 粉，粉末　vt. 抹粉
eyelash [ˈaɪlæʃ] n. 睫毛
curler [ˈkɜːlə] n. 卷发夹子
automatic [ˌɔːtəˈmætɪk] adj. 自动的，不假思索的，无意识的
waterproof [ˈwɔːtəpruːf] adj. 不透水的，防水的　vt. 使防水，使不透水
quartz [kwɔːts] n. 石英
alarm [əˈlɑːm] vt. 警告，使惊慌　n. 警钟，警报器，闹钟
certification [ˌsɜːtɪfɪˈkeɪʃən] n. 证明
ripe [raɪp] adj. 成熟的，时机成熟的
watermelon [ˈwɔːtəˌmelən] n. 西瓜
seedless [ˈsiːdləs] adj. 无核的
disagree [ˌdɪsəˈgriː] vi. 不同意，持不同意见
liquor [ˈlɪkə] n. 酒，烈性酒

Section 2　Text

Hong Kong—The Shopping Paradise

　　Millions of visitors come to Hong Kong every year, and shopping is high on their list of things to do. The territory's variety of goods has tempted visitors for decades and its reputation as a shopper's paradise is well deserved.

　　No matter why you come to Hong Kong, and whether or not you're a shopper by nature, it's highly unlikely that you'll leave here without having bought something. Indeed, Hong Kong does a roaring trade in bargain-priced luggage simply because so many travelers run out of space in their suitcases.

　　There are several good reasons for this. The first is Hong Kong's status as a free port, where everything other than alcohol, tobacco, perfumes, cosmetics, cars, and some petroleum products comes in without import duty. The second is that Hong Kong has access to a skilled and still relatively inexpensive labor force just across the border in Chinese mainland. Goods made on either side of the border are considerably cheaper than they will be when they reach shop shelves anywhere else in the world. The third factor is the highly competitive nature of the retail business—the result of a local policy of free trade, which encourages every store to try to undercut its neighbors. To this end, many shops, with the exception of those in the western and central districts, stay open until 10:00 p.m.. Shops also hum on Sunday and on all holidays apart from the Chinese New Year, when everything closes for at least three days.

扫码听短文

What else makes Hong Kong special? Because it's very small and very heavily populated, Hong Kong has had to grow upward and downward rather than outward—which means there are shops and small businesses in all sorts of unexpected places. You'll find a trendy fashion designer tucked away on the third floor of a scruffy building in an alleyway, a picture framer in the basement of a lighting shop, a tailor snipping and stitching in the back room of a shoe shop.

Many buildings will appear dingy and dirty, and you may be inclined to think that no self-respecting business can be carried on inside; but it can, and it is. These are the places where Hong Kongers do much of their own shopping. Prices for the same goods vary from sky-high to rock bottom within a 100-yard stretch.

Visitors will be delighted with a truly unique souvenir that reflects all the graceful charm of the city where East meets West! The six signature Hong Kong "Must-Buy" products selected by residents and visitors are truly representative of the myriad treasures of Hong Kong.

Travelers can check out the wide range of handicrafts with which Hong Kong has long been synonymous. A treasure trove for handicrafts and home furnishings produced locally and imported from Chinese provincial cities, Hong Kong specializes in quality products at reasonable prices. The same high quality is apparent in Chinese clothing. One of Asia's leading fashion centers, Hong Kong offers the best craftsmanship and widest range of styles and fabrics in fashionable Chinese and fashion-style clothes and accessories. Local tailors are renowned worldwide for their speedy tailor-made service.

Similarly, no visit to Hong Kong would be complete without refreshing Chinese tea. Tasting tea is an art and is believed to be good for your health. A wide selection of attractively packaged teas from different Chinese provinces is available in Hong Kong. Alternatively, tourists can spoil themselves with gold jewellery. Hong Kong's huge number of jewellery shops offer an unsurpassed selection of modern and traditional gold jewellery, accessories and ornaments; the purity of which is guaranteed.

Equally irresistible are scrumptious Chinese assorted cakes. Traditional Chinese cakes and festive delicacies such as "wife cake" and mini moon cakes are tasty treats for young and old alike. They'll taste even sweeter when served on fine Chinese tableware. Classic Chinese tableware, such as chopsticks, bowls, and dishes, are a lasting symbol of Hong Kong's exhilarating dining culture.

Hong Kong is a fusion of the eastern and western cultures; a diverse city where old and new meet at every turn. It is a unique experience shaped by a distinctive past and dreams of the future, an age-old synthesis of cultures and traditions that opens a window into what will be, while embracing what has passed.

Notes

(1) Shopping is high on their list of things to do. 购物在他们要做的事情中是很重要的。

(2) Its reputation as a shopper's paradise is well deserved. 作为购物者天堂的声誉是名副其实的。

(3) bargain-priced 廉价的，低廉的

(4) free port 自由港

(5) without import duty 没有进口税

(6) Chinese mainland 中国内地

(7) retail business 零售业

(8) to try to undercut its neighbors 尽量比相邻公司的价格低

(9) to this end 为此

(10) Shops also hum on Sunday and on all holidays apart from the Chinese New Year. 除了中国农历新年，在星期天和所有的节假日，商店也非常繁忙。

(11) Because it's very small and very heavily populated, Hong Kong has had to grow upward and downward rather than outward—which means there are shops and small businesses in all sorts of unexpected places. 由于香港地少人多，无法向外延伸，只能向上向下发展——这意味着商店和小店铺会出现在各种各样令人意想不到的地方。

(12) You'll find a trendy fashion designer tucked away on the third floor of a scruffy building in an alleyway, a picture framer in the basement of a lighting shop, a tailor snipping and stitching in the back room of a shoe shop. 你也许会在小街巷里某个外表陈旧的三楼上发现一家时髦的服装设计店，在某个灯具店的地下室里可能看到一位画框师，或在一家鞋店后部看到裁缝在裁剪、缝纫。

(13) Prices for the same goods vary from sky-high to rock bottom within a 100-yard stretch. 同样的商品在100码的距离内价格有时高得出奇，有时却低得离谱。

(14) the myriad treasures of Hong Kong 香港无数的珍宝

(15) A treasure trove for handicrafts and home furnishings produced locally and imported from Chinese provincial cities, Hong Kong specializes in quality products at reasonable prices. 香港像个聚宝盆，有各种来自本地和中国内地各省的手工艺品和家居饰品，专门提供质量上乘、价格合理的商品。

(16) The purity of which is guaranteed. 这些珠宝的纯度是可以得到保证的。

(17) Equally irresistible are scrumptious Chinese assorted cakes. Traditional Chinese cakes and festive delicacies such as "wife cake" and mini moon cakes are tasty treats for young and old alike. 同样令人垂垂涎欲滴、难以抵挡其诱惑的还有什锦饼。传统的中国糕饼和节日美食，如"老婆饼"和小月饼，都是老少皆宜的美味。

(18) Hong Kong's exhilarating dining culture 香港令人喜爱的餐饮文化

(19) Hong Kong is a fusion of the eastern and western cultures. 香港是东西方文化交融的城市。

PART II ENGLISH FOR OUTBOUND TOUR LEADERS

New Words & Expressions

territory [ˈterətri] n. 领土，管区，领域，地盘
variety [vəˈraɪəti] n. 品种，不同种类，各种，变化，多样化
tempt [tempt] vt. 引诱或怂恿(某人)干不正当的事
decade [ˈdekeɪd] n. 十年
deserve [dɪˈzɜːv] vt. 应受，应得，值得
run out of 用完
other than 除……以外
perfume [ˈpɜːfjuːm] n. 香水，芳香　vt. 使香气弥漫，在……喷香水
has access to 访问
considerably [kənˈsɪdərəbəli] adv. 非常，很，相当多地
undercut [ˌʌndəˈkʌt] vt. 以低于(竞争对手)的价格出售
apart from 除了
rather than 而非
trendy [ˈtrendi] adj. 时髦的，赶时髦的　n. 时髦人物，赶时髦的人
tuck away 使隐藏
scruffy [ˈskrʌfi] adj. 肮脏的，不整洁的
alleyway [ˈælɪweɪ] n. 小巷，窄道
basement [ˈbeɪsmənt] n. 地下室
snip [snɪp] vt. & n. 剪
dingy [ˈdɪndʒi] adj. 又黑又脏的，肮脏的
incline [ɪnˈklaɪn] v. (使)倾斜，(使)倾向于　n. 斜坡
sky-high [ˌskaɪˈhaɪ] adj. & adv. 极高的(地)
synonymous [sɪˈnɒnɪməs] adj. 同义的
trove [trəʊv] n. (物主不明的)发掘出来的金银财宝
furnishing [ˈfɜːnɪʃ] vt. 陈设，布置，提供
specialize in 专攻，专门研究，专注于
craftsmanship [ˈkræftsmənʃɪp] n. 手工，工艺，技能，技术
accessory [ækˈsesəri] n. 附件，配件，同谋，帮凶
refresh [rɪˈfreʃ] vt. 使恢复，使振作，使……记起
unsurpassed [ˌʌnsəˈpɑːst] adj. 未被超越的，非常卓越的
irresistible [ˌɪrɪˈzɪstəbl] adj. 无法抗拒的
scrumptious [ˈskrʌmpʃəs] adj. 可口的，美味的
assorted [əˈsɔːtɪd] adj. 各种各样的，五花八门的
delicacy [ˈdelɪkəsi] n. 精致，精美，娇嫩，精美的食物
tableware [ˈteɪblweə] n. 餐具
exhilarating [ɪɡˈzɪləreɪtɪŋ] adj. 令人兴奋的，使人愉快的
sophisticated [səˈfɪstɪkeɪtɪd] adj. 老练的，老于世故的，精密的，高雅的，有教养的

fusion ['fju:ʒən] n. 融合，核聚变，联合，合并
diverse [daɪ'vəs] adj. 不同的，多种多样的
synthesis ['sɪnθəsɪs] n. 综合，综合法，合成

Exercises

1. Read and recite the following special terms

（1）go shopping 购物

（2）pharmacy（drug）store 药店

（3）convenience store 便利店

（4）shopping mall 购物商场（商业街）

（5）shopping trolley 手推车

（6）business hours 营业时间

（7）advance payment 预付款

（8）cash payment 现金支付

（9）price tag 价格签

（10）retail price 零售价

（11）wholesale price 批发价

（12）on sale 降价出售

（13）bargain sale 大减价

（14）20% off (discount) 20%折扣

（15）VTA（value-added tax）附加税

（16）diamond ring 钻石戒指

（17）cosmetics 化妆品

（18）quality certificate 质量保证书

（19）duty-free shop 免税店

（20）flea market 跳蚤市场

2. Complete the following dialogues

At the Arts and Crafts Store

(At the arts and crafts store, the tour leader from CYTS helps his tourists to buy some arts and crafts.)

L＝Tour Leader　A＝Shop Assistant

A：Good morning! Can I help you?

L：_____(1)_____（我们想为这次法国之行买些纪念品），but we don't know what to buy. Would you mind doing us a favor?

A：Of course. _____(2)_____（我建议你们买一些与我们古代文明相关的东西）.

L：That's a good idea! What then?

A：How about this one? _____(3)_____（这件工艺品的历史可以追溯到一

百年以前).

L: I see. How much does it cost?

A: 40 euros.

L: OK. I'll take it.

A: What else would you like, sir?

L: _____(4)_____ (我对法国的绘画特别感兴趣). Do you have any good ones?

A: Certainly.

L: I see. Those ancient French paintings are an important part of your national culture, aren't they?

A: Yeah. _____(5)_____ (您觉得这幅名画的复制品怎样)?

L: Oh, I like them very much. How much?

A: _____(6)_____ (原价是50欧元). Now it is 30% off, it's 35 euros.

L: This is too much. _____(7)_____ (你能不能再给我们一个折扣啊)?

A: Sorry, this is the last price.

L: OK. I'll take it.

3. Translate the following sentences into English

(1) 他们的营业时间是从几点到几点?

(2) 你可以推荐一些适合当纪念品的东西吗?

(3) 慢慢看,你会发现你喜欢的东西。

(4) 在看过您所买的毛衣后,海关办公室会在这张表格上盖章。

(5) 同样的商品在100码的距离内价格有时高得出奇,有时却低得离谱。

Unit 13　Keys

Unit 14 Practicalities on Traffic and London's 5 Airports

Section 1 Situational Conversations

➢ Conversation 1 Taking a Taxi

(The tour leader from CTS and his tourists want to take a taxi to the airport.)

L＝Tour Leader　D＝Taxi Driver

L：Taxi! Are you engaged?

D：Where are you going, sir?

L：Please get us to the airport. How long does it take from here to the airport?

D：It depends on traffic conditions. Usually it takes one hour.

L：That means we can get there before 9:00.

D：I think we can, unless there is a traffic jam.

D：(50 minutes later) The traffic was not very heavy. We are here 10 minutes earlier.

L：Just drop us here. How much?

D：That's $ 33.5.

L：Here is $ 35. Keep the change.

D：Thank you.

Questions：

(1) Is the taxi engaged?

(2) How long does it take from here to the airport?

(3) When can the tour leader and his tourists normally arrive at the airport?

(4) Is there a traffic jam?

(5) How much is the fare?

Notes

(1) CTS 中国旅行社(China Travel Service)

(2) Are you engaged? 有人用车吗?

(3) It depends on traffic conditions. 要看交通状况。

(4) I think we can, unless there is a traffic jam. 如果不堵车,我想能按时赶到。

(5) Just drop us here. 就让我们在这里下车吧。

(6) Keep the change. 不用找了。

➢ Conversation 2   Taking a Bus

(The tour leader from CTS and his tourists want to take a bus to Chinatown.)

L=Tour Leader   T=Tourist   P=Porter

L: Let's have lunch in Chinatown.

T: Chinatown? Where is that?

L: It's on the Lower East Side.

T: Are we going to take a taxi there?

L: No, we aren't. We'll take a bus.

T: Does that go directly to Chinatown?

L: No. It's not that simple. We'll have to change downtown bus. I think we can change on Second Avenue. We can ask the driver later.

T: Do I need a ticket?

L: No. You'll have to pay the fare in coins.

(A porter comes over.)

L: Excuse me. Could you tell me how to get to the downtown by bus?

P: Go out of the entrance of our hotel, across the street, there is a bus stop. You can get on the yellow bus and get off at the terminal. But don't forget to signal to the driver as the bus comes, as they usually pass if passengers don't signal.

L: How much does it cost to get to the downtown?

P: 30 cents, I guess.

L: How frequent is the bus service?

P: Every ten minutes from 8:00 a.m. to 5:00 p.m. except on Sundays.

L: Thank you.

P: You're welcome.

Questions:

(1) Where will the tour leader and his tourists have lunch?

(2) Can they go directly to Chinatown by bus?

(3) How can they get to the downtown by bus?

(4) Why do they have to signal to the driver as the bus comes?

(5) How frequent is the bus service?

Notes

(1) Chinatown 唐人街

扫码听听力

(2) It's not that simple. 没那么简单。

(3) to change downtown bus 换乘市区的公共汽车

(4) You'll have to pay the fare in coins. 你得用硬币付车费。

(5) go out of the entrance of our hotel 出了饭店的门

(6) get off at the terminal 在终点站下车

(7) to signal to the driver 向司机招手

(8) How frequent is the bus service? 公共汽车多久来一趟？

➢ Conversation 3　Taking the Subway

(The tour leader from CTS and his tourists want to take the subway to 10th Street.)

L＝Tour Leader　　O＝Police Officer

L: Excuse me, officer. I wonder if you could help me out. I'm a little unsure about using the subway system here.

O: What would you like to know?

L: I need to get to 10th Street at 7th Avenue. I'm not sure where to change trains.

O: OK. You get on this train and go to Central Park. Central Park is the junction you want to get off at.

L: When I get off, where do I need to go to catch the other train?

O: When you get off you'll be on level 2. You need to go up to level 1 to catch your connecting train.

L: And the trains on that line go southbound, right?

O: Right. If you're unsure about what's north and what's south, ask someone, or look at the big maps of the subway system on the walls.

L: Thank you very much. Will it take long to get to 10th Street?

O: No more than 20 minutes. 5 minutes to get to Central Park, then another 15 minutes to get to 10th Street. If I remember correctly, there's a stop right at 10th Street.

L: Thank you very much for your time, officer.

O: Don't mention it.

Questions:

(1) What would the tour leader like to know?

(2) Where should the tour leader change trains?

(3) When the tour leader get off at Central Park, where does he need to go to catch the other train?

(4) What should he do if he is unsure about what's north and what's south?

(5) How long will it take to get to 10th Street?

PART II ENGLISH FOR OUTBOUND TOUR LEADERS

Notes

(1) I wonder if you could help me out. 不知道你是否能帮个忙。

(2) I'm a little unsure about using the subway system. 我不太清楚怎么搭乘地铁。

(3) Central Park is the junction you want to get off at. 中央公园就是你要下车的中转站。

(4) You need to go up to level 1 to catch your connecting train. 你必须走上一楼去转车。

(5) And the trains on that line go southbound, right? 那条线的地铁是向南的吧？

New Words & Expressions

depend on 依……而定，相信，依靠
jam [dʒæm] n. 拥挤，堵塞，窘境　vt. 堵塞
avenue ['ævənju:] n. 林荫道，大街，途径，手段
terminal ['tɜ:mɪnl] n. 终点站，终端　adj. 末端的，晚期的
frequent ['fri:kwənt] adj. 时常发生的，常见的 [fri'kwent] vt. 常到，光顾，常与……交往
subway ['sʌbweɪ] n. 地下人行道，地铁
junction ['dʒʌŋkʃən] n. 联结点，汇合点，枢纽
southbound ['saʊθbaʊnd] adj. 向南行的，往南去的

Section 2　Text

London's 5 Airports

London is serviced by 5 major airports, simply because of the huge number of tourists that visit the capital each year. Each of these airports offers good links to the city centre; a fact that makes them popular destinations for visitors and commuters alike.

Heathrow Airport—The majority of visitors to the UK fly into one of Heathrow's 5 terminals. The airport accommodates 90 individual airlines that fly in from over 170 major airports worldwide, making it the busiest for international travelers. Traveling into the city from Heathrow is quick and simple with the London Underground being on site. The journey is just short of 22 kilometers, it takes approximately 50 minutes and costs around $6.

Gatwick Airport—Gatwick is located slightly further from the centre of London (45 kilometers), however the transport network into the city is very good. If traveling by bus the journey can take up 90 minutes, depending on the time of day and

扫码听短文

traffic conditions. Alternatively Gatwick trains run regularly into London Victoria. Gatwick is smaller than Heathrow and is better known for its charter and discount flights.

Stansted Airport—Although not as big as the major airports, Stansted caters for a range of budget airlines, a fact that makes it a popular choice for tourists. The airport is located nearly 50 kilometers northeast of London's centre but the variety of transport links make commuting easy. Terravision, Stansted Bus and easyBus are reliable methods of travel into London with Marble Arch, Baker Street and Victoria Station being popular destinations.

Luton Airport—Luton Airport is located 56 kilometers north of London. It is a small airport (it has just a single runway) and it is predominantly used only by budget airlines flying to various destinations around Europe. As the airport is relatively far from central London, and involves going through busy areas, getting there by car or bus requires time and planning. There is a train station near the airport though, which will get you to the city center in less than an hour.

London City Airport—This small, central airport is situated just 11 kilometers from the centre of London and is suited to light aircraft that specialize in short take-offs and landings. Its location close to Canary Wharf makes it ideal for business flights and private travelers destined for the nearby financial district. In addition, the airport is well connected to London in its entirety through the Docklands Light Railway and a network of bus routes.

As an alternative, if you do not fancy flying directly to London, you can also fly to Birmingham Airport or Manchester Airport. Both of those international airports are centrally located in the UK, meaning that you can reach either London or the north of the country in just a few hours.

Notes

(1) London's 5 Airports 伦敦的5个机场（Heathrow, Gatwick, Stansted, Luton, London City）

(2) Each of these airports offers good links to the city centre. 这些机场都为往返市中心提供了良好的交通。

(3) commuter（远距离）上下班往返的人

(4) accommodate 容纳

(5) airline 航空公司

(6) London Underground 伦敦地铁

(7) being on site 在现场

(8) Alternatively Gatwick trains run regularly into London Victoria. 另外，盖特威克的火车定期开往伦敦的维多利亚火车站。

(9) is better known for its charter and discount flights 更是以它的包机航班和折扣航班闻名

PART II ENGLISH FOR OUTBOUND TOUR LEADERS

(10) Stansted caters for a range of budget airlines. 斯坦斯特德机场迎合了一系列廉价航空公司的需要。

(11) make commuting easy 使换乘很容易

(12) Terravision，Stansted Bus and easyBus 英国伦敦的三游览车企业

(13) Marble Arch，Baker Street and Victoria Station 大理石拱门、贝克街和维多利亚火车站

(14) runway 跑道

(15) involves going through busy areas 需要经过闹市区

(16) is suited to light aircraft that specialize in short take-offs and landings 适合专门短途起降的轻型飞机

(17) Canary Wharf 金丝雀码头（伦敦东二区金融中心）

(18) private travelers destined for the nearby financial district 以附近的金融区为目的地的个人旅游者

(19) the Docklands Light Railway 伦敦码头区轻轨

(20) as an alternative 作为一种替代方法

New Words & Expressions

commuter [kəˈmjuːtə] n. （远距离）上下班往返的人
alike [əˈlaɪk] adj. 相像的 adv. 同样地
worldwide [ˈwɜːldwaɪd] adj. 全世界的
take up 占用，着手处理，采纳，继续
charter [ˈtʃɑːtə] n. 许可证，宪章，包租 vt. 发给……许可证
cater for 迎合，投合，供应伙食
commuting [kəˈmjuːtɪŋ] n. 换乘，交换 adj. 交换的
runway [ˈrʌnweɪ] n. （机场的）跑道
predominant [prɪˈdɒmɪnənt] adj. 占主导地位的，显著的
budget [ˈbʌdʒɪt] n. 预算 adj. 价格低廉的 v. 把……编入预算
take off 起飞
wharf [hwɔːf] n. 码头，停泊处
be destined for 开往
entirety [ɪnˈtaɪərəti] n. 整体，全部
alternative [ɔːlˈtɜːnətɪv] adj. 两者择一的，供替代的 n. 抉择，可供选择的事物

Exercises

1. Read and recite the following special terms

(1) railway station 火车站
(2) highway 公路
(3) free way (express way) 高速公路
(4) rush hour 高峰时间
(5) traffic accident 交通事故

(6) pick up 接（人）

(7) make a detour to 绕道去

(8) ring road 环形路

(9) round trip 来回（双程）

(10) stop a taxi 拦出租车

(11) hang on 坐稳了

(12) pull over 靠边（停车）

(13) miss the stop 坐过站了

(14) go against the red light 闯红灯

(15) charge by meter 按表收费

(16) for-hire sign 空车标志

(17) underpass 地下通道

(18) initial charge 起步价

(19) zebra crossing 斑马线人行道

(20) overpass 过街天桥

2. Complete the following dialogues

Inquiring about the Public Transportation

（The tour leader from CTS is inquiring of the doorman about the public transportation.）

L＝Tour Leader   D＝Doorman of the Hotel

L：Excuse me.　　　　（1）　　　　（你能告诉我怎样去国家历史博物馆吗）?

D：Certainly, sir. It's near the Science Museum. 　　　　（2）　　　　（您熟悉这里的街道吗）?

L：No. I'm a tour leader from China. Today I'll go to visit the museum with some tourists.

D：I see. How would you like to go? Walking?

L：　　　　（3）　　　　（我完全不知道）. Is it far from the hotel?

D：Not really. 　　　　（4）　　　　（您沿着这条街往前走）, and after 6 blocks you'll see it on your left.

L：How long will that take?

D：About 30 minutes on foot.

L：　　　　（5）　　　　（要是乘坐地铁呢）?

D：Sure. It's only two stops. Do you know which train to take?

L：The A train, is it right? I just looked at the city map.

D：That's right. You get off at the second stop, Cromwell Road, 　　　　（6）　　　　（您就会看到这一站的对面就是国家历史博物馆）.

L：What if I take a bus?

D：Now it's rush hour. The traffic is very heavy. If you take a bus,　　　　（7）　　　　（您可能因交通堵塞被困）.

L: I see. Do you know where the nearest subway station is?
D: There is one at the corner. I'll take you there.
L: That's very kind of you. Thanks a lot.
D: You are welcome.

3. Translate the following sentences into English

(1) 你能告诉我该乘哪一班地铁到麦迪逊广场公园吗？
(2) 我应该到哪一个站台等火车？
(3) 我迷路了，要怎样才能去时代广场？
(4) 沿着这条路直走，然后在第三个十字路口右转。
(5) 别人告诉我这段路程15美元就可以到，60美元恐怕太贵了。

Unit 14　Keys

Unit 15 Practicalities on Sightseeing and Entertainment and the Floating City without Auto

Section 1　Situational Conversations

➢ Conversation 1　Buying Admission Tickets

扫码听听力

(The tour leader from CTS wants to buy tickets for his tour group.)

L＝Tour Leader　P＝Local People　C＝Clerk of the Ticket Office

L：Excuse me, sir. Where can I get a ticket?

P：Go across the park, at the left of the entrance of the scenic spot.

L：Thanks a lot.

L：Hello! We are a group of tourists. Can we buy the group ticket?

C：You can have 20％ discount if you buy the group ticket, but you must have over 15 persons.

L：We have 20 passengers. By the way, can the tour leader be free?

C：Yes, the guide and tour leader are free.

L：Thanks.

Questions：

(1) Where can the tour leader get a ticket?

(2) Can the tour leader buy the group ticket for his group?

(3) Is there any discount for the group ticket?

(4) What's the condition for buying the group ticket?

(5) Can the tour leader be free?

Notes

(1) admission tickets 门票

(2) Go across the park, at the left of the entrance of the scenic spot. 穿过停车场，在景区入口处的左边。

(3) the group ticket 团体票

PART II ENGLISH FOR OUTBOUND TOUR LEADERS

(4) You can have 20% discount if you buy the group ticket, but you must have over 15 persons. 购买团体票可以优惠20%，但需要15人以上。

▶ Conversation 2 Watching a Song and Dance

(Some tourists led by the tour leader from CTS want to go to downtown and watch a song and dance.)

L＝Tour Leader　D＝Driver

L: Sir, some of our tourists want to go to downtown and watch a song and dance.

D: No problem.

L: After supper, we will go back to the hotel first, send other tourists back. Then take these tourists to the downtown. Let's appoint a time, you come to pick us up.

D: The show begins at 8:00, and we'll arrive there at 7:30. No parking there, I'll pick you up at 10:00, OK?

L: It seems all right. Where shall we meet?

D: Just at the place where you get off. You'd better ask each passenger to take a hotel card. If he gets lost, he can take a taxi back with it.

L: Thank you. Let's make it.

Questions:

(1) What do some tourists of the tour group want to do?
(2) How does the tour leader arrange their schedule after supper?
(3) When will they arrive at the show place?
(4) Where shall they meet?
(5) What's the driver's advice to the tour leader?

Notes

(1) to go to downtown 到市中心去
(2) No problem. 没问题。
(3) Let's appoint a time, you come to pick us up. 我们约定一个时间，你来接我们。
(4) You'd better ask each passenger to take a hotel card. 你最好让每位客人拿一张酒店卡。
(5) If he gets lost, he can take a taxi back with it. 万一走散，可持酒店卡打的回去。
(6) Let's make it. 就这么说定了。

▶ Conversation 3 Taking a Group Picture

(The tour leader from CTS asks a passerby to take a group picture for his

扫码听听力

扫码听听力

group.)

L＝Tour Leader　P＝Passerby

L: Excuse me, sir. Could you please help us take a group picture?

P: Take a group picture?

L: Yes, everything is ready. Just press the shutter.

P: With pleasure, here we go.

L: I'd like to get Pattaya Beach in the background.

P: Ready? Say "cheers".

L: Once more, please.

P: No problem.

L: Thank you very much.

P: You're welcome.

Questions:

(1) What does the tour leader ask the passerby to do?

(2) How does the tour leader ask the passerby to take the picture?

(3) What would the tour leader like to get in the background?

Notes

(1) to take a group picture 照团体合影

(2) Just press the shutter. 只需按快门。

(3) I'd like to get Pattaya Beach in the background. 我想以芭堤雅海滩为背景。

➢ Conversation 4　Enjoying at the Recreational Center

(The tour leader from CTS wants to enjoy himself at the recreational center.)

L＝Tour Leader　S＝Staff of the Recreational Center

S: Can I help you, sir?

L: Yes, my doctor has told me that I must keep in good physical condition. Could you tell me what facilities you have here?

S: Well, you can enjoy yourself at the recreational center. We have a well-equipped gymnasium with all the latest recreational sports apparatus such as exercise bicycle, barbells, wall bars. And we have the billiards room and bowling center.

L: That sounds very interesting.

S: Then we have two excellent saunas. By the way, there's a free supply of towels and Finnish sauna soap.

L: Very good. And what about a swim?

S: Yes, you can have a dip in our heated swimming pool which contains a special salt in the water to stimulate the skin. The water is very clear and we change it every other day. You can also borrow swimming trunks free of charge.

PART II ENGLISH FOR OUTBOUND TOUR LEADERS

L: Oh, good. I've left mine at home.

S: And afterwards you can relax with beer or soft drinks and some pastries in the after-sauna room where there is a large open fireplace with birch logs.

L: Great.

S: Besides, if you like dancing, you can enjoy yourself in our modern dance hall.

L: Oh, I don't like disco. It's too noisy.

S: Well, we have all kinds of music. You can try waltz or tango if you like.

L: That's a good idea. How about outdoor activities?

S: We have a nine-hole golf course or if you prefer you can water-ski on the lake or hire a rowing boat if you feel energetic.

L: Do you have any tennis courts?

S: Oh yes. You can also play tennis. Rackets and balls are available at a small charge. And if that is not enough there is always croquet on the lawn.

L: Wonderful. Thanks a lot.

Questions:

(1) What facilities are there at the gymnasium?

(2) What about a swim at the recreational center?

(3) Does the tour leader intend to borrow swimming trunks?

(4) What can the tour leader do in the after-sauna room?

(5) How about outdoor activities at the recreational center?

Notes

(1) I must keep in good physical condition. 我必须保持良好的身体状况。

(2) We have a well-equipped gymnasium with all the latest recreational sports apparatus such as exercise bicycle, barbells, wall bars. 我们有一座装备完善的健身馆，里面有各种各样最新的体育器械，如供锻炼用的自行车、举重用的杠铃及肋木（靠墙安装的体操器械）。

(3) the billiards room and bowling center 台球房和保龄球中心

(4) By the way, there's a free supply of towels and Finnish sauna soap. 顺便说一下，供蒸汽浴用的毛巾及芬兰蒸汽浴皂都是免费提供的。

(5) You can have a dip in our heated swimming pool which contains a special salt in the water. 您可以到加温游泳池泡一泡，池里的水含有一种特殊的盐。

(6) to stimulate the skin 刺激你的皮肤

(7) swimming trunks 男式泳裤

(8) the after-sauna room 浴后休息室

(9) There is a large open fireplace with birch logs. 有一个很大的壁炉，旁边备有桦木条。

(10) You can try waltz or tango if you like. 如果您愿意，您可以跳华尔兹或

探戈。

(11) tennis courts 网球场

(12) Rackets and balls are available at a small charge. 球拍和球都低价出租。

(13) And if that is not enough there is always croquet on the lawn. 如果这些还不够，您可以到草坪上去，那儿总有槌球游戏。

(14) water-ski 用滑水橇滑行

New Words & Expressions

admission [əd'mɪʃən] n. 准许进入，入场费，入场券，承认
go across 穿越
pick up 接人，拾起，收拾，整理
get lost 迷路
shutter ['ʃʌtə] n. 百叶窗，（照相机的）快门
barbell ['bɑ:bel] n. 杠铃
Finnish ['fɪnɪʃ] adj. 芬兰的
birch [bɜ:tʃ] n. 桦树，桦木 vt. （用桦木条）抽打
trunk [trʌŋk] n. 树干，大旅行箱，象鼻
pastry ['peɪstri] n. 糕点
fireplace ['faɪəpleɪs] n. 壁炉
stimulate ['stɪmjʊleɪt] vt. 刺激，激励
waltz [wɔ:ls] n. 华尔兹舞，华尔兹舞曲 v. 跳华尔兹舞
disco ['dɪskəʊ] n. 迪斯科舞厅，迪斯科舞会
tango ['tæŋɡəʊ] n. 探戈舞，探戈舞曲
lawn [lɔ:n] n. 草地，草坪
energetic [ˌenə'dʒetɪk] adj. 精力充沛的，充满活力的
racket ['rækɪt] n. （网球等）球拍，吵闹声，敲诈，勒索，诈骗
croquet ['krəʊkeɪ] n. 槌球
ski [ski:] vi. 滑雪 n. 滑雪板

Section 2　Text

The Floating City without Auto

As the unique city without auto, Venice has long been the most attractive place in the world. It is one of the few cities in the world where the sound of cars is never heard. Instead, when it is quiet, one hears the lapping of waves against the city's magnificent Renaissance building. Venice is located in a lagoon in the Adriatic Sea, and it is composed of 180 canals and 118 islands linked by 378 bridges. The special geographical environment makes the special transportation. In Venice all

PART II   ENGLISH FOR OUTBOUND TOUR LEADERS

transportation is by boat or on foot.

Venice's most famous vehicles are gondolas, which drift slowly through the city's famed canals as the men steering the boats serenade passengers with arias from Italian operas. Gondola is a kind of black boat, which is 12 meters long, and 1.5 meters wide, with flat bottom and elegant decoration. Its fore and stern are both risen up, and the hooked-like fore is convenient to find the height of forward bridge arch. It's said that there are gondolas only in Venice. Gondolas are still made in Venice, but the government limits the number of them, the new one can be made only until the old one is worn out. Gondola is completely man-made, made of five different kinds of woods and 280 pieces of them. In order to keep gondola in a good state, it must be timely mended. And gondola is a shadow of once developed shipbuilding in Venice.

There are two important rules to remember about gondola rides in Venice: if the price bothers you, don't do it; if the price doesn't bother you, make sure you understand the gondolier correctly.

The fact is, a gondola ride is like a hansom cab ride in New York City: It can be delightful experience, but only if you're able to forget the price and focus on the scenery. The city of Venice sets official rates for gondola rides, but gondoliers may regard the official rates as a polite fiction. Special services, such as singing, can boost the fare even more. This means you should negotiate both the rate and the length of the ride before you get into the boat. Otherwise, your gondola ride may be memorable for reasons that have nothing to do with sightseeing.

Except romantic but expensive gondola, you can also choose other boats, such as water bus and water taxi. The water bus called vaporetti and motoscafi run almost constantly, and you'll seldom have to wait more than a few minutes for one to come along. The water bus you'll use most often is No. 1, the local that stops 13 times between the Piazza Roma and the Piazza San Marco. The standard water bus or autobus fare is a painfully steep €6. However, you can save money with a 1-day, 3-day, or 7-day Venice Card, which allows unlimited public transportation, travel on the Alilaguna airport boat, and other perks. There's also a *Cartavenezia* card for residents, students, and visitors who are planning to stay a while. This card offers big discounts on public transportation fares but it isn't practical for short-term visitors.

Water taxis are the limousines of Venice: with their spacious leather-upholstered cabins, open-air seating in the stern and private captains to chauffeur you up the Grand Canal or between the airport and your hotel, they offer an experience that you won't forget in a hurry. Still, water taxis can hold up to 10 people, and the cost per person can be reasonable if you're splitting the fare with family or friends. Water taxis are also faster than public airport transportation, since you don't have to transfer to a vaporetto or walk a long way to your hotel when you arrive in the city.

(It is only about half an hour for the trip between Venice Marco Polo Airport and a waterside hotel in the city center.)

If you are tired of the boat visit, then you can choose to visit the romantic city on foot. Venice is not big, so that you don't need to worry about being lost. But if you are missing in the city, take it easy, you can go after the stream of people and find the church, and then everything is all right!

When you want to go to a fixed destination without knowing the direction, you can ask the local resident. And the usual answer you get is "go through ×× bridges, and then turn..." Yes, the bridges are another important component of Venice transportation. Among those old and beautiful bridges, the most famous ones are the Ponte dei Sospiri and the Rialto. The Ponte dei Sospiri is behind the Palazzo Ducale. Centuries ago the Ponte dei Sospiri is the only way for the criminals sentenced by doge to be sent to the prison. Those criminals often sigh for the sake of confession. And the bridge is also named for this reason. The Rialto, which is made of white marble in 1592, is the most famous bridge in Venice. There are many stores without auto, not only brings us the sense of romantic, but also gives us the chance of being quiet and reflecting. All in all, the floating city on the sea is unique and attractive.

Notes

(1) When it is quiet, one hears the lapping of waves against the city's magnificent Renaissance building. 每当四周寂静的时候，人们就可听到海浪拍打这座城市里文艺复兴时期的宏伟建筑的声音。

(2) Venice is located in a lagoon in the Adriatic Sea. 威尼斯位于亚得里亚海的一个潟湖之中。

(3) gondolas 贡多拉（威尼斯的一种船身狭长、两头尖的平底船）

(4) The men steering the boats serenade passengers with arias from Italian operas. 船夫们为游客唱意大利歌剧中的咏叹调小夜曲。

(5) Its fore and stern are both risen up, and the hooked-like fore is convenient to find the height of forward bridge arch. 它的船头和船尾都高高地翘起，钩状的船头便于船夫们判断前面桥洞的高度。

(6) And gondola is a shadow of once developed shipbuilding in Venice. 贡多拉是威尼斯曾经发达的造船业的缩影。

(7) gondolier 贡多拉的船夫

(8) hansom（旧时由一匹马拉的）双轮双座马车

(9) But gondoliers may regard the official rates as a polite fiction. 但是贡多拉的船夫们也许会认为这种定价只不过是官方的一厢情愿。

(10) the water bus called vaporetti and motoscafi 被称作汽艇和摩托艇的水上巴士

(11) between the Piazza Roma and the Piazza San Marco 在罗马广场和圣马可广场之间

PART II   ENGLISH FOR OUTBOUND TOUR LEADERS

(12) a painfully steep €6 价格高达 6 欧元，令人心疼

(13) travel on the Alilaguna airport boat, and other perks 乘坐阿里拉古纳公司往返机场的交通船并享受其他方面的一些优惠

(14) short-term visitors 短期停留的游客

(15) spacious leather-upholstered cabins 宽敞的用皮革布置的船舱

(16) to chauffeur you up the Grand Canal or between the airport and your hotel 运送你沿运河而行或往来于机场和酒店之间

(17) water taxis 水上的士

(18) You can go after the stream of people. 你可以跟着人流走。

(19) the Ponte dei Sospiri and the Rialto 叹息桥和里亚尔托桥

(20) the criminals sentenced by doge 被威尼斯总督判决的罪犯

(21) Those criminals often sigh for the sake of confession. 犯人常常会因忏悔而叹息。

(22) There are many stores without auto, not only brings us the sense of romantic, but also gives us the chance of being quiet and reflecting. 这里没有汽车，只有许多商铺，这些不仅给我们带来浪漫，而且还让我们有机会平和内心，深刻思考。

New Words & Expressions

auto [ˈɔːtəʊ] n. 汽车
Venice [ˈvenɪs] n. 威尼斯（意大利港口城市）
lap [læp] vt. 轻拍，舔，舔食，领先一圈　n. 一圈
Renaissance [rɪˈneɪsns] n. 文艺复兴
Adriatic [ˌeɪdrɪˈætɪk] adj. 亚得里亚海的
be composed of 由……组成
gondola [ˈɡɒndələ] n. 贡多拉（威尼斯的一种船身狭长、两头尖的平底船）
serenade [ˌserɪˈneɪd] vt. 对……唱小夜曲　vi. 唱小夜曲　n. 小夜曲
aria [ˈɑːrɪə] n. 咏叹调
rise up 翘起，起来
shadow [ˈʃædəʊ] n. 阴影，影子
gondolier [ˌɡɒndəˈlɪə] n. 贡多拉船夫
hansom [ˈhænsəm]（旧时由一匹马拉的）双轮双座马车
cab [kæb] n. 出租车，（公共汽车、火车等的）驾驶室
fiction [ˈfɪkʃən] n. 小说，虚构的事
boost [buːst] vt. 向上推起，提高，促进，改善，激励，吹捧，大肆宣传
romantic [rəʊˈmæntɪk] adj. 浪漫的，富有浪漫色彩的　n. 浪漫的人，浪漫主义作家
memorable [ˈmemərəbl] adj. 值得纪念的
vaporetto [ˌvɑːpəʊˈretəʊ] n. 交通汽艇
motoscafo [ˌməʊtəʊˈskɑːfəʊ] n.（尤指在意大利威尼斯水道上航行的）摩托艇，汽艇

piazza [pi'ætsə] n. （尤指意大利城镇中的）广场
autobus [ˈɔːtəʊbʌs] n. 公共汽车
perk [pɜːk] v. 使振奋，活跃，快活 n. 额外津贴
upholstered [ʌpˈhəʊlstəd] adj. （椅子、座位等）铺软垫的
chauffeur [ˈʃəʊfə] vt. 为（某人）开车 n. 受雇于人的汽车司机
rialto [rɪˈæltəʊ] n. 市场，交易所
criminal [ˈkrɪmɪnəl] n. 罪犯，犯人 adj. 刑事的，犯罪的，不道德的
doge [dəʊdʒ] n. 共和国总督
confession [kənˈfeʃən] n. 忏悔，告解
palazzo [pəˈlɑːtsəʊ] n. 宫殿
ducale [ˈdjuːkəl] adj. 公爵的

Exercises

1. Read and recite the following special terms

（1）Notre Dame de Paris 巴黎圣母院
（2）Eiffel Tower 埃菲尔铁塔
（3）Arch of Triumph 凯旋门（巴黎）
（4）Louvre 卢浮宫
（5）Leaning Tower of Pisa 比萨斜塔
（6）Red Square 红场
（7）British Museum 大英博物馆
（8）Buckingham Palace 白金汉宫
（9）London Tower Bridge 伦敦塔桥
（10）Central Park 中央公园（位于美国纽约市中心）
（11）Statue of Liberty 自由女神像
（12）Yellowstone National Park 黄石国家公园
（13）Metropolitan Museum of Art 大都会艺术博物馆
（14）Great Lakes 五大湖
（15）Niagara Falls 尼亚加拉大瀑布
（16）Taj Mahal 泰姬陵
（17）Sydney Opera House 悉尼歌剧院
（18）nightclub 夜总会
（19）chest-expander(pull weights) 拉力器械
（20）to have one's hair done (to have hair set) 做头发

2. Complete the following dialogues

Discussing the Itinerary with the Local Guide

(The tour leader from CTS is discussing the itinerary with the local guide.)

L＝Tour Leader G＝Local Guide

L：Good afternoon, Mr. White. ＿＿＿＿＿＿（1）＿＿＿＿＿＿（让我们来谈谈行程，好吗）？

PART II ENGLISH FOR OUTBOUND TOUR LEADERS

G: Certainly, Mr. Wang. Do you have any good suggestions from your tourists or yourself?

L: Personally I like UK and France very much. _____(2)_____ （可是，由于我们只有5天的时间，我们不想错过这么多世界闻名的景点）. What shall we do?

G: Don't worry about that. I'll try my best and I'll make full use of the time.

L: Thank you very much. _____(3)_____ （你确实想得很周到）.

G: _____(4)_____ （我上星期初步设计了一个在英国旅游的行程）. Would you go through it?

L: Certainly. I think we'd better have a visit to Scotland.

G: Yes. _____(5)_____ （苏格兰的自然风光值得一看）. But the tour in Scotland takes two days.

L: That's all right. The tour in Scotland is popular in China. _____(6)_____ （绝大部分游客要求去那里参观）. And also perhaps Paris is another hot place.

G: Well. We'll visit Scotland from tomorrow morning, and two days later we'll pay a visit to Paris.

L: That's all right.

G: Is there anything else you want to change?

L: Here, why don't we spend more time in Cambridge and find a local restaurant in the city instead of fast food?

G: That's a good idea. However, there is a good local restaurant in the city and I'm sure you will feel impressed by its British characteristics. We could stop there for lunch. _____(7)_____ （一些旅行团成员可能喜欢在这座城市里逛一逛）.

L: I'm sure all the group members would be happy with that. What time shall we check out and leave for Scotland?

G: Perhaps eight o'clock.

L: That's all right. I'm quite satisfied with the itinerary. _____(8)_____ （好像每件事情都安排得很好）.

G: Good. I'll wake you up at 7:00 tomorrow morning. Hope you enjoy your stay here.

L: OK, thank you.

3. Translate the following sentences into English

(1) 女士们、先生们，早上好！欢迎大家来到巴黎，我是你们巴黎之行的导游威廉，今天我们将参观巴黎圣母院、埃菲尔铁塔、凯旋门及爱丽舍宫。

(2) 自由活动那天，有些游客想让我带他们到这座城市逛一逛。你能告诉我附近有哪些好玩的地方吗？

(3) 买团体票可以打七折，但必须15人以上。

(4) 威尼斯位于亚得里亚海的一个潟湖之中。它是由180条运河和被378座桥连接在一起的118个岛屿组成的。

(5) 她的演出是如此受欢迎，以至于门票通常两天内就卖完了。

Unit 15 Keys

Unit 16
Practicalities about the Safety Abroad and Safety Tips in Rome

Section 1 Situational Conversations

➢ Conversation 1 Reporting to the Police

(One tourist's money has been stolen, the tour leader asks the policeman for help.)

L＝Tour Leader　P＝Policeman

P: Hello. This is police station. What's the problem?

L: One of our tourist's money has been stolen.

P: Where are you?

L: We are at the corner of the First Street and the Green Avenue.

P: Don't move. Policemen will arrive soon.

(A few minutes later)

P: What time did it happen?

L: About twenty minutes ago.

P: What do they look like?

L: One is taller, with yellow hair and blue eyes. The other one is shorter. Oh, he is in a white jacket and black trousers.

P: OK. Please fill in the form. Don't forget your address and telephone number. We'll contact you as soon as possible.

L: Thank you, sir.

Questions:

(1) What's the problem with the tour leader?

(2) Where are the tour leader and his tourists?

(3) When did the theft happen?

(4) What do the thieves look like?

(5) What does the policeman ask the tour leader to do?

Notes

(1) police station 警察局

(2) the First Street 第一街道

(3) One is taller, with yellow hair and blue eyes. 其中一个个子较高，黄头发，蓝眼睛。

(4) We'll contact you as soon as possible. 我们将尽快与你联系。

➢ Conversation 2　About Security in the Hotel

(The security officer gives the tour leader Wang Gang from CTS some information on the security system in the hotel.)

L＝Tour Leader　O＝Security Officer

O: Please sit down, Mr. Wang. I'm Steven, the security officer of the security department in the hotel. I would like to give you some information on the security system in our hotel, mainly on fire prevention and guarding against burglary.

L: It's my pleasure. Please do.

O: All the rooms are equipped with smoke detectors and automatic sprinkler system. There are fire hydrants, fire hoses and fire extinguishers at each end of the corridor on each floor. The automatic fire alarm is also in the corridor. Fire exits are next to the elevators.

L: May I know if the pipes of the sprinkler systems are in the basement or on the mezzanine floor?

O: They are in the basement. I'll show you around after our talk if you like.

L: Thank you.

O: About guarding against burglary, guests are advised to deposit their valuables in the front office safe. In case of burglary or theft, you must report to the security office immediately and we'll take action right away.

L: Very well, Steven. May I know if there are some guards for the patrols?

O: Yes. Guards are required to patrol the compound every hour and punch the clocks.

L: Now I'm clear about the security system of your hotel. Thank you very much.

O: You're welcome.

Questions:

(1) What does Steven do in the hotel?

(2) What would Steven like to tell the tour leader Wang Gang?

(3) What are all the rooms equipped with?

(4) Where are the fire hydrants, fire hoses and fire extinguishers?

(5) Where are the pipes of the sprinkler systems?

(6) What does Steven advise the guests to do with their valuables?

(7) Are there some guards for the patrols?

Notes

(1) the security officer of the security department 保安部主任

(2) the security system 安全系统

(3) mainly on fire prevention and guarding against burglary 主要是关于防火防盗

(4) Please do. 请讲吧。

(5) All the rooms are equipped with smoke detectors and automatic sprinkler system. 所有房间都装有烟感器和自动喷水系统。

(6) There are fire hydrants, fire hoses and fire extinguishers at each end of the corridor on each floor. 每层楼面的走廊两端都有灭火消防龙头、消防救火软管和灭火器。

(7) The automatic fire alarm is also in the corridor. 走廊里还有火灾自动报警器。

(8) Fire exits are next to the elevators. 安全门就在电梯旁边。

(9) the basement 地下室

(10) the mezzanine floor 夹层楼面

(11) to deposit their valuables in the front office safe 把他们的贵重物品寄存在前厅的保险箱里

(12) May I know if there are some guards for the patrols? 有没有警卫人员巡逻啊？

(13) Guards are required to patrol the compound every hour and punch the clocks. 警卫人员需要每小时巡逻各处一遍，并在打卡钟上打卡。

➢ Conversation 3　The Passport of a Tourist Is Lost

(A tourist has lost his passport, the tour leader from Pleasure Travel Service and the local guide are dealing with the problem.)

L＝Tour Leader　G＝Local Guide

L: Frank, Mr. Liu, the tourist of our tour group has got a trouble. His passport was lost.

G: I'm sorry to hear that. In this case, you should go to my travel agency and the local police station for certificates for the loss first. Then, taking with the certificates, you can go to the Chinese Embassy for replacement.

L: But what about his visa?

G: I don't think that will be a problem. He had a tourist visa to begin with. The local police station will reissue his visa if he has the replacement of his passport.

L: You can help us with it, can't you, Frank?

G: Certainly. I'll accompany you to get all these documents.

L：You're the most helpful. Thank you so much.

G：Don't mention it. Now let's go.

Questions：

(1) What's the trouble Mr. Liu, the tourist of the tour group has got?

(2) What should Mr. Liu do?

(3) How about his visa?

(4) Who will accompany the tour leader and Mr. Liu to get all these documents?

Notes

(1) In this case, you should go to my travel agency and the local police station for certificates for the loss first. 在这种情况下，你们首先应该去我们旅行社和当地警察局开具遗失证明。

(2) the Chinese Embassy 中国大使馆

(3) I'll accompany you to get all these documents. 我将陪同你们办好所有这些证件。

New Words & Expressions

as soon as possible 尽快

prevention [prɪˈvenʃən] n. 防止，预防

burglary [ˈbɜːgləri] v. 入室行窃

equip with 配备

detector [dɪˈtektə] n. 探测器

sprinkler [ˈsprɪŋklə] n. 洒水器，喷洒器，（建筑物内的）自动喷水灭火装置

hydrant [ˈhaɪdrənt] n. 给水栓，消防龙头

extinguisher [ɪkˈstɪŋgwɪʃə] n. 灭火器

corridor [ˈkɒrɪdɔː] n. 走廊，通道

automatic [ˌɔːtəˈmætɪk] adj. 自动的，不假思索的，无意识的

basement [ˈbeɪsmənt] n. 地下室

mezzanine [ˈmezəniːn] n.（介于两层楼之间的）夹层

punch [pʌntʃ] vt. 用拳猛击，打孔 n. 猛击，拳打

deposit [dɪˈpɒzɪt] vt. 放置，放下，存放，交与……保管，付定金 n. 定金，存款

theft [θeft] n. 偷盗，偷窃，盗窃之物，失窃案例

take action 采取行动

patrol [pəˈtrəʊl] n. 巡逻，巡查，巡逻队 vt. & vi. 巡逻

compound [ˈkɒmpaʊnd] n. 化合物，（围起来的）场地 [kəmˈpaʊnd] vt. 使混合，使恶化

embassy [ˈembəsi] n. 大使馆

document [ˈdɒkjʊmənt] n. 公文，文件，文献 vt. 证明，记录，记载

replacement [rɪˈpleɪsmənt] n. 代替，替换，更换，替换的人（物）
reissue [ˌriːˈɪʃuː] vt. 再版，重新发行

Section 2　Text

Safety Tips in Rome

Rome is a safe city, as long as you follow common sense and take precautions. Learn about the customs and local laws of the country to which you are going. Remember that you are subject to their laws and are not protected by U. S. laws. In general, keep a low profile. In many countries Americans are not always viewed in a positive light. Once you have some time to adjust to your new location, you will have a better sense of how you wish to act in your new surroundings.

Always carry a copy of your passport with you. Carrying a personal document is mandatory by law, but it is always safer when you are coming to class, or just taking a walk, to carry the copy rather than the original. Note that if you will be traveling, or going to the bank to cash traveler's checks, you'll need your original. For lost or stolen passport, call your consulate.

Precaution

Beware of pickpockets. They are generally women and children, and have mastered the art of pickpocketing, and quickly take advantage of easily accessible purses or wallets in large crowds and packed buses. They are easy to be recognized, and concentrate near the main tourist attractions and museums; most of the children carry newspapers or pieces of cardboard to distract their targets.

Women should not walk alone late at night, especially if they have had too much to drink—it is unsafe and inappropriate. Call a taxi or walk with someone.

Although there is no drinking age limit in Italy, this does not mean that you can drink on the street any time, any day or night. If you're found in an inebriate state, the police can stop you, ask for documents and fine you (up to 350 Euros!). Also, in these conditions, you are at a greater risk of being physically or verbally attacked.

Notes

(1) take precautions 采取预防措施，未雨绸缪

(2) Remember that you are subject to their laws and are not protected by U. S. laws. 记住，你是受他们（罗马当地）法律的保护，而不是受美国法律的保护。

(3) In general, keep a low profile. 在一般情况下，保持低调。

(4) In many countries Americans are not always viewed in a positive light. 在许多国家，美国人并不总是被人以积极的眼光看待。

(5) Carrying a personal document is mandatory by law. 携带个人证明是法律规

定的义务。

(6) to carry the copy rather than the original 携带复印件而不是原件

(7) going to the bank to cash traveler's checks 去银行兑换旅行支票

(8) call your consulate 打电话给你的领事馆

(9) Beware of pickpockets. 当心扒手。

(10) packed buses 拥挤的公共汽车

(11) Most of the children carry newspapers or pieces of cardboard to distract their targets. 大多数儿童携带报纸或硬纸板，以分散他们的偷窃目标的注意力。

(12) in an inebriate state 处于醉酒状态

New Words & Expressions

be subject to 受……支配
profile ['prəʊfaɪl] n. 侧面，侧面像，轮廓，外形，简介，概况
positive ['pɒzɪtɪv] adj. 积极的
adjust [ə'dʒʌst] v. 调整，调节
mandatory ['mændətəri] adj. 强制性的，法定的，义务的
consulate ['kɒnsjələt] n. 领事馆
pickpocket ['pɪkpɒkɪt] n. 扒手
take advantage of 利用
accessible [ək'sesəbl] adj. 可到达的，可进入的，可使用的
purse [pɜːs] n. 钱包
cardboard ['kɑːdbɔːd] n. 硬纸板
distract [dɪs'trækt] vt. 使（人）分心，分散（注意力）
physically ['fɪzɪkli] adv. 身体上地
inebriate [ɪn'iːbrɪeɪt] v. 灌醉
verbally ['vɜːbəli] adv. 口头上
inappropriate [ˌɪnə'prəʊpriət] adj. 不恰当的，不适宜的

Exercises

1. Read and recite the following special terms

(1) pickpocket 扒手

(2) the security officer 保安主任

(3) the security system 安全系统

(4) fire prevention 防火

(5) guarding against burglary 防盗

(6) smoke sensor (detector) 烟感器

(7) automatic sprinkler system 自动喷水系统

(8) fire hydrant 消防龙头

(9) fire hose 救火软管

(10) fire extinguisher 灭火器

(11) the automatic fire alarm 火灾自动报警器

(12) the security check 安全检查

(13) get lost 迷路

(14) be stolen 被偷

(15) the police station 警察局

(16) traffic accident 交通事故

(17) keep the scene of the accident intact 保护好事故现场

(18) make a claim for lost passport 申报护照遗失

(19) the lost property form 失物单

(20) the lost certificate 遗失证明

2. Complete the following dialogues

Coping with a Traffic Accident

(When a traffic accident occurs, the tour leader from Pleasure Travel Service is calling the police station.)

L＝Tour Leader　　P＝Policeman

L：Hello. ＿＿＿＿＿(1)＿＿＿＿＿（警察局吗）?

P：Yes, What can I do for you?

L：＿＿＿＿＿(2)＿＿＿＿＿（我们这里发生了交通事故）.

P：Where did the accident happen?

L：The accident is at the intersection of 50th avenue and Park Road.

P：＿＿＿＿＿(3)＿＿＿＿＿（请保护好事故现场）. We'll come right now.

L：All right, sir.

(Now the policeman has arrived at the accident scene.)

P：Who called the police just now? What happened here?

L：It's me who called the police. We had a traffic accident. ＿＿＿＿＿(4)＿＿＿＿＿（一辆小汽车从后面撞上了我们的巴士逃走了）.

P：Did you stop at a red light?

L：Yes. ＿＿＿＿＿(5)＿＿＿＿＿（我可以肯定巴士司机没有违法）.

P：I see. Did you see the car's plate?

L：I'm sorry. ＿＿＿＿＿(6)＿＿＿＿＿（我那时吓坏了）.

P：Alright. How about the color or the model?

L：I think it was a white Volve.

P：Great. ＿＿＿＿＿(7)＿＿＿＿＿（我可以看看你的驾照吗）?

L：Sorry, sir. I'm not the diver. I'm the tour leader from China.

P：Where is the diver?

L：The driver is seriously injured. He broke his right arm. ＿＿＿＿＿(8)＿＿＿＿＿（我们叫了一辆救护车已将他送到了医院）.

P：Do you have your passport with you?

L: Yes, sir. It's right in my bag.

P: ＿＿＿＿＿＿（9）＿＿＿＿＿＿（请你跟我一起去警察局，好吗）?

L: Why?

P: Well, we need your help for the report.

L: Sure. I'll go now.

3. Translate the following sentences into English

（1）当我向导游问起我丢失的行李时，他态度很不友好，他不愿意帮我向机场查询。

（2）我的护照丢了，我可以做一下登记吗？

（3）那辆车突然从十字路口那边朝我冲来。

（4）我们遭遇了交通事故，一辆小汽车从后面撞上了我们的巴士逃走了。

（5）大多数扒手携带报纸或硬纸板，以分散他们的偷窃目标的注意力。

Unit 16　Keys

PART III
ENGLISH TOPICS FOR FOREIGN TOURISTS

Unit 17
Introduction to China

Position and Area

China is situated in the eastern part of Asia, on the west coast of the Pacific Ocean. China has a total land area of 9.6 million square kilometers, next only to Russia and Canada. From north to south, it measures some 5500 kilometres, stretching from the central line of the Heilong River north of the town of Mohe to the Zengmu Reef at the southernmost tip of the Nansha Islands. From west to east, the territory of China extends about 5200 kilometers from the Pamirs to the confluence of the Heilong and Wusuli rivers. China's land border is 22800 kilometres long. The nation is bordered by Korea in the east; Mongolia in the north; Russia in the northeast; Kazakhstan, Kirghizia and Tadzhikistan in the northwest; Afghanistan, Pakistan, India, Nepal and Bhutan in the west and southwest; and Myanmar, Laos and Vietnam in the south. Across the seas to the east and southeast are Japan, the Philippines, Brunei, Malaysia, and Indonesia. The Chinese mainland is flanked by the Bohai Sea, the Huanghai Sea (Yellow Sea), and the East China Sea and the South China Sea in the east and south. More than 5000 islands are scattered over China's vast territorial seas, the largest being Taiwan with an area of 36000 square kilometers, and the next largest, Hainan with an area of 34000 square kilometers. Taiwan and Hainan are two provinces of China. The coast of the mainland, 18000 kilometres long, is dotted with excellent harbours and ports, the most famous of them, from north to south, being Dalian, Qinhuangdao, Tianjin, Yantai, Qingdao, Lianyungang, Nantong, Shanghai, Ningbo, Wenzhou, Fuzhou, Xiamen, Guangzhou, Zhanjiang and Beihai. Among them Shanghai is the largest city in China with a population of about 24.87 million (until 2021) and well-developed industry, commerce and ocean transportation.

Administrative Divisions

The administrative divisions are basically a three-level system of provinces, counties (cities), and townships (towns). The country is divided into provinces, autonomous regions, municipalities and special administrative regions directly under the central government. The autonomous regions (equivalent to provinces in status), autonomous prefectures (consisting of several counties), and autonomous counties and townships are all national autonomous areas. China is divided into 23 provinces, 5 autonomous regions, 4 centrally administered municipalities and 2 special administrative regions. Beijing is the capital of the People's Republic of China, as well as the country's political and cultural centre. It has a population of about 21.89 million (until 2021). With a history of more than 800 years as a national capital, Beijing has many scenic attractions and historical landmarks.

Topography

China's surface slopes down from west to east in a four-step staircase. The top of the staircase is the Qinghai-Tibet Plateau, with an average elevation of more than 4000 meters and known as "the roof of the world". The Qinghai-Tibet Plateau is composed of rows of snowcapped peaks and glaciers. The major mountain ranges are the Kunlun, Gangdise and Himalaya. The second step consists of the Inner Mongolian, Loess and Yunnan-Guizhou plateaus, and the Tarim, Junggar and Sichuan basins, on an altitude of 1000-2000 meters. The third step, about 500—1000 metres in elevation, begins at the line from the Greater Hinggan, Taihang, Wushan and Xuefeng mountain ranges eastward to the sea coast. Here, running from north to south are the Northeast Plain, the North China Plain, and the Middle-lower Yangtze Plain. Interspersed amongst the plains are hills and foothills. To the east of the third step, the shallow waters of the continental shelf, an extension of the land into the ocean, form the fourth step of the staircase. The depth of the water here is less than 200 meters. Great quantities of mud and sand have been carried here by the rivers on the mainland.

Rivers and Lakes

Most of China's rivers flow from west to east into the Pacific Ocean except a few in southwest China that flow to the south. The rivers in China total 220000 kilometers in length and more than 1500 of them drain an area of 1000 square kilometers or larger each. The total flow of these rivers is 2600 billion cubic meters, almost the same as the total flow of the rivers in Europe, and their hydroelectric power reserves amount to 680 million kilowatts. The Yangtze River(Changjiang), 6363 kilometers long, is the longest river in China. It has a catchment area of 1800000 square kilometers, and is the major inland river transport artery in China. The Yellow River (Huanghe), stretching over 5464 kilometers, covering an area of more than 795000 square kilometers, is the birthplace of ancient Chinese civilization and has a wealth of historic sites and relics, many of them buried underground. China also has a famous man-made waterway, the Grand Canal, running from Beijing in the north to Hangzhou, Zhejiang in the south, totalling 1801 kilometers long. It was dug in the 5th century and extended and dredged by different subsequent dynasties. In ancient times, materials were transported from south to north and emperors went from north to south on pleasure trips through this canal. China has many natural lakes, most of them scattered in the Middle-lower Yangtze Plain and the Qinghai-Tibet Plateau. China's largest freshwater lake is Poyang Lake with an area of 2933 square kilometers and largest salt lake is Qinghai Lake in the west with an area of 4340 square kilometers.

Climate

Most of China is situated in the temperate zone. Some parts of South China are located in tropical and subtropical zones while the northern part is near the frigid zone. In North China, summers are warm and short while winter long and cold. In the tropical and subtropical South, trees and other vegetation remain green all year. The eastern coastal regions of China are warm and humid and have four distinct seasons. But the temperatures in the interior areas of Northwest China change greatly during the daytime. There is a saying, "People wear fur coats in the morning and silk at noon." Because of its high elevation, the Qinghai-Tibet Plateau area, a special alpine cold zone, has low temperatures all year round.

Land Resources

China has 134.9 million hectares of cultivated land, mostly in the Northeast, North China, and Middle-lower Yangtze Plains, the Zhujiang Delta and the Sichuan Basin. The Northeast Plain with fertile black soil is ideal for crop growth—wheat, maize, sorghum, soybeans, sugar beets and flax. The North China Plain has level terrain and deep topsoil, where major crops include wheat, maize, millet, sorghum and cotton, along with apples, pears, grapes, persimmons and other fruits.

The Middle-lower Yangtze Plain abounds in rice, rapeseed, broad beans, tangerines and freshwater fish. This area is called "land of fish and rice". China has 2.528 million square kilometers of forest cover. The Greater Hinggan Mountains, Lesser Hinggan Mountains and Changbai Mountains in northeast China are the largest natural forest areas that produce large stands of coniferous trees, such as Korean pine and larch and broad leaf trees, such as white birch, oak, northeast China ash, poplar and elm. Southwest China is another natural forest area, where the following varieties thrive: dragon spruce, fir, Yunnan pine, teak, red sandalwood, camphor wood, nanmu and padauk. Grasslands cover 219.3 million hectares. Grasslands stretch 3000 kilometers across China from the northeast to the southwest. Animal husbandry bases are located in the grasslands. Inner Mongolian grassland is the largest natural pastureland in China where the Sanhe horse, Sanhe cattle and Mongolian sheep are raised. South and north of the Tianshan Mountains in Xinjiang, there are also famous natural pastureland ideal for livestock. The famous Yili horse and the Xinjiang fine wool sheep are raised here.

Fauna and Flora

China has the greatest diversity of wildlife in the world. There are an estimated 2091 species of terrestrial vertebrates, 10 percent of the world's total. There are 1186 known species of birds, and more than 420 animal species. Among the wild animals, there are many rare species found only in China. These include the giant panda, golden monkey, white-lipped deer, takin, Chinese river dolphin and Chinese alligator. Giant pandas live in the remote mountain areas of Sichuan, Gansu and Shaanxi provinces and feed on bamboo. The panda, called a "living fossil," is a remnant species which thrived during the glacier period of the Quaternary. China has 7000 species of woody plants, of which 2800 are arbors. The metasequoia, China cypress, cathaya, silver fir, China fir, golden larch, Taiwan flousiana, Fujian cypress, and eucommia are trees found only in China. The metasequoia grows to 35 meters in height. Commonly found in East Asia, North America and Europe one hundred million years ago, it became extinct by the glacial period of the Quaternary. In 1941, China discovered more than a thousand metasequoia on the Sichuan-Hubei border. This was one of the greatest botanical discoveries of the twentieth century. After 1949, metasequoia were introduced to other countries of the world. To protect China's zoological and botanical resources, more than 600 nature reserves have been established covering more than 28 million hectares. The Wolong Nature Reserve in Sichuan, the Changbai Mountains Reserve in Jilin, the Dinghu Mountains Reserve in Guangdong, and four other reserves serve as bases for international scientific research.

Mineral Resources

China is rich in mineral resources. At present, geologists have verified reserves of 171 different minerals. In 2019, Coal reserves total 1718.2 billion tons. It is found mainly in Shanxi, Inner Mongolia, Liaoning and Heilongjiang. Some 246 oil and gas bearing basins have been discovered, of which more than 130 are being exploited. Progress has been made in offshore oil exploration since the 1980s. Large oil basins have been discovered in the Bohai Sea, Huanghai Sea, East China Sea, the Zhujiang River Estuary, and the Beibu Bay and Yinggehai in the South China Sea. Iron ore is wildly dispersed throughout China, with reserves estimated at 85.3 billion tons. China is among the countries that lead the world in such nonferrous metals as tungsten, tin, antimony, zinc, molybdenum, lead, and mercury, whereas its rare earth metal reserves far exceed the world's total.

Notes

(1) ...from the Pamirs to the confluence of the Heilong and Wusuli rivers……从帕米尔高原到黑龙江和乌苏里江的汇合处

(2) 4 centrally-administered municipalities 4个中央直接管辖的直辖市

(3) Gangdise and Himalaya 冈底斯山和喜马拉雅山

(4) Interspersed amongst the plains are hills and foothills. 山地和丘陵夹杂在平原之间。

PART Ⅲ ENGLISH TOPICS FOR FOREIGN TOURISTS

(5) hydroelectric power reserves 水力蕴藏量
(6) the frigid zone 寒带
(7) fauna and flora 动植物
(8) the glacier period of the Quaternary 第四纪冰期
(9) cathaya 银杉属
(10) flousiana 秃杉
(11) eucommia 杜仲
(12) special administrative region(SAR) 特别行政区

New Words & Expressions

territory ['terətri] n. 领土，领域，管区
confluence ['kɒnfluəns] n.（河流的）汇合处，（事物的）汇集
Pamirs [pə'miəz] n. 帕米尔高原
be bordered by 与……接壤
be flanked by 被……夹击的
scatter over 分布
be dotted with 点缀着……
administrative [əd'mɪnɪstrətɪv] adj. 管理的，行政的
autonomous region 自治区
municipality [mjuːˌnɪsɪ'pæləti] n. 市政当局，自治市
prefecture ['priːfektʃə] n.（法、意、日等国的）地方行政区域，省，县
landmark ['lændmɑːk] n. 陆标，地标，里程碑，有历史意义的建筑物（或遗址）
topography [tə'pɒɡrəfi] n. 地形，地势，地形学
plateau ['plætəʊ] n. 高原
elevation [ˌelɪ'veɪʃn] n. 高地，海拔，提高，立面图
glacier ['ɡlæsɪə] n. 冰川
loess ['ləʊɪs] n. 黄土
intersperse [ˌɪntə'spɜːs] vt. 散布，点缀
catchment ['kætʃmənt] n.（地理学上的）汇水
artery ['ɑːtəri] n. 动脉，干线，干道，主流
Grand Canal [kə'næl] 大运河
dredge [dredʒ] vt. 疏浚，捞取，挖掘，采捞
temperate ['tempərət] adj. 有节制的，适度的气候温和的
subtropical [sʌb'trɒpɪkl] adj. 亚热带的
frigid ['frɪdʒɪd] adj. 寒冷的
vegetation [ˌvedʒə'teɪʃn] n. 植被，（总称）植物
alpine ['ælpaɪn] adj. 高山的，阿尔卑斯山的
maize [meɪz] n. 玉米
sorghum ['sɔːɡəm] n. 高粱

flax [flæks] n. 亚麻
terrain [təˈreɪn] n. 地形，地势，地带
millet [ˈmɪlɪt] n. 粟，黍类
persimmon [pəˈsɪmən] n. 柿子，柿子树
abound [əˈbaʊnd] vi. 大量，大量存在
rapeseed [ˈreɪpsiːd] n. 油菜籽
tangerine [ˌtændʒəˈriːn] n. 橘子，橘色
coniferous [kəˈnɪfərəs] adj. 结球果的，松柏科的，松类的
larch [lɑːtʃ] n. 落叶松属植物，落叶松木材
northeast China ash 水曲柳
poplar [ˈpɒplə] n. 白杨，白杨木
elm [elm] n. 榆树
spruce [spruːs] n. 云杉，云杉木　adj. 整洁的
dragon spruce 云杉
teak [tiːk] n. 柚木树，柚木，泰柚
sandalwood [ˈsændlwʊd] n. 檀香，白檀
camphor [ˈkæmfə] n. 樟脑
padauk [pəˈdɔːk] n. 紫檀木
grassland [ˈɡrɑːslænd] n. 牧草地，草原
husbandry [ˈhʌzbəndri] n. 畜牧业
pastureland [ˈpɑːstʃəlænd] n. 牧场
Sanhe horse 三和马
fauna [ˈfɔːnə] n. 动物群
flora [ˈflɔːrə] n. 植物群
terrestrial [təˈrestriəl] adj. 陆地的
vertebrate [ˈvɜːtɪbrət] n. 脊椎动物　adj. 有脊椎的，脊椎动物的
takin [ˈtɑːkɪn] n. 羚牛，扭角羚
alligator [ˈælɪɡeɪtə] n. 产于美洲的鳄鱼
fossil [ˈfɒsl] n. 化石，僵化的事物，顽固不化的人　adj. 化石的，陈腐的，守旧的
remnant [ˈremnənt] n. 残余，剩余，零料　adj. 剩余的
arbor [ˈɑːbə] n. 藤架，凉亭，乔木
quaternary [kwəˈtɜːnəri] n. 四，四个一组　adj. 四进制的
metasequoia [ˌmetəsɪˈkwɔɪə] n. 水杉
cypress [ˈsaɪprəs] n. 柏树
botanical [bəˈtænɪkl] adj. 植物的，植物学的
zoological [ˌzəʊəˈlɒdʒɪkl] adj. 动物学的
nature reserve 自然保护区
verify [ˈverɪfaɪ] vt. 检验，校验，查证，核实
offshore [ˌɒfˈʃɔː] adj. 向海面吹的，离岸的，海面上的
estuary [ˈestjʊəri] n. 河口，江口

PART Ⅲ ENGLISH TOPICS FOR FOREIGN TOURISTS

nonferrous [nɒn'ferəs] adj. 不含铁的，非铁的
tungsten ['tʌŋstən] n. 钨
tin [tɪn] n. 锡
antimony ['æntɪməni] n. 锑
zinc [zɪŋk] n. 锌
molybdenum [mə'lɪbdənəm] n. 钼
lead [li:d] n. 铅
mercury ['mɜːkjəri] n. 水银，汞
earth metal 稀土金属

Exercises

1. Read and recite the following special terms

(1) the Pacific Ocean 太平洋
(2) the Mediterranean 地中海
(3) population density 人口密度
(4) ethnic group 民族
(5) freshwater lake 淡水湖泊
(6) saltwater lake 咸水湖泊
(7) the Nile 尼罗河
(8) the Amazon 亚马孙河
(9) the Mississippi 密西西比河
(10) the Danube 多瑙河
(11) the Qomolangma 珠穆朗玛峰
(12) tropical jungles 热带丛林
(13) time zone 时区
(14) longitude 经度
(15) latitude 纬度
(16) altitude (height) above sea level (elevation) 海拔高度
(17) precipitation 降雨量
(18) monsoon zone 季风带
(19) continental climate 大陆性气候
(20) oceanic climate 海洋性气候
(21) moderate temperature 气温适中

2. Translate the following sentences into English

(1) 中国是亚洲最大的国家，也是世界上人口最多的国家，国土面积为960万平方千米。
(2) 北京是中华人民共和国的首都，也是中国的政治和文化中心。
(3) 青藏高原的平均海拔高度为4000多米，有"世界屋脊"之称。
(4) 大运河是一条著名的人工水道，北起北京，南至浙江的杭州，全长1801千米，开凿于公元5世纪。

Unit 17 Keys

Unit 18
History of China

扫码听短文

Ancient Times (from Antiquity to 1840)

From archaeological findings we know that about 500000—1000000 years ago, there were primitive human beings such as Yuanmou Man, Lantian Man and Peking Man in the wide expanse known today as China. After the long period of primitive existence, the Xia Dynasty, the first in Chinese history, was established in the 21st century BC, heralding the beginning of a slave society in China. The following Shang (16th century BC-11th century BC) and the Western Zhou (11th century BC-771 BC) dynasties saw further development of the slave society. Then came the Spring and Autumn and Warring States Period (770 BC-221 BC), a period of transition from slave to feudal society.

In 221 BC, Qin Shi Huang, the First Emperor of the Qin Dynasty, ended the rivalry among the independent principalities in the Warring States Period and established the first centralized, unified, multi-national state in the Chinese history—the Qin Dynasty. Subsequently, one dynasty replaced another. They included the Han (206 BC-220 AD), Wei (220-265) and Jin (265-420), Southern and Northern Dynasties (420-589), Sui (581-618), Tang (618-907), Five Dynasties (907-960), Song (960-1279), Yuan (1206-1368), Ming (1368-1644) and Qing (1644-1911). Until the Opium War in 1840, China had been a feudal society for close to 2000 years.

Ancient China was fairly well developed in both economy and culture. During the apex of the Chinese feudal society—the Han and Tang dynasties—agriculture, handicrafts, weaving and shipbuilding were advanced. Transportation both by land and water was convenient; extensive economic and cultural relations were established with Japan, Korea, India, Persia, and Arabia.

Meanwhile, famous thinkers in ancient China such as Lao Zi and Confucius were influencing the traditional Chinese culture and even the world civilizations. Sun Zi's the *Art of War* remained an invaluable reference for people of the military and economic circles; Cao Xueqin's *Dream of Red Mansions* is considered the representative work of Chinese classical literature and continues to inspire research and study both at home and abroad. Great achievements were also made in the fields of astronomy, mathematics, geography and medicine. *The Gan Shi Xing Jing* (*Gan*

Shi Catalogue of Stars) of the Warring States Period is the earliest catalogue of fixed stars in the world. Zhang Heng of the Han Dynasty invented the armillary sphere and seismograph. During the Southern and Northern Dynasties Zu Chongzhi calculated the value of π to be between 3.1415926 and 3.1415927. He was the first person in the world who accurately calculated the value of π to seven decimal places. *The Ben Cao Gang Mu (Compendium of Materia Medica)* by Li Shizhen of the 16th century, records more than 1800 kinds of herbal medicines and over 10000 prescriptions.

Modern Period (1840-1919)

The Opium War, which started in 1840, was a turning point in Chinese history. In the 17th and 18th centuries the major countries of Europe were looking around for markets for their merchandise and colonies. To protect its opium trade, Britain launched the war of aggression against China in 1840. In 1842 the corrupt Qing court signed the humiliating Treaty of Nanking with Britain, bartering away China's national sovereignty. This marked the reduction of China to a semicolonial, semifeudal country. The revolution of 1911, a bourgeois democratic revolution led by Dr. Sun Yat-sen, ended the rule of the Qing Dynasty. Thus, the monarchy that had existed in China for 2000 years came to an end, and the provisional government of the Republic of China was founded. However, the fruits of the Revolution of 1911 were wrested away by Yuan Shikai, the head of the northern warlords who practiced autocracy at home and sought protection with imperialists abroad. The Chinese people had to live in an abyss of misery.

Contemporary Period (1919-1949)

In 1919 the May 4th Movement against imperialism and feudalism took place. In this movement, the Chinese working class for the first time appeared on the political scene and displayed its great potential. In 1921, at the First National Congress, delegates representing Communist groups from all parts of China including Mao Zedong, Dong Biwu, Chen Tanqiu, He Shuheng, Wang Jinmei, Deng Enming and Li Da, met in Shanghai and founded the Communist Party of China. The Chinese people led by the Communist Party participated in a bitter struggle for 28 years, which included four periods: the Northern Expedition (1924-1927), Agrarian Revolutionary War (1927-1937), War of Resistance Against Japan (1937-1945), and the National Liberation War (1945-1949). In 1949 the Chinese finally ended the rule of the Kuomintang headed by Chiang Kai-shek and liberated all of China except Taiwan and some other islands. On October 1, 1949 the founding of the People's Republic of China was proclaimed, marking the beginning of the historical period of socialist revolution and construction in China.

Notes

(1) archaeological findings 考古发现

（2）heralding the beginning of a slave society in China 预示着奴隶社会在中国的出现

（3）the independent principalities 独立的诸侯国

（4）during the apex of the Chinese feudal society 在中国封建社会的顶峰时期

（5）*Dream of Red Mansions*《红楼梦》

（6）the armillary sphere and seismograph 浑天仪和地震仪

（7）seven decimal places 七位小数

（8）the humiliating Treaty of Nanking 丧权辱国的《南京条约》

（9）bartering away China's national sovereignty 出卖中国的主权

（10）an abyss of misery 一个痛苦的深渊

（11）Agrarian Revolutionary War 土地革命战争

New Words & Expressions

antiquity [æn'tɪkwəti] n. 古代，古老，古代的遗物
archaeological [ˌɑːkɪə'lɒdʒɪkəl] adj. 考古学的，考古学上的
primitive ['prɪmɪtɪv] adj. 原始的，远古的
herald ['herəld] n. 预兆使者，传令官，通报者　vt. 预示，宣布
transition [træn'zɪʃn] n. 过渡
rivalry ['raɪvlri] n. 竞争，竞赛，敌对，敌对状态
subsequently ['sʌbsɪkwəntli] adv. 后来，随后
opium ['əʊpiəm] n. 鸦片
apex ['eɪpeks] n. 顶点
civilization [ˌsɪvəlaɪ'zeɪʃn] n. 文明
invaluable [ɪn'væljuəbl] adj. 无价的，价值无法衡量的
mansion ['mænʃn] n. 大厦，官邸，公寓
catalogue ['kætəlɒg] n. 目录
astronomy [ə'strɒnəmi] n. 天文学
armillary [ɑː'mɪləri] adj. 手镯的，环形的
sphere [sfɪə] n. 球，球体，范围，领域
seismograph ['saɪzməɡrɑːf] n. 地震仪，测震仪
decimal ['desɪml] adj. 十进制的，小数的　n. 小数
compendium [kəm'pendiəm] n. 汇编
merchandise ['mɜːtʃəndaɪz] n. 商品，货物
colony ['kɒləni] n. 殖民地
corrupt [kə'rʌpt] adj. 腐败的，贪污的　vt. 使腐烂，腐蚀，使恶化　vi. 腐烂，堕落
humiliating [hjuː'mɪlieɪtɪŋ] adj. 羞辱性的
barter ['bɑːtə] v. 以物易物
barter away 出卖
sovereignty ['sɒvrənti] n. 主权

monarchy ['mɒnəki] n. 君主制
provisional [prə'vɪʒənl] adj. 临时的
wrest away 夺取
autocracy [ɔː'tɒkrəsi] n. 独裁政体，专制制度
abyss [ə'bɪs] n. 深渊
expedition [ˌekspə'dɪʃn] n. 远征，探险
agrarian [ə'greəriən] adj. 农业的，耕地的
in the wide expanse [ɪks'pæns] 在这个广阔的区域里

Exercises

1. Read and recite the following special terms

(1) to make a raid upon 袭击，入侵

(2) BC 公元前

(3) AD 公元

(4) the Neolithic Age 新石器时代

(5) the Paleolithic Age 旧石器时代

(6) nomadic tribe 游牧部落

(7) coinage 货币制度

(8) weights and measures 度量衡

(9) at the mercy of... 听任……支配（摆布）

(10) feudal empire 封建王朝

(11) the Spring and Autumn Period 春秋时期

(12) the Warring States Period 战国时期

(13) a united feudal empire 统一的封建帝国

(14) the last emperor 末代皇帝

(15) the Qin fell to the Han 秦灭汉立

(16) dukedom 诸侯国

(17) the peasant uprising 农民起义

(18) thousands of years later 数千年后

(19) the Silk Road 丝绸之路

(20) a period of decline 衰落时期

(21) the Northern Expedition 北伐

2. Translate the following sentences into English

(1) 中国有文字记载的历史可以追溯到公元前20世纪。

(2) 早在公元前6000年就有新石器时代的居民在这个地区居住了。

(3) 秦始皇是中国历史上第一位建立统一封建王朝的君主。

(4) 1840年，英国为了保护其鸦片贸易，发动了侵略中国的战争。鸦片战争是中国历史的转折点。

(5) 中国共产党领导中国人民进行了28年艰苦卓绝的斗争，经历了4个时期，即北伐战争、土地革命战争、抗日战争和解放战争。

Unit 18 Keys

Unit 19
Population and Nationalities of China

Population Situation

China has more people than any other country. According to the results of the seventh national census published on May 11, 2021, China had a population of about 1.44349 billion (excluding Taiwan, Hong Kong and Macao), accounting for about 21.5 percent of the world's total population. China's population density (about 147 people per square kilometer) is relatively high. Distribution, however, is uneven: the coastal areas in the east are densely populated, with about 360 people per square kilometer; the plateau areas in the west are sparsely populated, with fewer than 10 people per square kilometer.

The table below shows, in general, the composition of population in China (published in 2021):

Sex		Region		Age		
Male	Female	Cities and towns	Countryside	0-14 years old	15-59 years old	60 years old and above
51.24%	48.76%	63.89%	36.11%	17.95%	63.35%	18.7%

Population Growth and Family Planning

In 1949 there were 541670000 people living on the mainland. Lacking controls, appropriate education on the subject and experience—and the improvement of people's living standards led to a rapid increase of China's population, which had reached 806710000 by 1969. Facing the serious problem of the over population, China has implemented family planning to control the population growth. Since it was initiated in the 1970s, the birth rate has declined each year. By 2003 the birth rate dropped to 14.39 per thousand from 34.11 per thousand in 1969, and the natural growth rate declined to 6.01 per thousand from 26.08 per thousand. By 2016 the birth rate dropped to 12.95 per thousand from 14.39 per thousand in 2003, and the natural growth rate declined to 5.86 per thousand from 6.01 per thousand in 2003. The birth population was 12 million in 2020, the birth rate was 8.50‰, and the birth population declined for three consecutive years, the lowest since the data existed in 1952.

The basic demands of previous family planning policy were late marriage and late childbirth—having fewer but healthier babies, specifically, one child for one couple. In rural areas, the couple with the shortage of labor power or other difficulties could have a second baby, but had to wait several years after the birth of the first child. In areas inhabited by minority peoples, a couple could have more children. At that time, family planning as a basic state policy was supported by a vast majority of the people.

In recent years, the problem of the aging population of China is getting worse. Therefore the Chinese government has modified the policy of family planing, one couple can have three children whether in cities or in rural areas. The proportion of children's population in China has gone up again, and the new fertility policy adjustment has achieved positive results. At the same time, the aging degree of the population is further deepened, and the coming period will continue to face the long-term pressure of the balanced population development.

Fifty-six Nationalities

China is a multi-national country with 56 ethnic groups. According to the seventh national census, there are about 1.28631 billion Han people, accounting for 91.11% of China's total population. The other 55 nationalities represent about 125.47 million people, or 8.89% of the total. Compared with 2010, the Han population increased by 4.93%, the population of various ethnic minorities increased by 10.26%, and the proportion of the ethnic minority population increased by 0.40 percentage points. The steady growth of the ethnic minority population fully reflects the all-round development and progress of all ethnic minorities under the leadership of the Communist Party of China. The 55 minorities are: Zhuang, Hui, Uygur, Yi, Miao, Manchu, Tibetan, Mongolian, Tujia, Bouyei, Korean, Dong, Yao, Bai, Hani, Kazak, Dai, Li, Lisu, She, Lahu, Va, Shui, Dongxiang, Naxi, Tu, Kirgiz, Qiang, Daur, Mulam, Gelo, Xibe, Jingpo, Salar, Blang, Maonan, Tajik, Pumi, Nu, Achang, Ewenki, Jino, Ozbek, Jing, Deang, Yugur, Bonan, Moinba, Drung, Oroqen, Tatar, Russian, Gaoshan, Hezhen, and Lhoba. The Zhuang nationality, the largest of the 55 ethnic groups, has 16.1788 million people. The Han nationality is found in all parts of the country, but mainly in the middle and lower reaches of the Yellow River(Huanghe), Yangtze River (Changjiang) and Pearl River (Zhujiang) and the Northeast Plain. The areas inhabited by the minority nationalities are mainly in the border regions of the North, Northeast, Northwest and Southwest China. The Han nationality has its own spoken and written language, known as the Chinese language, which is commonly used throughout China and a working language of the United Nations. The Hui and Manchu nationalities also use the Han (Chinese) language. The other 53 ethnic groups use the spoken languages of their own; 23 minority nationalities have their own written languages.

Regional Autonomy for Minority Peoples

Equality, unity and common prosperity are the fundamental objectives of the government in handling nationality relations. To this end, while maintaining unified leadership by the state, China exercises national regional autonomy, which allows the minority peoples living in compact communities to establish self-government and direct their own affairs. At present, altogether 5 autonomous regions, 30 autonomous prefectures and 24 autonomous counties (banners) have been established in the country. The central government provides the autonomous areas with financial and material support to promote the development of local economy and culture.

Life Styles

The unique customs and habits of the minorities have developed in the process of their long history and were influenced by their peculiar environment, social and economic conditions. Generally, people in South China like rice, while people in the North prefer noodles; the Uygur, Kazak and Ozbek nationalities like roast mutton kebab and crusty pancake; Mongolians like millet stir-fried in butter, fried sheep tail and tea with milk; Koreans like sticky rice cakes, cold noodles and kimchi (pickled vegetables); Tibetans eat zanba (roasted qingke barley flour) and buttered tea; the Lis, Jings and Dais chew betelnuts. Mongolians wear Mongolian robes and riding boots; Tibetans wear Tibetan robes; Uygurs wear embroidered skullcaps; Koreans wear boat-shaped rubber overshoes; Miao, Yi and Tibetan women wear gold or silver ornaments; Yis like to wear cha'erwa (woolen cloak). Courtyard type dwellings are universally adopted in the areas inhabited by the Hans; most minorities in the pastoral areas of Inner Mongolia, Xinjiang, Qinghai and Gansu live in Mongolian yurts; the Dais, Zhuangs and Bouyeis in South China often live in the ganlan (balustrade) style storeyed houses.

Traditional festivals of China include Spring Festival (Lunar New Year), Lantern Festival (15th day of the first lunar month), Dragon Boat Festival (5th day of the fifth lunar month), and Mid-Autumn Festival (15th day of the eighth lunar month). Spring Festival is the most important and ceremonious. During Spring Festival, in both urban and rural areas, every household will display Spring Festival couplets and pictures, and decorate the home. Spring Festival Eve is an important time for family reunions. Usually, in the evening of the last day of the twelfth month by the lunar calendar each year, the entire family gets together for a New Year's Eve dinner. After dinner, all family members sit together to chat or play games, staying up till early the next morning. At midnight, people let off firecrackers to ring out the old year and ring in the new. In the morning people pay New Year calls on relatives to extend congratulations. During Spring Festival, many people also attend traditional recreational activities, such as the lion dance, dragon-lantern dance and stilt-walking. Minority nationalities have also retained their own traditional festivals, including the

PART III　ENGLISH TOPICS FOR FOREIGN TOURISTS

Water Splashing Festival of the Dai nationality, the Nadam Fair of the Mongolian nationality, the Third Month Fair of the Bai nationality, the Antiphonal Singing Day of the Zhuang nationality, and the Tibetan New Year and Onghor (Expecting Good Harvest) Festival of the Tibetan nationality.

Notes

(1) population density 人口密度
(2) the composition of population 人口构成
(3) late marriage and late childbirth 晚婚晚育
(4) regional autonomy for minority peoples 少数民族区域自治
(5) unified leadership 统一领导
(6) to this end 为达此目的
(7) roast mutton kebab and crusty pancake 烤羊肉串和硬饼
(8) kimchi (pickled vegetables) 朝鲜泡菜
(9) courtyard-type dwellings 院落式住宅
(10) to ring out the old year and ring in the new 辞旧迎新
(11) stilt-walking 踩高跷
(12) the Antiphonal Singing 对歌

New Words & Expressions

exclude [ɪksˈkluːd] vt. 把……排除在外
density [ˈdensəti] n. 密度
account for 占……比例
sparsely [ˈspɑːsli] adv. 稀少地，稀疏地
composition [ˌkɒmpəˈzɪʃən] n. 写作，作文，成分，合成物
appropriate [əˈprəʊpriət] adj. 适当的
implement [ˈɪmplɪmənt] vt. 贯彻，执行，实施　n. 工具，器具
the birth rate 出生率
multi-national [mʌltiˈnæʃnəl] adj. 多民族的
census [ˈsensəs] n. 人口普查
ethnic [ˈeθnɪk] adj. 民族的，种族的
compact [kəmˈpækt] adj. 紧凑的，紧密的，袖珍的　[ˈkɒmpækt] n. 契约，带镜小粉盒
peculiar [pɪˈkjuːliə] adj. 奇特的，罕见的，特殊的
kebab [kɪˈbæb] n. 烤肉串
kimchi [ˈkɪmtʃi] n.（朝鲜语）朝鲜泡菜
barley [ˈbɑːli] n. 大麦
betelnut [ˈbiːtlˌnʌt] n. 槟榔
skullcap [ˈskʌlkæp] n. 无边便帽，并头草属的植物

dwelling ['dwelɪŋ] n. 住处

pastoral ['pɑːstərəl] adj. 牧师的，牧人的，田园生活的，乡村的 n. 牧歌，田园诗，田园景色

yurt [jɜːt] n. 蒙古包

balustrade [ˌbæləs'treɪd] n. 栏杆

ceremonious [ˌserə'məʊnɪəs] adj. 讲究仪式的，隆重的

couplet ['kʌplət] n. 对联，对句，两行诗

let off 放（鞭炮）

firecracker ['faɪəkrækə] n. 爆竹，鞭炮

stilt [stɪlt] n. 高跷，支柱

splash [splæʃ] n. 溅，飞溅，斑点 v. 溅，泼，溅湿

antiphonal [æn'tɪfənəl] adj. 交互轮唱的

Exercises

1. Read and recite the following special terms

（1）densely populated area (thickly inhabited area) 人口稠密的地区

（2）sparsely populated area 人口稀少的地区

（3）population explosion 人口爆炸

（4）population distribution 人口分布

（5）over population 人口过剩

（6）population base 人口基数

（7）aging of population 人口老龄化

（8）population census 人口普查

（9）population statistics 人口统计

（10）population growth 人口增长

（11）population quality 人口质量

（12）natural growth rate of population 人口的自然增长率

（13）family planning 计划生育

（14）the birth rate 出生率

（15）a multi-national country 多民族国家

（16）the Han nationality 汉族

（17）regional autonomy 区域自治

（18）minority people 少数民族

（19）Mongolian yurt 蒙古包

（20）nationality relations 民族关系

2. Translate the following sentences into English

（1）根据2021年第七次全国人口普查的结果，中国人口已经达到14.1178亿，占世界总人口的21.5%。

PART Ⅲ ENGLISH TOPICS FOR FOREIGN TOURISTS

（2）中国是一个拥有56个民族的多民族国家，汉族人口占全国总人口的90%以上。

（3）民族平等、民族团结和共同繁荣是我国处理民族关系的基本方针。

（4）在汉族居住区，人们大多住在院落式的住所里；在草原地区，绝大多数少数民族住在蒙古包里；南方的傣族、壮族和布依族住在杆栏式的房子里。

Unit 19　Keys

Unit 20
Political System of China

Constitution

Four constitutions have been formulated and promulgated since the establishment of the People's Republic of China, in 1954, 1975, 1978 and 1982. Included in the present Constitution are 138 articles. Apart from the preamble, it is divided into the following chapters: General Principles, the Fundamental Rights and Duties of Citizens, the Structure of the State, and the National Flag, the National Emblem, the National Anthem, and the Capital. The Constitution provides for the fundamental rights of citizens. They are the right to vote and stand for election; freedom of speech, the press, assembly, association, procession and demonstration; freedom of religious belief; freedom of the person, the personal dignity of citizens and the inviolability of their homes; freedom and privacy of correspondence as protected by law; the right to criticize, make suggestions to and supervise any state organ or functionary; the right to work and to rest and the right to material assistance from the state and society when they are old, ill or disabled; the right to receive education; and freedom to engage in scientific research, literary and artistic creation and other cultural pursuits.

The People's Congress System

All power in the People's Republic of China belongs to the people. The organs through which the people exercise state power are the National People's Congress and the local people's congresses. Therefore, the people's congress system is China's fundamental political system.

Deputies to the people's congresses at various levels are elected by the people, they are responsible to the people and accept supervision from the people. The deputies are broadly representative; they include people from all nationalities, all walks of life, all regions, classes and strata. As they come from the people, they maintain close ties with their respective constituencies and the people and earnestly listen to their views and demands. When the congresses meet to discuss issues of major policies and principles they can air their views fully and carry out the decisions after they have been made. Hence, the people's views can be collected and the people can exercise the right to manage their state, economic and social affairs through the people's congresses.

The Multi-Party Cooperation and Political Consultation System

China is a multi-national and multi-party country. Before the state adopts important measures or makes decisions on major issues bearing on the national economy and the people's livelihood, the Communist Party of China, as the party in power, consults with all nationalities, political parties, all circles and non-party democrats in order to reach a common understanding. This system, called multi-party cooperation and political consultation system led by the CPC, is also a basic political system of China.

The multi-party cooperation and political consultation system adopts two main forms. One is the Chinese People's Political Consultative Conference (CPPCC) and the other is the consultative meetings and forums of democratic parties and non-party personages held by the CPC Central Committee or local party committees at different levels.

The CPPCC has a national committee and local committees at the provincial (autonomous regional or municipal) level and at the county (city) level, which consists of representatives from the CPC, democratic parties, non-party democrats, people's organizations, minority nationalities and all walks of life, compatriots from Taiwan, Hong Kong and Macao, returned overseas Chinese and specially invited individuals. The committees at various levels hold a plenary session once a year and, when the committee is not in session, it organizes the committee members to conduct special activities, to go on inspection tours to various localities, to hold consultations on major issues relating to major state policies, important local affairs, people's lives and the united front work and to exercise democratic supervision over the work of state organs and the implementation of the state constitution and laws by offering opinions, proposals and criticisms. The consultative meetings participated in by leader of democratic parties and representatives of non-party democrats at the invitation of leaders of the CPC Central Committee are held once a year and the forums are held once every other month, the former mainly to discuss state major policies along the democratic line and the latter mainly to exchange information, hear proposals on policy or discuss certain subjects.

The National Flag, National Anthem and National Emblem

The national flag of the People's Republic of China is red in color, rectangular in shape, with five stars. The proportion between the length and height of the flag is three to two. The five five-pointed yellow stars are located in the upper left corner. One of them, which is bigger, appears on the left, while the other four hem it in on the right.

The red color of the flag symbolizes revolution; the stars take on the yellow color in order to bring out their brightness on the red ground. The larger star represents the CPC, while the four smaller ones, the Chinese people. The relationship between the stars means the great unity of the Chinese people under the leadership of the CPC.

The national emblem of the People's Republic of China is Tian'anmen in the centre illuminated by five stars and encircled by ears of grain and a cogwheel. The ears of grain, stars, Tian'anmen and cogwheel are painted golden, and the inner part of the circle and hanging ribbons are painted red because these two colors are traditional Chinese colors representing auspiciousness and happiness.

Tian'anmen symbolizes the unyielding national spirit of the Chinese people in their fight against imperialism and feudalism; the ear of grain and cogwheel represent the working class and the peasantry; and the five stars stand for the great unity of the Chinese people under the leadership of the CPC.

The national anthem was created in 1935, the lyrics by Tian Han, a famous poet, and the music by Nie Er, a famous composer. The lyrics are as follows: "Arise, who refuse to be slaves; with our very flesh and blood let us build our new Great Wall! The peoples of China are in the most critical time, everybody must roar his defiance. Arise! Arise! Arise! Millions of hearts with one mind, brave the enemy's gunfire. March on! Brave the enemy's gunfire, march on! March on! March on, on!" This song, originally named *March of the Volunteers*, is the theme song of the film, *Young Heroes and Heroines in Stormy Years*. The film describes the people who went to the front to fight against the invaders in the 1930s when Japan invaded Northeast China and the fate of the Chinese nation was hanging in the balance.

March of the Volunteers, inspiring and forceful, expresses the determination of the Chinese people to sacrifice themselves for national liberation, and their fine tradition of bravery, firmness and unity in their fight against aggression. It was for this reason that the CPPCC on September 27, 1949 decided to adopt the song as the national anthem of the People's Republic of China.

Notes

(1) Four constitutions have been formulated and promulgated 制定和公布了四部宪法

(2) apart from the preamble 除序言以外

(3) China's fundamental political system 中国的基本政治制度

(4) They can air their views fully. 他们能够充分表达他们的观点。

(5) to make decisions on major issues bearing on the national economy and the people's livelihood 对关系国计民生的重大问题做出决定

(6) the Chinese People's Political Consultative Conference (CPPCC) 中国人民政治协商会议

(7) the CPC Central Committee 中国共产党中央委员会

(8) The national anthem was created in 1935, the lyrics by the famous poet Tian

Han and music by the Nie Er, a famous composer. 国歌创作于 1935 年，由著名的诗人田汉作词，由著名的作曲家聂耳作曲。

（9）*March of the Volunteers*《义勇军进行曲》

（10）the fate of the Chinese nation was hanging in the balance 中华民族的命运危在旦夕

New Words & Expressions

  constitution [ˌkɒnstɪˈtjuːʃn] n. 宪法，章程，体质，构造
  formulate [ˈfɔːmjuleɪt] vt. 规划，制定
  promulgate [ˈprɒməlgeɪt] vt. 公布，传播，发表，颁布
  apart from 远离，除……之外
  preamble [priːˈæmbl] n. 序言　vi. 作序
  anthem [ˈænθəm] n. 国歌
  emblem [ˈembləm] n. 徽章，象征
  inviolability [ɪnˌvaɪələˈbɪləti] n. 不可侵犯，神圣，不可亵渎
  correspondence [ˌkɒrəˈspɒndəns] n. 通信，一致
  functionary [ˈfʌŋkʃənəri] n. 官员，公务员
  pursuit [pəˈsjuːt] n. 追赶，追求
  supervision [ˌsjuːpəˈvɪʒn] n. 监督，管理，监控，监视
  stratum [ˈstrɑːtəm] n. 层，地层，社会阶层
  constituency [kənˈstɪtjuənsi] n.（选区的）选民，选区，选民区，支持者
  earnestly [ˈɜːnɪstli] adv. 认真地，诚挚地
  consultation [ˌkɒnslˈteɪʃn] n. 咨询，磋商，会诊，讨论会
  livelihood [ˈlaɪvlihʊd] n. 生计，生活，营生
  democrat [ˈdeməkræt] n. 民主党人
  forum [ˈfɔːrəm] n. 论坛
  personage [ˈpɜːsənɪdʒ] n. 要人，名人
  compatriot [kəmˈpætriət] n. 同胞，同国人　adj. 同胞的，同国的
  plenary [ˈpliːnəri] n. 全体会议　adj. 全体参加的
  inspection [ɪnˈspekʃn] n. 视察，检查
  rectangular [rekˈtæŋgjələ] adj. 矩形的
  hem [hem] n.（衣服等的）褶边　vt. 给……缝边
  take on 承担，呈现，具有，流行，接纳，雇用，穿上
  lyric [ˈlɪrɪk] n. 歌词
  composer [kəmˈpəʊzə] n. 作曲家
  volunteer [ˌvɒlənˈtɪə] n. 志愿者
  to hang in the balance 悬而未决，不能确定，尚未决定
  firmness [ˈfɜːmnəs] n. 坚定，坚固
  sacrifice [ˈsækrɪfaɪs] n. 牺牲，祭品，供奉　vt. 牺牲

illuminate [ɪˈluːmɪneɪt] vt. 阐明，照明，照亮，用灯装饰
cogwheel [ˈkɒɡwiːl] n. 齿轮
auspiciousness [ɔːˈspɪʃəsnəs] n. 吉兆，吉祥
unyielding [ʌnˈjiːldɪŋ] adj. 不屈的，坚强的，不弯曲的
peasantry [ˈpezntri] n.（总称）农民

Exercises

1. Read and recite the following special terms

（1）the National People's Congress 全国人民代表大会
（2）the multi-party cooperation and political consultation system 多党合作和政治协商制度
（3）the fundamental rights and duties of citizens 公民的基本权利和义务
（4）the national flag 国旗
（5）the national anthem 国歌
（6）the national emblem 国徽
（7）all walks of life 各界人士
（8）the national economy 国民经济
（9）the people's livelihood 人民生活
（10）the Communist Party of China（CPC）中国共产党
（11）the party in power 执政党
（12）a party not in office 在野党
（13）non-party personages 无党派人士
（14）the Chinese People's Political Consultative Conference（CPPCC）中国人民政治协商会议
（15）central committee 中央委员会
（16）the Chinese nation 中华民族
（17）the unyielding national spirit 不屈不挠的民族精神
（18）imperialism and feudalism 帝国主义和封建主义
（19）the working class and peasantry 工人阶级和农民

2. Translate the following sentences into English

（1）宗教信仰自由和人身自由是我国宪法赋予公民的基本权利。
（2）人民代表大会制度是我国的基本政治制度，人民通过全国人民代表大会和地方各级人民代表大会行使国家权力。
（3）中国共产党领导下的多党合作和政治协商制度也是我国的一个基本政治制度。
（4）中华人民共和国的国旗是五星红旗，国歌是《义勇军进行曲》。
（5）中华人民共和国国徽中间是五星照耀下的天安门，周围是谷穗和齿轮。

Unit 21
The Present Status of Education & Public Health in China

Education

Education has always been given great priority in China. The ancient Chinese sage Confucius said that nothing is lofty except reading books. In modern China, the Communist Party and Chinese government attach great importance to education. Deng Xiaoping has often said that science and technology are crucial to the realization of modernization, and that education provides a solid foundation for the target. In his words, China must, if necessary, sacrifice speedy development in other sectors in order to solve problems related to education.

扫码听短文

New progress had been made in educational undertakings. Compulsory education is the cornerstone of basic educational development. With the implementation of the nine-year compulsory education program, in 2018, the enrollment of primary-school-age children was about 99.95%, and the proportion entering junior middle schools reached about 100%, the proportion entering senior middle schools reached about 88.8%. A nationwide "Hope Project" has been carried out to help the dropouts to go back to school with donations and encouragement by individuals and enterprises. In 2018, the enrollment rate of new college students was about 38.33 million, the proportion entering institutions of higher learning reached about 48.1%, the scale has already exceeded that of America and ranks first all over the world.

According to the state's law on compulsory education, primary education is the universal. The main body of early education is the full-time primary school, a six-year program. The curriculum includes moral character, Chinese, arithmetic, nature, history, geography, computer, drawing, music and physical culture.

Secondary education includes ordinary middle school education and vocational secondary education. The ordinary middle school is composed of junior and senior high schools, each with a length of study of three years. The courses offered in the ordinary middle school include Chinese, mathematics, foreign language, politics, history, geography, physics, chemistry biology, physical culture, music, fine arts, physiology and work skills.

Vocational education offers a special secondary, technical and vocational curriculum; the length of schooling ranging from two to three years or from three to four years. The special secondary schools and technical schools offer courses in engineering, agriculture, forestry, medicine, finance and economics, teacher training, physical culture, arts, political science and law, culture, tourism, cooking, navigation and industrial art. Technical schools mainly train the middle-level technical workers.

Institutions of higher learning in China include universities and institutes or colleges for professional training. The length of study for regular undergraduates in institutions of higher learning is four years; for some majors such as medicine, the period is five years. Colleges for professional training require three years; a few, two years. The well-known institutions of higher learning include Beijing University, Tsinghua University, Fudan University, Nankai University, Chinese University of Science and Technology, Wuhan University and Tongji University, etc. Generally speaking, universities and colleges conduct national unified entrance examinations, now there are also some exceptions. Students are selected on the basis of their test results, health and personal choice. Outstanding college graduates are selected for state positions. Work units may select and employ top students based on their special skills and training, personal choice, society's need and the school's recommendation. Postgraduates are trained mainly by institutions of higher learning and research institutes.

Adult education is flourishing in China at radio and TV universities, workers' colleges, farmers' colleges, correspondence colleges, evening universities, colleges giving in-service training to government employees or secondary school teachers, vocational secondary schools, technical schools, literacy classes, classes for making up primary education, and technical classes. People taking adult education courses do so to improve their professional and vocational skills, expand their knowledge of social and cultural affairs or prepare for new careers.

Schools at all levels in China must follow the principles that education should serve the drive for socialist modernization, be combined with labor production, and builders and successors should be trained morally, intellectually and physically. In recent years, *Outline of National Medium-and long-Term Program for Education Reform and Development* (2010-2020), *Teachers' Law* and *Education Law* have been adopted. Those documents will guarantee the duties and the rights of the teacher, and ensure the healthy and rapid development of education in China.

Notes

(1) Nothing is lofty except reading books. 万般皆下品，唯有读书高。

(2) compulsory education 义务教育

(3) the dropout rates for students 失学率

(4) the dropouts 辍学学生

PART III ENGLISH TOPICS FOR FOREIGN TOURISTS

(5) undergraduate students 在读大学生

(6) vocational education 职业教育

(7) institutions of higher learning 高等教育机构

(8) postgraduate 研究生

(9) adult education 成人教育

(10) in-service training 在职培训

(11) correspondence colleges 函授大学

(12) Education should serve the drive for socialist modernization. 教育应该为社会主义现代化建设服务。

New Words & Expressions

priority [praɪˈɒrəti] n. 优先，优先权

sage [seɪdʒ] adj. 贤明的，明智的 n. 贤人，圣人，德高望重的人

crucial [ˈkruːʃl] adj. 至关紧要的

relate to 与……有关

undertaking [ˌʌndəˈteɪkɪŋ] n. 事业，企业，承诺，保证，殡仪业

compulsory [kəmˈpʌlsəri] n.（花样滑冰、竞技体操等的）规定动作 adj. 义务的，必修的，被强制的

cornerstone [ˈkɔːnəstəun] n. 墙角石，基础

implementation [ˌɪmplɪmenˈteɪʃn] n. 执行

enrollment [ɪnˈrəulmənt] n. 登记，注册，入伍，入会，入学

dropout [ˈdrɒpaut] n. 退学学生，中途退学，辍学学生

nationwide [ˈneɪʃnˈwaɪd] adj. 全国性的

undergraduate [ˌʌndəˈɡrædʒuət] n. 大学生，本科生

illiteracy [ɪˈlɪtərəsi] n. 文盲

intellectually [ˌɪntɪˈlektʃuəli] adv. 智力上，理智地

Public Health

Good health is a fundamental goal of people throughout the world, and the Chinese people are of no exception. The average life expectancy of Chinese people was 45 before 1949, now has increased to over 70. The infant mortality rate for the whole country fell from 200 per 1000 in 1949 to 81 per 1000 in 1956. Today, the rate has dropped to less than 10 per 1000. All this is due to the improvements in medical care and living standards of the Chinese people.

Prevention always comes first. The Chinese government and people have time and again launched nationwide Patriotic Public Hygiene Campaigns so that epidemics have been brought under control. Medical treatment has also been improved. By the end of 2018, there were about 6.56 million hospital beds in the country and over 9.5 million full-time health workers. There are general hospitals, hospitals for special diseases, western medicine hospitals and traditional Chinese medicine hospitals and

扫码听短文

institutions emphasizing scientific research. Besides numerous hospitals at provincial, city, and county levels, there is always a clinic in every factory, every school and every community with well-trained doctors and nurses on hand to help.

Medical program is changing in China today. Originally, the government employees enjoy free medical care; they are teachers, doctors, factory workers, office workers and army men. Others have to buy insurance to help them meet medical expenses. According to the new medical policy, everyone has to buy insurance to help him meet medical expenses.

Problems in medical care stem from the huge population. There are not enough funds and doctors so that diagnosis and treatment are sometimes hurried. There is a long way to go before all the Chinese people are well-covered by a satisfactory health plan.

In past years, great progress has been made in promoting traditional Chinese medicine and combining it with western medicine. Chinese medicine has its own system of theories, therapeutic principles and methods of treatment. Efforts to study and explain them in a modern approach and in connection with clinical experience have led to some new successes. In acupuncture and moxibustion, for example, a number of new acupuncture points and new methods have been discovered so that more than 300 types of ailments can be treated now, 100 of which with good or very good results, including coronary heart disease, acute bacterial dysentery, gall stones and neural paralysis. Public health means more than medical care. The Ministry of Public Health of China has launched many campaigns to raise the level of China's public health. Some of those campaigns aim to improve public hygiene and medical services in the rural areas and in the remote border regions, to fight against increasingly serious environmental pollution, to ban smoking in certain places, to cure eating disorders, to lay down requirements and standards for food processing. Naturally the list seems endless.

Notes

(1) the Chinese people are of no exception 中国人民也不例外

(2) the average life expectancy 平均寿命

(3) Patriotic Public Hygiene Campaigns 爱国卫生运动

(4) Problems in medical care stem from the huge population. 人口众多引起了医疗保健方面的一些问题。

(5) coronary heart disease, acute bacterial dysentery, gall stones and neural paralysis 冠心病、急性痢疾、胆结石和神经麻痹

(6) to lay down requirements and standards for food processing 给食品加工制定了相关要求和规定

PART III ENGLISH TOPICS FOR FOREIGN TOURISTS

New Words & Expressions

expectancy [ɪkˈspektənsi] n. 期待，期望
mortality [mɔːˈtæləti] 死亡数量
patriotic [ˌpætriˈɒtɪk] adj. 爱国的
hygiene [ˈhaɪdʒiːn] n. 卫生，卫生学
campaign [kæmˈpeɪn] n. 战役，（政治或商业性）活动　vi. 参加活动，领导运动
epidemic [ˌepɪˈdemɪk] adj. 流行的，传染的，流行性的　n. 流行病
on hand 在场，到场，在手头
stem from 起源
diagnosis [ˌdaɪəgˈnəʊsɪs] n. 诊断
satisfactory [ˌsætɪsˈfæktəri] adj. 满意的
therapeutic [ˌθerəˈpjuːtɪk] adj. 治疗的，治疗学的　n. 治疗剂，治疗学家
acupuncture [ˈækjupʌŋktʃə] n. 针刺，针刺疗法　vt. 对施行针刺疗法
moxibustion [mɒksɪˈbʌstʃn] n. 艾灸，灸术，灸法
ailment [ˈeɪlmənt] n. 小病，不安，病痛，疾病
coronary [ˈkɒrənri] adj. 冠的，花冠的，冠状的
acute [əˈkjuːt] adj. 敏锐的，急性的，剧烈的
dysentery [ˈdɪsəntri] n. 痢疾
gall [gɔːl] n. 胆汁，恶毒，肿痛，恼怒　vt. 磨伤，烦恼，屈辱
neural [ˈnjʊərəl] adj. 神经系统的，神经中枢的，背侧的
paralysis [pəˈræləsɪs] n. 瘫痪，麻痹
ban [bæn] n. 禁令　vt. 禁止，取缔（书刊等）
lay down 制定

Exercises

1. Read and recite the following special terms

(1) liberal arts 文科
(2) science 理科
(3) schooling 学制
(4) undergraduate 本科生
(5) graduate student 研究生
(6) full-professor 教授
(7) doctorate 博士学位
(8) audio-visual center 视听中心
(9) academic exchange 学术交流
(10) scholarship 奖学金
(11) press publication 出版物
(12) adult education 成人教育

(13) public health 公共卫生
(14) life expectancy 寿命
(15) the infant mortality rate 婴儿死亡率
(16) the Patriotic Public Hygiene Campaign 爱国卫生运动
(17) free medical care 免费医疗
(18) medical expense 医疗费
(19) coronary heart disease 冠心病
(20) cooperative medical service 合作医疗

2. Translate the following sentences into English

(1) 目前，中国政府在全国范围内开展"希望工程"来帮助失学学生重返校园。

(2) 职业教育开设一些专门的职业和技术课程，学制2—3年或3—4年。

(3) 近年来，大学的教学、科研设备条件得到了改善，与国外高等学校间的国际学术交流十分频繁。

(4) 1949年以前中国人的人均寿命是45岁，现在已提高至70岁以上。

(5) 中国政府多次开展爱国卫生运动来控制流行性疾病，医疗条件得到了很大的改善。

Unit 21　Keys

Unit 22
Traditional Chinese Medicine

扫码听短文

Chinese medicine is a great treasure-house which has been drawing much attention in the world. The origins of Chinese medicine are lost in legend, but it is said that in ancient times a man named Shen Nong sampled hundreds of herbs in order to find cures for illnesses prevalent at that time. Medical specialization developed early in China. As early as the Shang Dynasty, some Chinese doctors became nutritional specialists while others were physicians, surgeons, or veterinarians. The theoretical system of Chinese medicine took shape from the Warring States Period to the Three Kingdoms (475BC-265AD). During the Warring States Period, an important medical book *Nei Jing* came into being. *Nei Jing*, also known as *Huang Di Nei Jing*, in eighteen volumes, is the oldest medical book existing in China. It was probably written collectively by many doctors. The book reflects the medical theory and experience of the time. It laid the foundation of Chinese medicine. At the end of the Han Dynasty, the distinguished doctor Zhang Zhongjing wrote *Treatise on Febrile and Other Diseases*, this is the first important work on clinical treatment. In sixteen volumes, the book sums up medical experience in diagnosing and treating typhoid and other mainly internal diseases. During the Western Jin, Tang, and Song dynasties (265-1279) great achievements were made in Chinese medicine. Among the renowned doctors of the Tang Dynasty, Sun Simiao was probably the greatest. Enjoying a long life of one hundred and one years (581-682), he wrote two important medical books: *The Thousand Golden Formula* and *Supplement to the Thousand Golden Formula*. In these books he discusses the treatment of diseases, especially the diseases of women and children. The Ming Dynasty marked another peak in the development of Chinese medicine. A significant medical book *Compendium of Materia Medica* written by Li Shizhen was completed in this period. This book includes 1892 medicines, 11096 prescriptions, and 1160 illustrations. The compendium sums up Chinese medical knowledge before the 16th century and corrects the mistakes of many earlier medical books. It is a great contribution to the development of medicine. The basic characteristics of Chinese medicine can be summarized the following aspects.

Firstly, the concept of viewing the organism as a whole. In Chinese medicine, the doctor studies the human body. The human body is an organic whole with five internal organs (the heart, liver, spleen, lungs and kidneys) as the center, all organs in human body are physically related by channels and affect each other pathologically. The failure of an internal organ will reveal itself in an outer organ, and the failure of an outer organ will affect an internal organ. For example, the doctor treats pinkeye with an antipyretic remedy to liver. The doctor also studies the relationship between the spirit and body. Irritation and depression will affect the normal physical function of the human body. *Nei Jing* says "anger harms liver", "thinking harms spleen", "worry harms lungs", "fear harms kidney".

In Chinese medicine, the doctor also views the human and nature as a whole and studies the relation between man and nature. The human can't separate from nature, his food and air are from nature. Nature has four seasons, the human meets the changes of nature through his body function's regulation. If the human can't meet the changes of nature, he will become ill. For example, in spring, seasonal febrile diseases spread around. In summer, heatstroke diseases spread around. In autumn, malaria diseases spread around. While in winter, typhoid diseases spread around. So the function of the human body is at every moment affected by nature and the patient must be treated according to nature's changes.

Secondly, the basic principle of diagnosis is to analyze the symptoms of the patient before drawing conclusions and prescribing treatment. In practice, detailed questions are asked about the history of the illness. Attention is paid to the quality of the voice and the color of the face. The patient's pulse is examined. On the basis of all these examinations, a set of principles in medical treatment is made. To cite a few principles: "to cure a person, the root of the disease must be found out", "symptomatic treatment in acute condition and radical treatment in chronic condition" and "prevention is more important than treatment." For thousands of years these principles proved to be scientific and effective.

Symptoms refer to all clinical manifestations. In Chinese medicine, disease is an indication of a contradiction between "vital energy" and "evil energy" within the human body. "Vital energy" refers to the ability to resist diseases while "evil energy" refers to the factors that incur illness. When evil energy attacks the human body, vital energy will respond or resist the attack, thus give us indications. The foremost task is to analyze symptoms, because only when symptoms are correctly analyzed can a doctor prescribe suitable medicines or use some other method to cure the patient. There are eight principles in the general method of analyzing symptoms. The eight principles refer to eight kinds of syndromes. They are "Yin, Yang, external, internal, hot, cold, insufficient and excessive". In addition, symptoms can also be analyzed according to the state of vital energy, blood, body fluid, viscera, and other indications. All these methods are different in nature and are used in different situations, but they are associated with each other.

The Yang symptom is treated with inhibition; Yin, with excitation; external, with diaphoresis; internal, with a laxative remedy; hot, with an antipyretic remedy; cold, with a warming remedy; insufficient with a tonic remedy; excessive, with laxative remedy. However, symptoms are usually not simple, they interweave. A disease could be cold on the surface but hot internally. Sometimes it could be excessive on the surface, but actually insufficient, or the other way around. Consequently compound treatment is likely to be adopted.

In a word, Chinese medicine focuses on the essence of diseases. The surface sign and the root cause of the disease must be distinguished. The doctor should abide by principles but also be flexible. Medical measures are taken according to time, place and the patient. This is the diagnosis and treatment based on an overall analysis of the illness and the patient's condition.

Chinese medicine focuses on the analysis of symptoms to find the cause of the disease. Disease is under dynamic observation. The object of analysis is the patient and internal causes. This method reflects the principle that diseases are general in nature. While western medicine, on the other hand, focuses on the analysis of the specific disease itself, or pathogeny. The object is disease and external causes. The individuality of diseases is the key principle. This is the major difference between Chinese medicine and western medicine. As time and science advance, Chinese medicine and western medicine will combine and complement each other.

Notes

(1) Shen Nong sampled hundreds of herbs. 神农尝百草。
(2) Medical specialization developed early in China. 医学专业在中国发展得很早。
(3) *treatise on Febrile and Miscellaneous Diseases*《伤寒杂病论》
(4) *The Thousand Golden Formula*《千金方》
(5) *Compendium of Materia Medica*《本草纲目》
(6) the concept of viewing the organism as a whole 视人体为有机整体的观念
(7) seasonal febrile diseases 季节性的热病
(8) heatstroke diseases 中暑
(9) malaria diseases 疟疾
(10) typhoid diseases 伤寒
(11) to cite a few principles 引用几个原理
(12) all clinical manifestations 所有的临床表现
(13) vital energy 正气，生命力，活力
(14) evil energy 邪气
(15) Yin, Yang, external, internal, hot, cold, insufficient and excessive 阴、阳、表、里、热、寒、虚、实
(16) compound treatment 综合治疗

(17) The doctor should abide by principles but also be flexible. 医生在遵守原则的同时也应该表现出一定的灵活性。

New Words & Expressions

prevalent [ˈprevələnt] adj. 普遍的，流行的
surgeon [ˈsɜːdʒən] n. 外科医生
veterinarian [ˌvetərɪˈneərɪən] n. 兽医
come into being 形成
treatise [ˈtriːtɪz] n. 论文，论述
febrile [ˈfiːbraɪl] adj. 发烧的，热病的
clinical [ˈklɪnɪkl] adj. 临床的，病房用的
sum up 总结
typhoid [ˈtaɪfɔɪd] n. 伤寒症 adj. 伤寒的，斑疹伤寒症的
formula [ˈfɔːmjələ] n. 公式，规则，客套语，配方，处方
compendium [kəmˈpendiəm] n. 纲要，概略
prescription [prɪˈskrɪpʃn] n. 指示，规定，命令，处方，药方
illustration [ˌɪləsˈtreɪʃn] n. 说明，例证，例子，图表，插图，图解
spleen [spliːn] n. 脾
kidney [ˈkɪdni] n. 肾
pathologically [ˌpæθəˈlɒdʒɪkəli] adv. 病理地，病态地
pinkeye [ˈpɪŋkaɪ] n. 传染性急性结膜炎（火眼），红眼病
antipyretic [ˌæntipaɪˈretɪk] adj. 退热的 n. 退热剂
remedy [ˈremədi] n. 补救，治疗，赔偿
heatstroke [ˈhiːtstrəʊk] n. 中暑
malaria [məˈleərɪə] n. 疟疾，瘴气
symptom [ˈsɪmptəm] n. 症状，征兆
draw conclusions 得出结论
prescribe [prɪˈskraɪb] v. 指示，规定，处(方)，开(药)
on the basis of 在……基础上
find out 找到，发现，认识到
acute [əˈkjuːt] adj. 敏锐的，急性的，剧烈的
radical [ˈrædɪkl] adj. 根本的，基本的，激进的
chronic [ˈkrɒnɪk] adj. 慢性的，延续很长的
manifestation [ˌmænɪfesˈteɪʃn] n. 显示，表现，示威运动
contradiction [ˌkɒntrəˈdɪkʃn] n. 矛盾
foremost [ˈfɔːməʊst] adj. （位置或时间）最先的，最重要的 adv. 首要地，首先
syndrome [ˈsɪndrəʊm] n. 综合征
insufficient [ˌɪnsəˈfɪʃnt] adj. 不足的，不够的，虚的
excessive [ɪkˈsesɪv] adj. 过多的，过分的，实的

viscera [ˈvɪsərə] n. 内脏
inhibition [ˌɪnhɪˈbɪʃn] n. 禁止，阻止，禁制，压抑
excitation [ˌeksɪˈteɪʃn] n. 刺激，兴奋，激动，激励，鼓舞
diaphoresis [ˌdaɪəfəˈriːsɪs] n. 发汗
laxative [ˈlæksətɪv] n. 泻药，缓泻药　adj. 通便的
tonic [ˈtɒnɪk] adj. 激励的，滋补的　n. 滋补剂，滋补品
interweave [ˌɪntəˈwiːv] v.（使）交织，织进，（使）混杂
essence [ˈesns] n. 基本，本质，香精
dynamic [daiˈnæmik] adj. 动力的，动力学的，动态的
pathogeny [pəˈθɒdʒini] n. 生病，病原
individuality [ˌindiˌvidjuˈæliti] n. 个性，个人的特性，个人的嗜好

Exercises

1. Read and recite the following special terms

（1）traditional Chinese medicine 中医
（2）western medicine 西医
（3）channel and collateral 经络
（4）the five internal organs (heart, liver, spleen, lung and kidney) 五脏（心、肝、脾、肺、肾）
（5）the six hollow organs (gallbladder, stomach, small intestine, large intestine, bladder and the three visceral cavities) 六腑（胆、胃、小肠、大肠、膀胱、三焦）
（6）deficiency of vital energy 气虚
（7）five elements (water, fire, metal, wood and earth) 五行（水、火、金、木、土）
（8）six evils (wind, cold, heat, wetness, dryness and fire) 六淫（风、寒、暑、湿、燥、火）
（9）seven passions (joy, anger, grief, meditation, sorrow, terror and fright) 七情（喜、怒、忧、思、悲、恐、惊）
（10）to invigorate the circulation of blood 活血
（11）the Yellow Emperor's Classic of Internal Medicine《黄帝内经》
（12）acupuncture and moxibustion 针灸
（13）cupping 拔火罐
（14）acupuncture point 穴位
（15）a treatment for some diseases by scraping the patient's neck, chest or back with a coin or something of the like moistened with water or vegetable oil 刮痧
（16）to reinforce body fluid and nourish the blood 滋阴
（17）collapsing pulse 沉脉
（18）to regulate the flow of vital energy and to remove obstruction to it 理气
（19）to feel the pulse 诊脉
（20）stagnant pulse 涩脉

2. Translate the following sentences into English

（1）中国医药学是在实践中产生并在实践中不断发展的医学科学，是我国劳动人民同疾病做斗争的经验总结，是一个伟大的医学宝库。

（2）中医学的特点概括起来主要有两个方面，一是整体观念，二是辨证论治。

（3）整体观念包含两个内容，即人是一个统一的整体和人与自然是相统一的。

（4）辨证论治是中医认识疾病和治疗疾病的基本原则，是中医学对疾病的一种特殊的研究和处理方法。

（5）针灸疗法是通过针灸和艾灸刺激穴位以调整阴阳，疏通经络气血，从而达到预防和治疗疾病的两种不同疗法。

Unit 22 Keys

Unit 23
Wushu and Taijiquan

Wushu

Wushu, Chinese martial arts, known in the west as Kungfu, is a cultural heritage of the Chinese people which has been enriched down through the ages. With its graceful movements and salubrious effects on health, it has a strong appeal to a vast multitude of people.

The origin of Wushu may be traced back to prehistoric times when our ancestors used stones and wooden clubs in hunting, both for subsistence and self-defence. In tribal strifes they used their tools of production as weapons of war. During the Shang (1600BC-1046BC) and Zhou (1046BC-256BC) dynasties, with the development of productive forces, especially that of the techniques in bronze casting, the variety of weapons increased and their quality improved.

In the Jin and Southern and Northern Dynasties, Wushu came under the influence of Buddhism and Taoism. Ge Hong, a famous physician and Taoist philosopher, integrated Wushu with Qigong, an important branch of traditional Chinese medicine. His theories of "external and internal work" in Wushu are still universally accepted today.

The court examination system initiated in the Tang Dynasty required both military men and scholars to practice Wushu.

Because of its long history incorporating differences in culture, ideology, region and usage, Wushu has developed into a great variety of schools and styles. There are over one hundred schools of boxing in the Yellow River valley area and about eighty in the Yangtze River basin. Each school has its own characteristics. Changquan demands quickness and valour, and it is liked by young people. Taijiquan, characterized by its slow rhythm and gentle movements, is suitable for people of all ages, especially elderly people. Xingyiquan, vigorous in its balanced motions and poise steps, is popular with young and middle-aged people. Nanquan is widely spread in China's southern areas. Its practitioners utter shouts and cries now and then to make their movements more forceful. Shaolinquan, popular in the North, is known for its short routines of movements and swiftness and vigour. In certain styles such as Tanglangquan (the Mantis Boxing) and Zuiquan (the Drunkard Boxing), the practitioners imitate animals and birds as well as the drunk.

In spite of its rich variety, Wushu has four main types: barehanded boxing, the wielding of weapons, combat, and collective performances. The weapons used in Wushu fall into three categories: long weapons including spears and broadswords; short weapons such as short swords, daggers and hooks; and flexible weapons which include nine-section cudgels and three-section cudgels.

However, Wushu is by no means limited to the external movement, but also emphasizes the full display of the internal temperament, mental attitude and potential of the human being. The practice of Wushu not only strengthens the bones and muscles but also the internal organs and intelligence. To be more specific, Wushu stresses that the mind directs the circulation of air flow (Qi) within the body and that the inner circulation of air generates the external strength, so demonstrating the combination of external and internal forces. Cultivating air flows inside the body in order to improve the basic structures inside the body is an important purpose of Wushu exercises.

The implication of Chinese Wushu is broader than that of Kungfu. It embodies a profound philosophy and a sense of human life and social values. It is the summation of the code of conduct for the adjustment of the relationships between man and man and between man and nature. Wushu emphasizes traditions, experience and rational knowledge, all of which are clearly reflected in the martial ethics of Wushu. Martial ethics advocates respect for human life. In ancient China, human beings were regarded as the most valuable treasure of nature. Man is called one of the "four greats", together with the heaven, earth and truth, or law of natural activities. Martial ethics requires that a person exercises self-restraint, never abusing his abilities for personal gratification or oppressing those weaker than himself. He should seek to uphold justice, remain fearless in the face of brutality, and cultivate modesty and a spirit of cooperation.

Wushu is not only a way to enhance one's health and skills. Its long association with dance has lent an enriching artistic quality. At the same time, its emphasis on posture, composure, self-control, spirit and lively exercise imbues it with a beautifying effect on the physique, and a positive effect on the character. These qualities turn Wushu into Wuyi—martial artistry.

Wushu enjoys great popularity in China, and it is captivating the attention of more and more people in the world, because of its uniqueness and charisma originating from the traditional oriental culture.

Notes

(1) Kungfu 功夫

(2) a vast multitude of people 广大人民

PART III ENGLISH TOPICS FOR FOREIGN TOURISTS

(3) the court examination system 殿试制度

(4) barehanded boxing, the wielding of weapons, combat, and collective performances 拳术、器械、格斗和集体表演

(5) Shang and Zhou Dynasties 商朝和周朝

(6) Jin and Southern and Northern Dynasties 晋朝和南北朝

(7) Tanglangquan and Zuiquan 螳螂拳和醉拳

(8) nine-section cudgels and three-section cudgels 九节棍和三节棍

(9) martial ethics 武德

(10) Wuyi 武艺

New Words & Expressions

martial ['mɑːʃl] adj. 战争的，军事的，尚武的，威武的
salubrious [sə'luːbriəs] adj. 清爽的，健康的，健全的，气候有益健康的
appeal [ə'piːl] n. 呼吁　vi. 求助，上诉
multitude ['mʌltɪtjuːd] n. 多数，群众
prehistoric [ˌpriːhɪs'tɒrɪk] adj. 史前的
subsistence [səb'sɪstəns] n. 生存，生活，留存
strife [straɪf] n. 斗争，冲突，竞争
initiate [ɪ'nɪʃieɪt] vt. 开始，发动，传授　v. 开始，发起
ideology [ˌaɪdi'ɒlədʒi] n. 意识形态，思想意识，观念学
valour ['vælə] n. 英勇，勇猛
poise [pɔɪz] n. 平衡，均衡，姿势　vt. 使平衡，使悬着，保持……姿势　vi. 平衡
routine [ruː'tiːn] n. 例行公事，常规，日常事务，程序
mantis ['mæntɪs] n. 螳螂
wield [wiːld] vt. 使用，行使，挥舞
spear [spɪə] n. 矛，长矛，叶片　vt. 用矛刺
broadsword ['brɔːdsɔːd] n. 阔刀，腰刀
dagger ['dægə] n. 匕首，短剑　vt. 用剑刺
cudgel ['kʌdʒəl] n. 棍棒　vt. 用棍棒打
temperament ['temprəmənt] n. 气质，性情，易激动，急躁
implication [ˌɪmplɪ'keɪʃən] n. 含义，暗示，牵连，卷入
summation [sʌ'meɪʃən] n. 总和，和，合计
advocate ['ædvəkeɪt] vt. 提倡，主张，拥护　n. 提倡者，律师
gratification [ˌgrætɪfɪ'keɪʃən] n. 满意，满足
oppress [ə'pres] vt. 压迫
uphold [ʌp'həʊld] vt. 支持，赞成
brutality [bruː'tæləti] n. 残忍，野蛮的行为
imbue [ɪm'bjuː] v. 使充满，灌输，激发（强烈的感情）
physique [fɪ'ziːk] n. 体格，体形

captivate ['kæptɪveɪt] vt. 迷住，迷惑
charisma [kə'rɪzmə] n. 超凡魅力，感召力
originate [ə'rɪdʒɪneɪt] v. 起源，发源
oriental [ˌɔːri'entl] n. 东方人　adj. 东方的，东方人的

Taijiquan

Brief History of Taijiquan

Taijiquan, a branch of Chinese boxing arts, dates back to more than three hundred years and forms part of China's cultural legacy. In the seventeenth century, when the Qing Dynasty was about to replace the Ming Dynasty, wars were continually breaking out and Wushu (martial arts) became extremely popular among the people. At that time, based on various folk boxing arts, a new style of Chinese boxing emerged. This new style overcame strength with gentleness and won victory through cleverness. At the end of the eighteenth century Wang Zongyue, a famous martial arts master, consolidated it and called it Taijiquan. At first, Taijiquan was popular in the rural areas of Henan Province, then, in the middle of the nineteenth century, it spread to Beijing and finally to all parts of the country.

Taijiquan involves whole sets of exercises, including the bare-hand exercise, the two-man push-hand exercise and exercise with apparatus such as sword, cudgel, and spear. Over the past hundred years, along with changes in society, Taijiquan changed from a fighting to a keep-fit and medical exercise; jumping and explosive movements decreased. Finally it became a gentle, steady physical exercise.

In the process of evolving and developing, Taijiquan formed different schools. The four main schools, Yang, Wu, Sun and Chen, all have their own characteristics. The movements of Yang-style Taijiquan, originated by Yang Chengpu, are extended and steady; those of the Wu-style, originated by Wu Jianquan, are well organized and gentle; Sun-style movements, originated by Sun Lutang, are small and exquisite; Chen-style movements, originated by Chen Fake, are both firm and gentle, preserving more of the ancient exercises. The most popular of the four is Yang-style.

Though differing in style, the various schools have the same basic principles and features. Two important principles in performing Taijiquan are relaxation and stillness. Relaxation means to keep the body relaxed and natural, the movements mild, gentle and coherent, with no strong force. Stillness means concentration and serenity. As a whole-body exercise, combining physical and mental control, Taijiquan stresses the domination of meditation over the body, paying more attention to mental than to physical strength. Thus it is not surprising that some people liken Taijiquan to mental exercises. Since the founding of New China in 1949 the government has attached importance to this old sport. Now Taijiquan has become a favorite exercise in China. Every morning millions of people in cities and villages throughout the country attentively practise Taijiquan. Some people also practise Taijijian (Taiji swordplay).

To meet the needs of the general public the State Physical Culture and Sports Commission now General Administration of Sport of China compiled simplified Taijiquan (twenty-four movements) on the basis of Yang-style Taijiquan. Simplified Taijiquan omits all the difficult and repeated movements. Several routines combining characteristics of various styles and consisting of forty-eight, sixty-six, eighty-eight, etc. movements were also created, greatly enriching Taijiquan.

The Salubrious Effects of Taijiquan

A relaxed, gentle kind of physical activity, Taijiquan conforms to physiological laws and can help people keep fit. According to medical science, it is also good for health care and medical treatment, having positive effect in curing and preventing diseases. The physiological effects of Taijiquan on various body systems can be explained as follows:

(1) Improving central nervous system;

(2) Improving cardiovascular and respiratory system;

(3) Improving digestive system.

Simplified Taijiquan

Simplified Taijiquan is based on a popular form of Taijiquan. It is easy to master and practise. Simplified Taijiquan's twenty-four movements are divided into eight sections. Practitioners can do the whole set or select a single movement or section. The following points should be remembered:

(1) Keep an even tempo. For beginners the tempo should be a bit slow. At normal speed it takes four to six minutes to complete the whole set. Some people move more slowly, taking eight or nine minutes. However, do not move too slowly.

(2) Keep movements at same level. The height of the movements is decided by the commencing movement. Keep the same level throughout, except for the movement of pushing down. People who have a poor physique should take a little higher level. After a period of practice, when they get familiar with the movements and become stronger, they can take a medium or lower level.

(3) Keep to the proper amount of exercise. Duration, repetition and intensity depend on the individual's fitness. Healthy adults may practise about one hour every day. Old people should do Taijiquan in the morning. Beginners and people who have a poor physique should do only as much as their physical condition allows. They may practise one or two sets continually, practise one or several sections, or only a certain movement, such as Grasp the Bird's Tail or Wave Hands Like Clouds, for the ill the amount of exercise depends on their condition. For instance, arthritis sufferers may perform more movements, but with less intensity in each session; patients suffering from indigestion can practise more movements and increase the amount of exercise in each session to improve the functioning of the digestive system.

The names of the movements in simplified Taijiquan are:

Section One

(1) Commencing Movement

(2) Part the Wild Horse's Mane on Both Sides

(3) The White Crane Spreads Its Wings

Section Two

(4) Brush Knee and Twist Step on Both Sides

(5) Strumming the Lute

(6) Step Back and Whirl Arms on Both Sides

Section Three

(7) Grasp the Bird's Tail—Left

(8) Grasp the Bird's Tail—Right

Section Four

(9) Single Whip (Form 1)

(10) Wave Hands Like Clouds—Left

(11) Single Whip (Form 2)

Section Five

(12) High Pat on Horse

(13) Kick with Right Heel

(14) Strike Opponent's Ears with Both Fists

(15) Turn and Kick with Left Heel

Section Six

(16) Push Down and Stand on One Leg—Left

(17) Push Down and Stand on One Leg—Right

Section Seven

(18) Work Shuttles on Both Sides

(19) Needle at Sea Bottom

(20) Flash the Arm

Section Eight

(21) Turn, Deflect Downward, Parry and Punch

(22) Apparent Close up

(23) Cross Hands

(24) Closing Movement

Notes

(1) This new style overcame strength with gentleness and won victory through cleverness. 这种新式武术以柔克刚，通过机智取胜。

(2) Jumping and explosive movements decreased. 跳跃和爆发性的动作减少了。

(3) Taijiquan stresses the domination of meditation over the body. 太极拳强调意念对整个身体的控制。

PART III ENGLISH TOPICS FOR FOREIGN TOURISTS

（4）the State Physical Culture and Sports Commission 国家体育运动委员会

（5）Taijiquan conforms to physiological laws and can help people keep fit. 太极拳符合生理规律，能帮助人们保健。

（6）cardiovascular and respiratory system 心血管和呼吸系统

（7）Dantian (about one inch below the navel) 丹田（位于肚脐下面大约一英寸，即2.54厘米的地方）

（8）Keep an even tempo. 保持一个均匀的速度。

（9）the commencing movement 开始动作

（10）depend on the individual's fitness 取决于每个人的健康状况

（11）arthritis sufferers 关节炎患者

New Words & Expressions

break out 爆发
consolidate [kən'sɒlɪdeɪt] v. 巩固
apparatus [ˌæpə'reɪtəs] n. 器械，设备，仪器
keep-fit ['kiːpˌfɪt] adj. 保健的
stillness ['stɪlnəs] n. 静止，沉静
coherent [kəʊ'hɪərənt] adj. 连贯的，一致的，明了的，清晰的，凝聚性的
serenity [sə'renəti] n. 平静，宁静，晴朗，风和日丽
liken ['laɪkən] vt. 比拟，把……比作
swordplay ['sɔːdpleɪ] n. 击剑，剑术，针锋相对的争论
compile [kəm'paɪl] vt. 编译，编制，汇编
conform [kən'fɔːm] v. 使一致，使遵守，使顺从，符合
physiological [ˌfɪziə'lɒdʒɪkəl] adj. 生理学的，生理学上的
cardiovascular [ˌkɑːdiəʊ'væskjələ] adj. 心血管的
respiratory [rə'spɪrətri] adj. 呼吸的
tempo ['tempəʊ] n.（音乐）速度，拍子，发展速度
commence [kə'mens] vi. 使开始，使得学位 vt. 开始，着手
except for 除……外，若无
repetition [ˌrepə'tɪʃn] n. 重复，循环
intensity [ɪn'tensəti] n. 强烈，剧烈，强度，亮度
arthritis [ɑː'θraɪtɪs] n. 关节炎
mane [meɪn] n. 鬃毛
strum [strʌm] n. 乱弹的声音 v. 乱弹，乱奏
lute [luːt] n. 琉特琴，诗琴
whirl [wɜːl] v.（使）旋转，急动，急走 n. 旋转，一连串快速的活动
opponent [ə'pəʊnənt] adj. 对立的，对抗的 n. 对手，反对者
deflect [dɪ'flekt] v.（使）偏斜，（使）偏转
downward ['daʊnwəd] adj. 向下的

parry ['pæri] n. 躲避

punch [pʌntʃ] n. 冲压机，冲床，打孔机　vt. 冲孔，打孔

apparent [ə'pærənt] adj. 显然的，表面上的

Exercises

1. Read and recite the following special terms

（1）traditional Chinese martial arts（Wushu）武术

（2）traditional Chinese boxing（Quanshu）拳术

（3）traditional Chinese Taiji boxing（Taijiquan）太极拳

（4）five-animal exercises 五禽戏

（5）beginning form 起势

（6）closing form 收势

（7）flowing movement 绵绵不断的动作

（8）soft weapon 软兵器

（9）three-section cudgel 三节棍

（10）nine-section cudgel 九节鞭

（11）Qigong 气功

（12）the cerebral cortex 大脑皮层

（13）channels and collaterals 经络

（14）foot position 腿法

（15）driving leg 蹬腿

（16）kicking with heel leading 蹬脚

（17）pushing the palm 推掌

（18）bare-handed practice 徒手练习

（19）empty hands against cudgel 空手对棍

（20）required routine 规定套路

2. Translate the following sentences into English

（1）武术起源于我们远古祖先的生产劳动。那时为了生存和自卫，他们在狩猎中使用石器和棍棒，在部落冲突中使用生产工具作为战争的武器，逐步形成了徒手或持械的格斗技能。

（2）武术并不局限于外在的动作，也注重个人内在气质、精神状态和潜能的充分展现。

（3）武术可以分为四个主要的类型，即拳术、器械、格斗和集体表演。

（4）气功又叫吐纳，实践证明它在治疗慢性疾病和疑难杂症方面效果尤为突出。

（5）太极拳是中国拳术的一部分，其历史可追溯到300多年以前。在其演化和发展过程中，太极拳形成了不同的流派，其中的四个主要流派是杨氏、吴氏、孙氏和陈氏太极拳，它们都各有特点。

Unit 23　Keys

Unit 24
Religions of China

扫码听短文

China is a country with many religious beliefs and the major religions are Buddhism, Taoism, Islam, Catholicism and Protestantism. There are over a hundred million religious followers of Taoism, Buddhism, Islam, Catholicism and Protestantism in China. Among the 56 ethnic groups, some 20 minority groups are composed almost entirely of followers of the same religion. In China, citizens enjoy freedom of religious belief, and all normal religious activities are protected by the Constitution. The Buddhist, Islamic, Catholic, Protestant and Taoist organizations have been established at national and local levels, independently dealing with their own religious affairs.

Buddhism

There are now about 13000 Buddhist temples and some 200000 monks and nuns. Buddhism also still has strong appeal to numerous elderly people, who turn to the Buddha for help. Lamaism, a blend of Buddhism and indigenous religion, is followed by the overwhelming majority of Tibetans. Buddhism is said to be founded in India in the 6th century BC by Siddhartha Gautama, the son of a nobleman and member of the Kshatriya caste near the present borders of India and Nepal. He is also known by the titles Sakyamuni (the sage of the Sakya family) and Tathagata (the follower of truth). The main doctrine of Buddhism is the Four Noble Truths and the Noble Eightfold Path. The Four Noble Truths preached by Gautama Buddha are:

(1) First, that sorrow is the universal experience of mankind, and everyone is subjected to the trauma of birth, decrepitude, sickness and death.

(2) Second, that the cause of sorrow is desire, especially the desire of the body and the desire for personal fulfilment, and the cycle of birth is perpetuated by the desire for existence.

(3) Third, that the removal of sorrow can only come from the removal of desire, that is to say, that happiness can only be achieved if these desires are overcome.

(4) Fourth, that desire can be systematically abandoned if one follows the Noble Eightfold Path.

The Noble Eightfold Path includes the following eight tenets: the "Right Knowledge", the "Right Aspiration", the "Right Speech", the "Right Behaviour", the "Right Livelihood", the "Right Effort", the "Right Mindfulness" and the "Right Absorption". By following the Noble Eightfold the Buddhist aims to attain "nirvana", a condition beyond the limits of the mind, thoughts, feelings, desire, the will, and a state of bliss, ecstasy.

Buddhism was introduced into China in the first century, and spreaded widely after the 4th century, becoming the most influential religion in China. There are three types of Buddhism in China, Mahayana (Big Raft) Buddhism and Hinayana (Little Raft) Buddhism and Lamaism.

Mahayana Buddhism was introduced into China in the first century. The earliest Buddhist temple, the Baima Temple (White Horse Temple), was built in Luoyang during the reign of Emperor Ming Di of the Eastern Han Dynasty in 68 AD with the help of two Indian monks. Mahayana Buddhism reached its peaks of popularity during the Sui and Tang dynasties. Mahayana Buddhism emphasizes the existence of many Buddhas. It focuses attention on Buddhas in heaven and on people who will become Buddhas in the future. It believes that these present and future Buddhas can save people through compassion and grace. Today there are eight main sects of Mahayana Buddhism. These are the Sanlun Sect, the Faxiang Sect, the Tiantai Sect, the Huayan Sect, the Jingtu Sect, the Chan (Zen) Sect, the Ritsugaku Sect, and the Esoteric Sect.

Hinayana (also called Pali) Buddhism was introduced from Myanmar in the 7th century, into regions inhabited by the Dai, Bulang, Achang ethnic minorities in Yunnan Province. Today its followers are mainly people from these ethnic minorities. In China it is called Pali Buddhism because Pali is the language of ancient India that is spoken in the temples. Hinayana Buddhism emphasizes the importance of Buddha as a historical figure, the virtues of monastic life, and the authority of the Tripitaka.

Lamaism is a form of Buddhism intermingled with indigenous Tibetan religion. Lamaism mainly gained its Buddhist knowledge from Han Mahayana Buddhist sources. Of the various sects that eventually developed within Lamaist Buddhism, the main ones are Nyingma, Sakya, Kagyu and Gelug. By far the most powerful of the Lamaist sects is the Gelug, or the "Yellow Sect", called so because the monks wear yellow hats. Ganden, Sera, Drepung, Tashilhunpo, Ta'er and Labrang are the principal monasteries of this sect.

Taoism

There are now about 1500 Taoist temples in China with some 250000 Taoist priests and nuns.

Taoism, a native Chinese religion, originated at the end of the Eastern Han Dynasty(25-220 AD). Taoists regard Lao Zi as their founder. His world-famous 5000 characters *Dao De Jing* is their canon. In this book, Lao Zi says that the basic principle is: first, be benevolent; second, be pure; and third, do not act in advance of other people. Being benevolent means assuming an amiable attitude toward everything in the universe and maintaining universal harmony. Being pure means getting rid of extravagant hopes and being plain in mind and body. Not daring to act in advance of other people means being modest, and holding the self in check, instead of assuming attitude of strength and dominance.

The word "Dao" (Tao), translates as "the way". In its broadest sense, the Tao is the way the universe functions, the path taken by all natural events. The Tao is nature's way, expressed in effortless action. Taoists often use the image of water to illustrate such effortless action. Water always settles to the lowest level and yet can wear away even the hardest of substances.

According to Taoism, the cosmos is a magnitude of harmony and order. It is active, not static. Its state is one of change and variation, perpetually becoming and fading away, contracting and expanding. The Tao guides its function as an ordering principle. Within the Tao, the two elementary powers, Yin and Yang, function by reciprocal action. Yin and Yang are the two polar opposites into which all things can be classified. Thus dark and light, death and life, female and male, evil and good, weak and strong are all manifestations of Yin and Yang.

In China, various sects of Taoism appeared in different periods. During the reign of Emperor Shun Di of the Han Dynasty, Zhang Ling established the Heavenly Teacher Sect, also known as the Five Picules of Rice Sect. Toward the end of the Eastern Han Dynasty, Zhang Jiao, a peasant rebel leader, set up another Taoist sect named Tai Ping Tao. By the Western and Eastern Jin Dynasties, the Five Picules of Rice Sect had become a major religion. During the Southern and Northern Dynasties, the ruling class tried to reform Taoism so that it would help them in controlling the peasants. In the North, the Northern Heavenly Teacher Sect was established and in the South, the Southern Heavenly Teacher Sect. During the Yuan Dynasty, the northern and southern sects merged into two major sects of Taoism, known as the True Unity Sect and the Complete Unity Sect.

The True Unity Sect believed in "driving out devils by calling in the gods" and "averting disasters by prayer". Its priests could marry and have meat and wine except during the special fasting periods; the Complete Unity Sect emphasizes self-cultivation and immortality, and its priests had to renounce home life, practice vegetarianism, and remain unmarried.

After 1949, however, the Complete Unity Sect and the True Unity Sect, and other different Taoist sects gradually merged into one, especially after the Chinese Taoist Association was founded in 1957.

All religions have equal status. As a result, harmony reigns among religions in China. In fact, in the course of the country's long history, the various religions have become part of Chinese tradition, thought and culture. Since 1949, the advocacy of patriotism, national equality and mutual respect has further enhanced this religious harmony.

Notes

About Buddhism

(1) Siddhatha Gautama 乔达摩·悉达多

(2) the Kshatriya caste 刹帝利种姓

(3) Tathagata 如来

(4) bo tree 菩提树

(5) the Four Noble Truths: buddhism suffering, the cause of suffering, the extinction of suffering, the way leading to the extinction of suffering 四谛：苦谛、集谛、灭谛、道谛

(6) Noble Eightfold Path 八正道

(7) Right Knowledge 正见

(8) Right Aspiration 正思维

(9) Right Speech 正语

(10) Right Behaviour 正业

(11) Right Livelihood 正命

(12) Right Effort 正精进

(13) Right Mindfulness 正念

(14) Right Absorption 正定

(15) Do not kill; do not steal; do not lie; do not be unchaste; do not drink intoxicants. 不杀生、不偷盗、不妄语、不邪淫、不饮酒。

(16) Mahayana Buddhism 大乘佛教（主要是汉传佛教，佛教三大派别之一）

(17) Hinayana Buddhism 小乘佛教（主要分布在中国西南各省，佛教三大派别之一）

(18) Sanlun Sect 三论宗

(19) Faxiang Sect 法相宗

(20) Tiantai Sect 天台宗

(21) Huayan Sect 华严宗

(22) Jingtu Sect 净土宗

(23) Chan (Zen) Sect 禅宗

(24) Ritsugaku Sect 律宗

(25) Esoteric Sect 密宗

(26) Pali Buddhism 巴利佛教

(27) Dai 傣族

(28) Bulang 布朗族

(29) Achang 阿昌族

(30) Nyingma 宁玛派

(31) Sakya 萨迦派

(32) Kagyu 噶举派

(33) Bon 苯教

(34) Gelug 格鲁派

(35) Padmasambhava (Indian master of Esoteric Buddhism) 莲花生

(36) Tsongkapa 宗喀巴

(37) Ganden, Sera, Drepung, Tashilhunpo, Ta'er, and Labrang 甘丹寺、色拉寺、哲蚌寺（这三座寺院位于拉萨附近，合称拉萨三大寺），扎什伦布寺（位于西藏的日喀则），塔尔寺（位于青海省西宁市附近），拉卜楞寺（位于甘肃省甘南藏族自治州夏河县）

About Taoism

(1) Lao Zi (Lao Tzu) 老子（春秋末年思想家，道宗创始人）

(2) *Dao De Jing*《道德经》（即《老子》，道家主要经典）

(3) First, be benevolent; second, be pure; and third, do not act in advance of other people. 一曰慈，二曰俭，三曰不敢为天下先。

(4) Emperor Shun Di of the Han Dynasty 汉顺帝（126—144 年）

(5) canon 经

(6) Yin and Yang 阴与阳

(7) Zhang Ling 张陵（天师道创始人）

(8) Heavenly Teacher Sect (Five Piculs of Rice Sect) 天师道（也称五斗米道）

(9) Zhang Jiao 张角（太平道创始人）

(10) Tai Ping Tao 太平道

(11) True Unity Sect 正一教

(12) Complete Unity Sect 全真教

(13) achieve the way 得道

(14) The Eight Immortals Crossing the Sea 八仙过海

(15) Supreme Patriarch 太上老君

(16) God of Wealth 财神

(17) God of the Door 门神

(18) in charge of every household's fortune and misfortune 掌管居家祸福

(19) *Collection of Taoist Classics*《道藏》

(20) *Canon of Quietism*《清静经》

(21) *Yellow Yard Classics*《黄庭经》

(22) Wu Wei 无为

New Words & Expressions

catholicism [kəˈθɒləsɪzəm] n. 天主教

protestantism [ˈprɒtɪstəntɪzəm] n. 新教，新教徒，新教教义

Hinayana [ˌhiːnəˈjɑːnə] n. 小乘佛教

indigenous [ɪnˈdɪdʒənəs] adj. 本土的，土著的，国产的

Lamaism [ˈlɑːmeɪzəm] n. 喇嘛教，藏传佛教
Siddhartha [siˈdɑːrtʌ] n. 悉达多（佛教创始人释迦牟尼的本名），释迦牟尼佛
Gautama [ˈɡaʊtəmə] n. 乔达摩（释迦牟尼的俗姓）
Kshatriya [ˈkʃætrijə] n. 刹帝利（印度四种教之一）
caste [kɑːst] n. 种姓社会阶层，社会等级制度
Sakyamuni [ˈsɑːkjəmuni] n. 释迦牟尼
sage [seɪdʒ] n. 圣人，贤人，哲人 adj. 明智的，贤明的，审慎的
Sakya [ˈsɑːkjə] n.（印度北部古代的）萨克耶人，释迦
trauma [ˈtrɔːmə] n. 创伤，精神创伤
decrepitude [dɪˈkrepɪtjuːd] n. 衰老，老朽，老耄
perpetuate [pəˈpetjueɪt] vt. 使永存，使不朽
tenet [ˈtenɪt] n. 原则，教义，信条
aspiration [ˌæspəˈreɪʃn] n. 热望，渴望
absorption [əbˈsɔːpʃn] n. 吸收，全神贯注，专心致志
nirvana [nɪəˈvɑːnə] n. 涅槃
bliss [blɪs] n. 福佑，天赐的福
ecstasy [ˈekstəsi] n. 入迷
Mahayana [ˌmɑːhəˈjɑːnə] n. 大乘佛教
sect [sekt] n. 宗派，门派
zen [zen] n. 禅，禅宗
esoteric [ˌesəˈterɪk] adj. 秘传的，限于圈内人的，难懂的
Myanmar [ˈmaɪænˌmɑː] n. 缅甸
Pali [ˈpɑːli] n. 巴利语
monastic [məˈnæstɪk] n. 僧侣，修道士 adj. 修道院的，僧尼的，庙宇的
Tripitaka [ˌtripiˈtɑːkə] n. 三藏经
intermingle [ˌɪntəˈmɪŋɡl] vt. 使混合 vi. 混合，掺杂
canon [ˈkænən] n. 标准，教规
benevolent [bəˈnevələnt] adj. 仁慈的，慈善的，亲切的
amiable [ˈeɪmiəbl] adj. 和蔼可亲的，亲切的
extravagant [ɪkˈstrævəɡənt] adj. 奢侈的，浪费的，过度的，放纵的
dominance [ˈdɒmɪnəns] n. 支配地位，统治
cosmos [ˈkɒzmɒs] n. 宇宙
magnitude [ˈmæɡnɪtjuːd] n. 巨大，重大，重要性，地震震级，重要，星的亮度
static [ˈstætɪk] adj. 静态的，静力的，静止的
perpetually [pəˈpetʃuəli] adv. 永恒地，持久地
fade away 逐渐消失
reciprocal [rɪˈsɪprəkl] adj. 互惠的，相互的 n. 倒数，互相关联的事物
manifestation [ˌmænɪfesˈteɪʃn] n. 显示，表现，示威运动
picul [ˈpɪkʌl] n. 担（重量单位）

merge into 并入

avert [əˈvɜːt] vt. 避免，防止，转移

self-cultivation [ˈselfˌkʌltɪˈveɪʃn] n. 修养，修身，自我修养，道德修养

immortality [ɪmɔːˈtæləti] n. 不朽，不朽的声名，不灭，长生不老

renounce [rɪˈnaʊns] vt. 宣布放弃，与断绝关系，垫牌

vegetarianism [vedʒɪˈteərɪənɪzəm] n. 素食主义

predominate [prɪˈdɒmɪneɪt] vt. 支配，主宰，在……中占优势　vi. 占主导（或支配）地位

Confucianism [kənˈfjuːʃənɪzəm] n. 儒家思想

patriotism [ˈpætrɪətɪzəm] n. 爱国主义

Exercises

1. Read and recite the following special terms

(1) religious belief 宗教信仰

(2) religious rites 宗教仪式

(3) the holy land 圣地

(4) the underworld 阴世

(5) to pay homage 朝拜

(6) the Goddess of Mercy (the Guanyin Bodhisattva) 观音

(7) Maitreya 弥勒

(8) the temple guardian Wei Tuo 韦驮

(9) arhat (Buddhist Saint) 罗汉

(10) the Four Devarajas (Heavenly Guardians) 四大天王

(11) Sakyamuni 释迦牟尼

(12) the Emperor of Heaven (the Supreme Deity of Taoism) 玉皇大帝

(13) celestial fairy 天仙

(14) on a pilgrimage to Mecca 去麦加朝觐

(15) Festival of Fast-Breaking 开斋节

(16) Fast of Ramadan 斋月

(17) the Saviour 救世主

(18) the Holy Bible 圣经

(19) missionary 传教士

(20) Taoist monastic name 道号

2. Translate the following sentences into English

(1) 中国是一个多宗教的国家，其主要的宗教有道教、佛教、伊斯兰教和基督教。

(2) 中国佛教分为大乘佛教、藏传佛教和小乘佛教。大乘佛教于公元1世纪传入汉族居住地，藏传佛教于公元7世纪传入西藏，小乘佛教于公元7世纪从缅甸传入西南少数民族居住地。

（3）基督教于唐代传入中国。基督教以耶稣基督为最高神和救世主，奉《旧约全书》《新约全书》为圣经。它包括天主教、新教和东正教三个主要分支。

（4）道教产生于东汉末年，它是根植于中国古代社会、土生土长的宗教，又是一种多神教，具有鲜明的中国特色。

（5）公元651年，伊斯兰教正式进入中国。在中国，主要的伊斯兰教节日是圣纪节、开斋节和古尔邦节。

Unit 24　Keys

Unit 25
Local Products

Chinese Tea

Of hundreds of varieties of Chinese tea, there are six major types. They are green tea, black tea, Oolong tea, white tea, scented tea, and tightly pressed tea.

Green tea has the longest history and still ranks first in output and variety today. People like its freshness and natural fragrance. Famous green tea includes Longjing (Dragon Well) Tea from the West Lake in Hangzhou, Maofeng Tea from Huangshan Mountain, Yinzhen (Silver Needle) Tea from Junshan Mountain and Yunwu (Cloud and Mist) Tea from Lushan Mountain.

Black tea is also popular both at home and abroad. Different from green tea, black tea is thoroughly fermented. In the fermentation, the tea turns from green to black.

Oolong tea possesses the freshness of green tea and the fragrance of black tea. In recent years, it has become popular with more and more people for its properties in helping body building and dieting. Oolong tea is found in Fujian, Guangdong and Taiwan. Because the tea grows on cliffs, it is difficult to pick. For this reason, Oolong tea is considered the most precious.

White tea is as white as silver and its water is clear. It is mainly produced in Fujian's Zhenhe and Fuding. Famous varieties include "silver needle" and White Peony.

Scented tea, which smells of flowers, is a variety unique to China. Scented tea is made by mixing green tea with flower petals through an elaborate process. Sweet osmanthus, jasmine, rose, orchid and plum flowers can all be used.

Another special tea is called tightly-pressed tea lumps. The black tea or green tea is pressed into brick, cake, or ball shapes. The tea lump is convenient to store and transport and is popular with minority people in border regions, especially nomadic herdsmen. This kind of tea is mainly produced in Hunan, Hubei, Sichuan, Yunnan and Guangxi Zhuang Autonomous Region.

In recent years, newly appeared bag tea, instant tea, and medicated tea, and health tea have also become popular.

The Chinese people were the first to find tea as well as the first to find its medical and health-preserving functions. According to modern scientific analysis, tea contains many mineral elements such as iron, manganese, aluminium, potassium, sodium calcium, phosphorus and magnesium. It also contains such organic compounds as phenol, alkaloid, sugar, protein, amino acid, aromatic, pigment, vitamins and enzymes, which are good for people's health.

Water is very important for making tea because too many foreign substances in the water will spoil the tea. Spring water is ideal. Other good-quality water includes unpolluted snow water, water from flowing wells or from rivers far from habitation.

Tea-houses in China are traditional leisure places for men. Customers to the tea-house pay a small amount for a place to sit, a cup of tea, and as many refills as they like. Many tea-houses provide entertainment as well, from musicians, singers and storytellers. Tea-houses are also places for people to talk business, mediate disputes, exchange gossips, or simply sit and relax.

Tea also makes a good present when you visit friends. In return, hosts also entertain guests with tea. The standard Chinese invitation to tea is normally an invitation to drink hot water with tea leaves in it. In Guangdong, however, an invitation to tea may suggest having some snacks as well as tea water.

When the Chinese make tea, they pour in water that is not at boiling point, so that leaves tend to float in the tea. Usually tea is pot-brewed but the first pot is not prized. Tea is considered the best at the second infusion. Then infusion after infusion is made and connoisseurs observe how the taste and fragrance change until it is very weak.

Presently, more than 50 countries produce tea, which is a sure sign of its popularity.

Notes

(1) green tea 绿茶

(2) black tea 红茶

(3) oolong tea 乌龙茶

(4) white tea 白茶

(5) scented tea 花茶

(6) pressed tea 砖茶

(7) Longjing Tea 龙井茶

(8) Maofeng Tea 毛峰

(9) Silver Needle Tea 银针茶

(10) Yunwu (Cloud and Mist) Tea 云雾茶

(11) White Peony 白牡丹

(12) sweet osmanthus 桂花

(13) bag tea 袋茶

PART III ENGLISH TOPICS FOR FOREIGN TOURISTS

(14) instant tea 速溶茶

(15) medicated tea 药茶

(16) health tea 保健茶

(17) amino acid 氨基酸

(18) aromatic pigment 芳香料（色素）

New Words & Expressions

variety [vəˈraɪəti] n. 多样，种类

oolong [ˈuːlɒŋ] n. 乌龙，乌龙茶（中国名茶之一）

freshness [ˈfreʃnəs] n. 新，新鲜，精神饱满

fragrance [ˈfreɪɡrəns] n. 香味，芬芳，香水

ferment [ˈfɜːmənt] vt. 使发酵，酝酿，使动乱   n. 发酵，酵素，动乱

properties [ˈprɒpətɪz] n.（property 的复数形式）性能，道具，财产属性，特性，性质

diet [ˈdaɪət] n. 饮食，食物，规定饮食，日常饮食   vi. 节食

peony [ˈpiːəni] n. 牡丹，芍药

petal [ˈpetl] n. 花瓣

elaborate [ɪˈlæbərət] adj. 精心制作的   v. 详细描述，精心制作，详细阐述

osmanthus [ɒzˈmænθəs] n. 木犀属植物，桂花

jasmine [ˈdʒæsmɪn] n. 茉莉花，淡黄色

orchid [ˈɔːkɪd] n. 兰花，兰科植物，淡紫色   adj. 淡紫色的

plum [plʌm] n. 梅子，李子，紫红色

plum flower 梅花

lump [lʌmp] n. 块，肿块   vt. 混在一起，使成块状

nomadic [nəʊˈmædɪk] adj. 游牧的，游牧民族的，流浪的，漂泊的

herdsmen [ˈhɜːdzmən] n. 牧人

medicate [ˈmedɪkeɪt] vt. 用药治疗

manganese [ˈmæŋɡəniːz] n. 锰

aluminium [ˌæljəˈmɪniəm] n. 铝

potassium [pəˈtæsiəm] n. 钾

sodium [ˈsəʊdiəm] n. 钠

calcium [ˈkælsiəm] n. 钙

phosphorus [ˈfɒsfərəs] n. 磷

magnesium [mæɡˈniːziəm] n. 镁

phenol [ˈfiːnɒl] n. 石碳酸，苯酚

alkaloid [ˈælkəlɒɪd] n. 生物碱

protein [ˈprəʊtiːn] n. 蛋白质

amino [əˈmiːnəʊ] n. 氨基

acid [ˈæsɪd] n. 酸   adj. 酸的，酸性的，尖酸的

aromatic [ˌærəʊˈmætɪk] n. 芳香植物，芳香剂　adj. 芳香的，芬芳的，芳香族的
pigment [ˈpɪɡmənt] n. 色素，颜料，色料　vt. 给……着色　vi. 呈现颜色
vitamin [ˈvɪtəmɪn] n. 维生素
enzyme [ˈenzaɪm] n. 酶
habitation [ˌhæbɪˈteɪʃən] n. 居住，住所，聚居地
refuge [ˈrefjuːdʒ] n. 避难，避难所，庇护　vt. 给予……庇护，接纳……避难　vi. 避难
refill [riːˈfɪl] n. 替换物，再注满　vt. 再装满，再充满　vi. 被再注满
mediate [ˈmiːdieɪt] adj. 间接的，居间的　vi. 调解，斡旋，居中　vt. 调停，传达
gossip [ˈɡɒsɪp] n. 小道传闻，随笔，爱说长道短的人，闲话，流言　vi. 闲聊，传播流言蜚语
brew [bruː] n. 啤酒，质地　vi. 酿酒，被冲泡，即将发生　vt. 酿造，酝酿
infusion [ɪnˈfjuːʒən] n. 灌输，浸泡，注入物，激励
connoisseur [ˌkɒnəˈsɜː] n. 鉴赏家，内行，行家

The Chinese Porcelain

The fine Chinese porcelain known as "china" in the West was brought to Europe in the 13th century. The Chinese people began to produce porcelain in the Han Dynasty some two thousand years ago. But the zenith of Chinese ceramics came during the Song Dynasty (960-1279) when China had an unprecedented number of kilns and potters.

The most famous ones were those at Jingdezhen in Jiangxi Province and Yixing in Jiangsu Province, which have been known as the capitals of porcelain and pottery respectively. Jingdezhen's original name was Changnanzhen. The ancient pottery center was transformed when an early Song emperor established a kiln there to manufacture porcelain for daily use in the imperial household. In honour of this event, which took place during the Jingde reign (1004-1007), the name of the town was changed into Jingdezhen (the town of Jingde).

The imperial kilns have turned out over 3000 varieties of porcelain. Song potters produced beautiful monochrome porcelain and also discovered the secret of making "crackled" pottery and porcelain, which appeared so delicate that it seems it would break at a mere touch. Connoisseurs both at home and abroad consider monochrome Song porcelain among the finest of porcelain making.

The technique of making blue-and-white porcelain in the Yuan Dynasty invigorated and transformed Chinese porcelain making-previously potters had never been able to apply colours successfully to a piece of unfired porcelain. The dignified blue-and-white porcelain is painted with cobalt-blue designs and covered with a transparent glaze. A variation is to pierce the body with a rice grain pattern and fill in with glaze, producing a translucent effect. Blue-and-white porcelain was exported to Europe, India, and Africa. The feather-light eggshell porcelain is so translucent that the painted designs can also be seen from the reverse side as though veiled in mask.

The "Five Colours" in which the five colours were outlined in blue, were developments of the Ming Dynasty. In the Qing Dynasty, the "Famille Rose", characterized by its contrasting colour intensity, was created.

Many of the traditional styles represent the cream of the art of Chinese porcelain makers through the ages. The glazes fired at Jingdezhen were so numerous that to distinguish one from another the potters gave them elaborate names such as sacrificial red, kiln red and peacock green.

Today more than 28 large and medium-sized porcelain factories, as well as 50 small workshops, are based in Jingdezhen. At present, there are about 300000 people at Jingdezhen nearly one-fifth of them work either in porcelain industry or related businesses. The varieties of traditional ware, tableware have increased from 375 in 1949 to over 1200 now. Nearly three hundred million pieces of porcelain are exported every year to more than 100 countries.

To ensure its continuing growth, the ceramics industry developed an extensive training program. A ceramics college with a wide range of specialization was set up in Jingdezhen. Many factories in major ceramic centers have their own research institutes. And the Central Academy of Fine Arts in Beijing now offers courses on ceramic art. The government encourages veteran artisans in famous porcelain centers to take on apprentices and pass on their special skills.

Notes

(1) kilns and potters 窑和陶工

(2) Jingdezhen 景德镇

(3) Yixin 宜兴

(4) Changnanzhen 昌南镇

(5) monochrome porcelain 单色瓷

(6) "crackled" porcelain 细裂纹瓷

(7) the reverse side 反面

(8) Five Colour porcelain 五彩瓷

(9) Famille Rose porcelain 粉彩瓷

(10) characterized by its contrasting colour intensity 以其强烈的色彩对比度为特点

(11) sacrificial red 祭红

(12) kiln red 窑红

(13) peacock green 孔雀绿

(14) Central Academy of Fine Arts 中央美术学院

(15) to take on apprentices and pass on their special skills 收徒传授他们的专业技术

New Words & Expressions

porcelain [ˈpɔːsəlɪn] n. 瓷，瓷器　adj. 瓷制的，精美的
zenith [ˈzenɪθ] n. 顶峰，顶点，最高点
ceramics [sɪˈræmɪks] n. 制陶术，陶艺，制陶业（ceramic 的复数），陶瓷
unprecedented [ʌnˈpresɪdentɪd] adj. 空前的，无前例的
kiln [kɪln] vt. 烧窑，在干燥炉干燥　n.（砖、石灰等的）窑，炉，干燥炉
potter [ˈpɒtə] n. 陶艺家，制陶工人　vt. 闲混，虚度　vi. 闲逛，慢条斯理地做事
in honour of 为纪念，为庆祝
monochrome [ˈmɒnəkrəʊm] n. 单色，单色画　adj. 单色的，黑白的
crackled [ˈkrækld] adj. 有裂痕的，有脆皮的，表皮松脆的
delicate [ˈdelɪkət] adj. 微妙的，精美的，雅致的，柔和的
invigorate [ɪnˈvɪɡəreɪt] vt. 鼓舞，使精力充沛
transform [trænsˈfɔːm] vt. 改变，使变形，转换
dignify [ˈdɪɡnɪfaɪ] vt. 使高贵，增威严，授以荣誉
cobalt [kəʊˈbɔːlt] n. [化]钴，钴类颜料，由钴制的深蓝色
cobalt-blue adj. 钴蓝色的
glaze [ɡleɪz] n. 釉，光滑面　vt. 给……装玻璃，给……上釉　vi. 变呆滞，变得光滑
transparent [trænsˈperənt] adj. 透明的，显然的，坦率的，易懂的
variation [ˌveəriˈeɪʃn] n. 变化，变异，变种
pierce [pɪəs] vt. 刺穿，洞察，响彻，深深地打动　vi. 进入，透入
translucent [trænzˈluːsnt] adj. 透明的，半透明的
featherlight [feðəˈlaɪt] adj. 轻如羽毛的
eggshell [ˈeɡʃel] n. 蛋壳，薄而易碎的东西
veil [veɪl] n. 面纱，面罩，遮蔽物，托词　vt. 遮蔽，掩饰　vi. 蒙上面纱，出现轻度灰雾
mask [mɑːsk] n. 面具，口罩，掩饰　vt. 掩饰，戴面具
famille rose 粉彩，胭脂红
intensity [ɪnˈtensəti] n. 强度，强烈
elaborate [ɪˈlæbərət] adj. 精心制作的，详尽的　v. 精心制作，详细阐述，详细描述
tableware [ˈteɪblweə] n. 餐具
specialization [ˌspeʃəlaɪˈzeɪʃn] n. 专门化，特殊化
veteran [ˈvetərən] n. 老兵，老手，富有经验的人，老运动员　adj. 经验丰富的，老兵的
artisan [ɑːtɪˈzæn] n. 工匠，技工
apprentice [əˈprentɪs] n. 学徒
pass on 传递，继续

PART III ENGLISH TOPICS FOR FOREIGN TOURISTS

扫码听短文

The Chinese Embroidery

Embroidery is done with coloured silk thread in different stitches. There are many kinds of hand-embroidery. Some of them use seven or eight different stitches and more than one hundred varieties of coloured thread. Sometimes the thread has to be split into many thin filaments. The finer the thread, the better the effect. To become a good embroiderer, one has to learn first of all how to divide a thread into a fine floss.

There are four important embroidery centers in China. They are Hunan, Sichuan, Jiangsu, and Guangdong, each famous for its own particular style. Therefore Xiang (Hunan), Shu (Sichuan), Su (Jiangsu), and Yue (Guangdong) have become the four most famous styles of embroidery.

Xiang embroidery has a history spanning more than 2500 years. It was first developed by local women to decorate skirts, pouches and other articles. The designs show birds, animals, flowers and landscapes. Originally Xiang embroidery was done on a single side of a piece of fabric. Later craftsmen adopted the technique of double-sided embroidery in which both sides display the same design in the same colour. In 1980, a new breakthrough was made: embroidery experts succeeced in embroidering pictures that were different in design, colour and stitches on either side of a piece of silk.

Su embroidery is famous for its delicate workmanship, beautiful designs, and tasteful colours. Suzhou's double-sided embroidery has a distinct pattern on either side. The two sides bear different patterns with different stitches and colours.

Yue embroidery, which is usually done in bright colours, includes the woollen needlepoint, cotton embroidery and embroidery with gold and silver thread. The superb workmanship of the Yue embroidery enables it to win prizes at international fairs in Panama and London in 1915 and 1923.

The last type is Shu embroidery. A typical example is "Hibiscus and Carp". Smooth, beautiful and exquisitely stitched, it shows a hibiscus tree growing on the river bank and carps swimming in the clear water.

Notes

(1) in different stitches 使用不同的针法

(2) hand-embroidery 手绣

(3) Xiang embroidery 湘绣

(4) Shu embroidery 蜀绣

(5) Su embroidery 苏绣

(6) Yue embroidery 粤绣

(7) double-sided embroidery 双面绣

(8) Suzhou's double-sided embroidery has a distinct pattern on either side. 苏州

的双面绣在任何一面都有一个截然不同的图案。

(9) to win prizes at international fairs in Panama and London 在巴拿马和伦敦的国际博览会上获奖

New Words & Expressions

embroidery [ɪmˈbrɔɪdəri] n. 刺绣,刺绣品
stitch [stɪtʃ] n. 针脚,线迹,一针　vt. 缝,缝合　vi. 缝,缝合
filament [ˈfɪləmənt] n. 灯丝,细丝,细线,单纤维
embroiderer [ɪmˈbrɔɪdərə] n. 绣花机,刺绣工
floss [ˈflɒs] n. 牙线,丝线　vt. 用牙线洁牙
pouch [paʊtʃ] n. 小袋,(有袋目动物腹部的)育儿袋　vt. 把……装入袋中
breakthrough [ˈbreɪkˈθruː] n. 突破,突破性进展
workmanship [ˈwɜːkmənʃɪp] n. 手艺,工艺,技巧
tasteful [ˈteɪstful] adj. 高雅的,雅致的,优美的
double-sided adj. 有两面的,两面派的
distinct [dɪsˈtɪŋkt] adj. 明显的,独特的,清楚的,有区别的
needlepoint [ˈniːdlpɔɪnt] n. 针尖,针绣
superb [sjuˈpɜːb] adj. 极好的,华丽的,宏伟的
to win prize 得奖,赢得奖品,获奖,赢得了奖金
international fair 国际博览会
Panama [ˌpænəˈmɑː] n. 巴拿马共和国(位于拉丁美洲)
hibiscus [hɪˈbɪskəs] n. 木槿,木槿属,芙蓉花
carp [kɑːp] n. 鲤鱼　vi. 吹毛求疵
exquisitely [ekˈskwɪzɪtli] adv. 精致地,精巧地,敏锐地

The Cloisonne Enamel of China

Cloisonne is a famous traditional enamelware, known as the "Blue of Jingtai" in China. It was so called because "blue" was the typical colour used for enamelling and "Jingtai" was the reign title of the 7th Ming emperor's reign.

The making of cloisonne requires rather elaborate and complicated processes: base-hammering, copper-strip inlay and soldering, enamel-fillng, enamel-firing, polishing and gilding.

Base-hammering is the first step in the making of cloisonne. The material for making the body is copper, because copper is easily hammered and stretched. Copper is hammered into the desired shape such as a vase, jar, bowl, plate, box, ash-tray or some ornamental objects.

The second step is copper-strip inlay and soldering. Delicate copper strips are bent into designs and soldered on to the surface of a metal art object. This requires great care and creativity: the artisan has a blueprint in mind and makes full use of his

扫码听短文

experience, imagination, and aesthetic perspectives in mapping out the patterns, which include everyday objects such as grasshoppers, frogs, horses, and flowers as well as dragons and phoenixes.

The third step is to apply colour which is known as enamel-filling. The colour of enamel is like the glaze on ceramics. It is called falang. Its basic elements are boric acid, saltpetre and alkaline. Owing to the difference in the minerals added, the colour differs accordingly. Usually one with much iron will turn grey; with uranium, yellow; with chromium, green; with zinc, white; with bronze, blue; with gold or iodine, red. All the colours, ground into fine powder and mixed into a kind of paste are applied to the little compartments separated by filigree.

The fourth step is enamel-firing. This is done by putting the article, with its enamel filling, to the crucible. After a short moment, the copper body will turn red and the enamel in the little compartments will sink down and fuse onto the copper base. Usually, a cloisonne piece has to be fired at least five times and a new coat of enamel is added each time until the compartments are finally filled.

The fifth step is polishing. The first polish is with emery. It aims at making the filigree and the filled compartments smooth. The whole piece is again put to fire, then polished once more with a whet-stone. Finally, a piece of hard carbon is used to polish it again to obtain lustre on the surface of the article.

The final step is gilding. The exposed parts of the filigree and the metal fringes of the article again undergo an electroplating and a slight polish.

Notes

(1) rather elaborate and complicated processes 相当细致和复杂的加工程序
(2) base-hammering 制胎
(3) copper-strip inlay and soldering 铜丝的镶嵌和焊接
(4) enamel-filling 点蓝
(5) enamel-firing 烧蓝
(6) boric acid 硼酸
(7) whet-stone 磨石

New Words & Expressions

cloisonne [klwɑːˈzɒnei] n. 景泰蓝瓷器 adj. 景泰蓝制的
enamel [ɪˈnæml] n. 搪瓷，珐琅，瓷釉 vt. 给……上珐琅，涂以瓷釉
enamelware [ɪˈnæmlweə] n. 搪瓷炊具，搪瓷器具
enameling [ɪˈnæməlɪŋ] n. 上釉，施釉，上漆 v. 涂以瓷釉（enamel 的现在分词）
hammer [ˈhæmə] v. 锤击，敲打 n. 铁锤，链球，锤骨，音锤
copper [ˈkɒpə] n. 铜
copper-strip 铜带，铜条

inlay [ˌɪnˈleɪ] n. 镶嵌，镶嵌物 vt. 把……嵌入，把……镶入
solder [ˈsəʊldə] n. 焊料，接合物 vt. 焊接
polishing [ˈpɒlɪʃɪŋ] v. 磨光，擦亮，（文章）润色（polish 的现在分词） n. 抛光，磨光
gilding [ˈɡɪldɪŋ] v. 镀金（gild 的现在分词） n. 镀金层，金色涂层
ornamental [ˌɔːnəˈmentl] adj. 装饰的，装饰性的 n. 观赏植物，装饰品
blueprint [ˈbluːˌprɪnt] n. 蓝图，设计图，计划 vt. 为……制订计划，为……制蓝图
aesthetic [iːsˈθetɪk] adj. 美的，美学的，审美的，具有审美趣味的
perspective [pəˈspektɪv] n. 观点，远景，透视图 adj. 透视的
map out 在地图上标出，筹划
grasshopper [ˈɡrɑːshɒpə(r)] n. 蚱蜢，蝗虫
boric [ˈbɔːrɪk] adj. 硼的，含硼的
boric acid [ˈbɔːrɪk ˈæsɪd] 硼酸
saltpetre [ˈsɔːltˌpiːtə] n. 硝石，硝酸钠，钾硝
alkaline [ˈælkəlaɪn] adj. 碱性的，含碱的
uranium [juˈreɪniəm] n. 铀
chromium [ˈkrəʊmiəm] n. 铬
zinc [zɪŋk] n. 锌 vt. 镀锌于……
iodine [ˈaɪədiːn] n. 碘
filigree [ˈfɪlɪɡriː] n. 金银丝饰品 adj. 金银丝工艺的 vt. 用金银丝装饰，掐丝
crucible [ˈkruːsɪbl] n. 坩埚，炉缸，严酷的考验
fuse [fjuːz] n. 保险丝，导火线，雷管 vt. 使融合，使熔化
emery [ˈeməri] n. 金刚砂，刚玉砂
whet-stone 磨刀轮
lustre [ˈlʌstə(r)] n. 光泽，光彩
undergo [ˌʌndəˈɡəʊ] vt. 经历，经受，忍受
fringe [frɪndʒ] n. 边缘，穗，刘海 adj. 边缘的，附加的 vt. 形成……的边缘
electroplating [ɪˈlektrəʊˌpleɪtɪŋ] n. 电镀，电镀术 adj. 电镀的

The Chinese Painting

Chinese traditional painting dates back to the Neolithic Period about 6000 years ago. The colored pottery with painted animals, fish, deer in those unearthed ancient tombs indicates that the Chinese had already started to use brushes to paint during the Neolithic Period. Chinese traditional painting is done with a soft brush, Xuan paper which is very absorbent and ink, so sometimes it is called ink-and-wash painting. In ancient time, scholars had Four Treasures of the Study, they are ink slab, ink stick, brush and Xuan paper.

Chinese traditional painting is highly regarded throughout the world for its theory, expression and techniques. According to the means of expressions, Chinese painting can be divided into two kinds: Xieyi school and Gongbi school. Xieyi school is marked by freehand brush work or sketch, and it's little abstract. Freehand brush painting emphasizes the sentiments, "make the form show the spirit". Gongbi is characterized by fine brush work and close attention to detail. It's meticulous and appreciated more for the technique than the expression. According to the subjects, Chinese painting is divided into three kinds: landscape, flower and bird, figure or portrait.

Chinese painting is hard. You must know very well about Chinese seal-engraving, calligraphy and poems. Actually, Chinese painting and calligraphy are closely related to each other because lines are used in both. Chinese people have turned simple lines into a highly developed form of art. Lines are not only to draw the contours, but also to express the artist's concept and feelings. They may be straight or curved, hard or soft, thick or thin, pale or dark and the ink may be dry or running. The use of lines and strokes is one of the elements which gives Chinese painting its unique qualities. It's also a combination in the same picture of the arts of poetry, calligraphy, painting, and seal-engraving. They help to explain the painters' ideas and sentiments and also add decorative beauty to the painting. Ancient artists liked to paint pines, bamboo and plum blossoms. They are meant to embody the qualities of people who are upright and ready to help each other in hard environments. Many artists often choose significant subjects which can embody some deep meanings or implications, such as fish—remainder of plentiful life, have ample food and clothing. Two fish—keep forging ahead, show courage to somebody. Flowers in blossom and full moon—to show perfect matching. Peony—to show wealth and high rank.

The different cultural backgrounds in China and the western countries have created different aesthetics. Western-style painting follows the principle of depicting the real world, stressing an exact and scientific representation. Its composition uses linear perspective to scientifically locate the object and produce a three-dimensional effect. To express color, it lookes to the light source and the environment. Chinese painting, however, influenced by Chinese traditional thinking, focuses on revealing the painter's inner feelings instead of outer objects and does not adhere rigidly to time and space. The painter expresses his own feelings and understanding of an object, approaching it from various angles instead of a fixed angle as in western-style painting. Color is used for contrast, without concern for the light source or the environment. The spirit and essence of an object are more important than its outer form.

Ink in Chinese traditional painting makes a unique contribution. Its dilution indicates space. Light ink represents the foreground and thick ink indicates the distance. An apparent performance on the stage usually shows the years of experiences which help to achieve the perfection.

Notes

(1) traditional Chinese painting 中国画
(2) the Neolithic Period 新石器时代
(3) Four Treasures of the Study 文房四宝
(4) Xieyi school and Gongbi school 写意派和工笔派
(5) making the form show the spirit 以形传神
(6) produce a three-dimensional effect 产生立体效果
(7) to show perfect matching 表现出完美的结合

New Words & Expressions

neolithic [ˌniːəˈlɪθɪk] adj. 新石器时代的
unearthed [ʌnˈɜːθt] v. 发掘，（偶然）发现（unearth 的过去分词）
brush [brʌʃ] n. 刷子，画笔，毛笔　vi. 刷，擦过，掠过　vt. 刷，画
absorbent [əbˈsɔːbənt] n. 吸收剂　adj. 易吸收的
ink-and-wash painting 水墨画
freehand brush work or sketch 写意画
sentiment [ˈsentɪmənt] n. 感情，情绪，情操，观点，多愁善感
be characterized by 具有……的特性，以……为特征
meticulous [məˈtɪkjələs] adj. 一丝不苟的，小心翼翼的
portrait [ˈpɔːtreɪt] n. 肖像，半身画像
engraving [ɪnˈɡreɪvɪŋ] n. 雕刻，雕刻术，雕刻品　v. 在……上雕刻
contour [ˈkɒntʊə] n. 轮廓，等高线，概要
curved [kɜːvd] adj. 弯曲的，曲线的
stroke [strəʊk] n. 中风，行程，笔画，打击　vi. 击球，敲击键盘　vt. 抚摸，敲击
embody [ɪmˈbɒdi] vt. 体现，使具体化，具体表达
upright [ˈʌpraɪt] n. 垂直，竖立，支柱，立柱　adj. 正直的，诚实的，垂直的，合乎正道的
implication [ˌɪmplɪˈkeɪʃn] n. 含义，暗示，牵连，卷入
remainder [rɪˈmeɪndə] n. 余数，残余，剩余物　adj. 剩余的　vt. 廉价出售
keep forging ahead 不断开拓进取
depict [dɪˈpɪkt] vt. 描述，描画，描写
linear [ˈlɪniə] adj. 线的，线型的，直线的，线状的，长度的
three-dimensional effect 3D 效果
adhere [ədˈhɪə] vi. 坚持，依附，粘着
dilution [daɪˈluːʃn] n. 稀释，冲淡，冲淡物
foreground [ˈfɔːɡraʊnd] n. 前景，最显著的位置，前台
perfection [pəˈfekʃn] n. 完善，完美

PART III ENGLISH TOPICS FOR FOREIGN TOURISTS

扫码听短文

Silk

With a history of 5000 years, China was the earliest producer of silk in the world. Silk cocoons and bits of silk have been found among relics from 4700 BC.

In ancient China, men tilled and women looked after textile production. They raised the silkworms, spun the thread, wove it and then embroidered it.

Silk has always been prized for its transparency and luminosity. Chinese silk and production techniques spread to other countries quickly. The Greeks called China the Silk Country. Imperial Rome referred to the Chinese as the silk people. Silk fabrics travelled to Europe and the Mideast along the "Silk Route" 2000 years ago.

The imperial court was a protector and patron of sericiculture. In the Qing Dynasty, a weaving bureau was set up in Nanjing exclusively to supply the court's silk. Today, silk technology is much advanced and silk fabric comes in several hundred varieties; the best known include georgette crepe, damask, satin, silk gauze, crepe silk, raw silk, velvet, tough silk, embroidered silk and painted silk. China's centuries-old experience in weaving silk gave it the expertise and technology necessary to expand its interests into the garment trade. Today, many of the western most famous designers have their products cut and sewn in China.

The traditional silk centers of Zhejiang and Jiangsu Provinces are still the two major producers of raw silk and silk fabrics in China with a combined output that makes up more than half of the national total. All the 62 counties in Zhejiang Province breed mulberry silkworms and produce among them one-third of China's cocoons. There are more than 250 silk mills throughout the province. The most important silk center in Zhejiang Province is Hangzhou, which produces more silk fabrics than any other place in the country. Hangzhou produces half of Zhejiang's silk and silk fabrics and more than 80% of the province's exports, which are sold to more than 160 countries and regions. The Hangzhou Silk Printing and Dyeing Complex, built in 1958, is China's largest enterprise combining reeling, weaving, printing and dyeing. Its production capacity is equivalent to the combined capacity of all silk mills in the city at the time of liberation. China's three best known brocades are: the Song brocade made in Hangzhou of Zhejiang Province, the Nanjing brocade made in Nanjing of Jiangsu Province and the Sichuan brocade made in Chengdu of Sichuan Province.

Notes

(1) spin the thread 纺线
(2) georgette crepe 乔其纱
(3) silk gauze 真丝绢
(4) crepe silk 绉绸
(5) raw silk 生丝
(6) the Hangzhou Silk Printing and Dyeing Complex 杭州丝绸印染厂

New Words & Expressions

cocoon [kəˈkuːn] n. 蚕茧
till [tɪl] n. 备用现金　vt. 耕种，犁地
silkworm [ˈsɪlkˌwɜːm] n. 蚕，桑蚕，家蚕
spin [spɪn] n. 旋转，疾驰　vi. 旋转，纺纱，吐丝　vt. 使旋转，纺纱，编造
transparency [trænsˈpærənsi] n. 透明，透明度，幻灯片
luminosity [ˌluːmɪˈnɒsəti] n. 发光度
sericiculture [ˈserɪsɪˌkʌltʃə] n. 养蚕业
georgette [ˌdʒɔːˈdʒet] n. 乔其纱
crepe [kreɪp] n. 绉纱，绉绸
damask [ˈdæməsk] n. 花缎，锦缎
satin [ˈsætɪn] n. 缎子，绸缎　adj. 绸缎做的，缎子一般的，光滑（似缎）的
gauze [ɡɔːz] n. 薄纱，纱布
velvet [ˈvelvɪt] n. 天鹅绒　adj. 天鹅绒的，柔软的
expertise [ˌekspɜːˈtiːz] n. 专门知识，专门技术
garment [ˈɡɑːmənt] n. 衣服，外衣
mulberry [ˈmʌlbəri] n. 桑树，桑葚，深紫红色
reel [riːl] n. 卷轴　vi. 蹒跚，眩晕
mill [mɪl] n. 磨坊，磨粉机，工厂，制造厂　vt. 碾磨，磨成粉
brocade [brəˈkeɪd] n. 织有金银丝浮花的，织锦，锦缎

Exercises

1. Read and recite the following special terms

（1）black tea 红茶
（2）scented tea 花茶
（3）chrysanthemum tea 菊花茶
（4）congou 工夫茶
（5）Su embroidery 苏绣
（6）hand embroidery 刺绣
（7）hand-stitching work 挑花
（8）silk gauze 真丝绢
（9）raw silk 生丝
（10）crepe silk 绉绸
（11）Jingdezhen porcelain wares 景德镇瓷器
（12）Tri-coloured glazed pottery of the Tang Dynasty 唐三彩
（13）underglaze color 釉下彩
（14）base-hammering 制胎
（15）filigree soldering 掐丝

(16) Suzhou rosewood furniture 苏州红木家具

(17) lacquerware 漆器

(18) potted lanscape (bonzai) 盆景

(19) Burma jade 缅甸玉

(20) stone carving 石雕

2. Translate the following sentences into English

(1) 中国是茶树的原产地，又是最早发现茶叶功效、栽培茶树和制成茶叶的国家。茶叶自古以来就是我国的三大特产之一，也是世界三大饮料（茶叶、咖啡、可可）之一。

(2) 苏州的苏绣、湖南的湘绣、广东的粤绣及四川的蜀绣，既继承了古老的优良传统，又有所创新，各具特色，被喻为我国"四大名绣"。

(3) 江西省景德镇市是我国的"瓷都"，所产瓷器素有"白如玉、薄如纸、明如镜、声如磬"的美誉。

(4) 东阳木雕产于浙江省东阳市，是我国古老的民间木雕工艺品之一。

(5) 景泰蓝是我国著名的工艺品，它的制作过程相当复杂，主要包括制胎、掐丝、镶丝、点蓝、烧蓝、抛光和点金七个步骤。

Unit 25　Keys

PART IV

Appendixes

This part consists of three appendixes: List of National Parks of China, List of National Famous Historical and Cultural Cities, List of World Heritage Sites in China.

Appendix 1　List of National Parks of China

（国家级风景名胜区）

Appendix 2　List of National Famous Historical and Cultural Cities

（国家历史文化名城名单）

Appendix 3　List of World Heritage Sites in China

（中国世界遗产名录）

参考文献
References

[1] 袁智敏,仉向明.领队英语[M].2版.北京:旅游教育出版社,2009.
[2] 夏林根.旅游目的地概述[M].北京:旅游教育出版社,2005.
[3] 郭兆康.实用饭店情景英语[M].上海:复旦大学出版社,2010.
[4] 崔玉范.英语领队实务[M].吉林:吉林出版集团股份有限公司,2010.
[5] 王健民.出境旅游领队实务[M].北京:旅游教育出版社,2010.
[6] 程丛喜.实用旅游英语听说教程[M].武汉:武汉大学出版社,2012.
[7] 冯玮.新编导游英语[M].武汉:武汉大学出版社,2003.
[8] 周玮.旅行社英语[M].广州:广东旅游出版社,2003.
[9] 段开成.导游英语听与说[M].天津:南开大学出版社,2001.
[10] 刘爱服.英语北京导游[M].北京:中国旅游出版社,2003.
[11] 程丛喜.导游英语阅读[M].武汉:武汉大学出版社,2007.
[12] 周保国.商务交际英语[M].武汉:武汉大学出版社,2004.
[13] 史爱华,顾宝珠.旅游英语[M].北京:机械工业出版社,2009.
[14] 姚宝荣,韩琪,曹锋.旅游管理英语[M].北京:旅游教育出版社,2007.
[15] 程丛喜,等.导游英语——湖北旅游热点[M].武汉:武汉大学出版社,2005.
[16] 莫红英.旅游基础英语[M].北京:旅游教育出版社,2007.
[17] 朱葆琛.最新汉英旅游词典[M].北京:旅游教育出版社,1992.
[18] 何道宽.英语创意导游[M].重庆:重庆出版社,1995.
[19] 朱歧新,张秀桂.英语导游翻译必读[M].北京:中国旅游出版社,1999.
[20] 程丛喜.导游英语[M].武汉:武汉大学出版社,2005.
[21] 程丛喜.导游英语[M].2版.武汉:武汉大学出版社,2013.

教学支持说明

普通高等学校"十四五"规划旅游管理类精品教材系华中科技大学出版社"十四五"规划重点教材。

为了改善教学效果,提高教材的使用效率,满足高校授课教师的教学需求,本套教材备有与纸质教材配套的教学课件和拓展资源。

为保证本教学课件及相关教学资料仅为教材使用者所得,我们将向使用本套教材的高校授课教师免费赠送教学课件或者相关教学资料,烦请授课教师通过电话、邮件或加入旅游专家俱乐部QQ群等方式与我们联系,获取"电子资源申请表"文档并认真准确填写后发给我们,我们的联系方式如下:

地址:湖北省武汉市东湖新技术开发区华工科技园华工园六路

邮编:430223

电话:027-81321911

E-mail:lyzjjlb@163.com

旅游专家俱乐部QQ群号:758712998

旅游专家俱乐部QQ群二维码:

群名称:旅游专家俱乐部5群
群　号:758712998

电子资源申请表

填表时间：_____年___月___日

1. 以下内容请教师按实际情况写，★为必填项。
2. 相关内容可以酌情调整提交。

★姓名		★性别	□男 □女	出生年月		★职务	
						★职称	□教授 □副教授 □讲师 □助教

★学校		★院/系	
★教研室		★专业	
★办公电话		家庭电话		★移动电话	
★E-mail（请填写清晰）				★QQ号/微信号	
★联系地址				★邮编	

★现在主授课程情况	学生人数	教材所属出版社	教材满意度
课程一			□满意 □一般 □不满意
课程二			□满意 □一般 □不满意
课程三			□满意 □一般 □不满意
其他			□满意 □一般 □不满意

教材出版信息						
方向一		□准备写	□写作中	□已成稿	□已出版待修订	□有讲义
方向二		□准备写	□写作中	□已成稿	□已出版待修订	□有讲义
方向三		□准备写	□写作中	□已成稿	□已出版待修订	□有讲义

　　请教师认真填写表格下列内容，提供索取课件配套教材的相关信息，我社根据每位教师填表信息的完整性、授课情况与索取课件的相关性，以及教材使用的情况赠送教材的配套课件及相关教学资源。

ISBN（书号）	书名	作者	索取课件简要说明	学生人数（如选作教材）
			□教学 □参考	
			□教学 □参考	

★您对与课件配套的纸质教材的意见和建议，希望提供哪些配套教学资源：